Eastern Christians

in the Habsburg Monarchy

Eastern Christians

in the Habsburg Monarchy

edited by

John-Paul Himka and Franz A. J. Szabo

Canadian Institute of Ukrainian Studies Press
Edmonton   •   2021   •   Toronto
Published in cooperation with the Wirth Institute for Austrian
and Central European Studies, University of Alberta

Canadian Institute of Ukrainian Studies Press

University of Alberta
Edmonton, Alberta
Canada T6G 2H8

University of Toronto
Toronto, Ontario
Canada M5S 2C3

Copyright © 2021 Canadian Institute of Ukrainian Studies
ISBN: 978-1-894865-64-7 (pbk.)

Library and Archives Canada Cataloguing in Publication
Title: Eastern Christians in the Habsburg monarchy / edited by John-Paul Himka and
Franz A. J. Szabo.
Names: International Conference on Eastern Christians in the Habsburg Monarchy (2009:
Edmonton, Alta.), author. | Himka, John-Paul, 1949- editor. | Szabo, Franz A. J., editor.
Description: International Conference on Eastern Christians in the Habsburg Monarchy,
jointly organized by the Wirth Institute for Austrian and Central European Studies and
by the Research Program on Religion and Culture of the Canadian Institute of Ukrainian
Studies of the University of Alberta, and held September, 11-12, 2009 in Edmonton,
Alberta. | Includes bibliographical references.
Identifiers: Canadiana 20210213590 | ISBN 9781894865647 (softcover)
Subjects: LCSH: Orthodox Eastern Church—Europe, Central—History—Congresses. |
LCSH: Europe, Central—Church history—Congresses.
Classification: LCC BX310.I58 2021 | DDC 281.943—dc23

This book has been published in cooperation with the Wirth Institute for Austrian and
Central European Studies, University of Alberta. A grant for this publication has been
provided by the Nestor Peczeniuk Memorial Endowment Fund at the Canadian Institute of
Ukrainian Studies (CIUS), University of Alberta. The publication of this book has also been
generously supported by the Father Hryhorij Fil and Olga Fil Endowment Fund and the
Yurkiwsky Family Memorial Endowment Fund at the CIUS.

Cover illustration: Tadei Spalinsky, an icon of the Protection of the Mother of God,
Hunkovce, 1781, National Gallery, Budapest.

Cover design by Christine Kurys Obbema.

Printed in Canada

Table of Contents

List of Illustrations / vi

Introduction / *John-Paul Himka and Franz A.J. Szabo* / x

Historical Overview

    Eastern Christians in the Habsburg Monarchy, 1526-1918 / *Paul Robert Magocsi* / 1

Historical Studies

    Politics, Religion, and Confessional Identity among the Romanians of Bistriţa: A Case Study / *Sever Cristian Oancea* / 24

    Aspects of Confessional Alterity in Transylvania: The Uniate – Non-Uniate Polemic in the Eighteenth Century / *Ciprian Ghişa* / 44

    Josephinist Reforms in the Metropolis of Karlovci and the Orthodox Hierarchy / *Marija Petrović* / 63

    Transnational Conversions: Migrants in America and Greek Catholic Conversion Movements to Eastern Orthodoxy in the Habsburg Empire, 1890-1914 / *Joel Brady* / 84

Sacral Culture

    The Art of the Greek Catholic Eparchy of Mukachevo: Sacral Painting of the Eighteenth Century / *Bernadett Puskás* / 102

    Sacred and Heraldic Images on Ukrainian Banners of the Eighteenth and Nineteenth Centuries / *Roksolana Kosiv* / 137

    Facing East: References to Eastern Christianity in Lviv's Representational Public Space ca. 1900 / *Andriy Zayarnyuk* / 170

    The Sacred Art of Modest Sosenko: Lost and Preserved / *Olesya Semchyshyn-Huzner* / 206

    Sacral Needlework in Eastern Galicia: Social and Cultural Aspects (Late Nineteenth and Early Twentieth Centuries) / *Natalia Dmytryshyn* / 239

List of Illustrations

Illustration 6.1: Flight into Egypt, predella of the iconostasis in Uzhok. / 107

Illustration 6.2: Apostles, including St. Peter, from the iconostasis of Kolodne. / 109

Illustration 6.3: Transfer of the Relics of St. Nicholas to Bari, from the iconostasis of Kolodne. / 110

Illustration 6.4: Crucifixion, Abaújszolnok. /113

Illustration 6.5: Mykhail Spalinsky, "Blessed Are the Poor in Spirit," from Malyi Bereznyi monastery. / 115

Illustration 6.6: Mykhail and Tadei Spalinsky, St. Mark, iconostasis of Máriapócs. / 116

Illustration 6.7: Mykhail and Tadei Spalinsky, iconostasis in Sátoraljaújhely. / 119

Illustration 6.8: Mykhail and Tadei Spalinsky, principal icon of the Mother of God, iconostasis in Sátoraljaújhely. / 120

Illustration 6.9: Mykhail and Tadei Spalinsky, St. Bartholomew, iconsostasis in the cathedral church in Uzhhorod. / 121

Illustration 6.10: Descent of the Holy Spirit with coat of arms of Austria, iconostasis in Huklyvyi. / 123

Illustration 6.11: Iconostasis in Hajdúdorog. / 124

Illustration 6.12: Ecce Homo, altar icon in Nyirderzs. / 129

Illustration 7.1: Church banners in a procession. Detail of the icon "Transfer of the Relics of St. Nicholas." Eighteenth century. / 142

Illustration 7.2: Church banner of the Mother of God Mater Misericordiae. 1712. From the church of St. George or the church of the Transfiguration in Drohobych. Author: Ivan Medytsky (?). / 145

Illustration 7.3: Church banner of the Mother of God Mater Misericordiae, with a scene of the communion of St. Onuphrius as well as St. John the Baptist. Early eighteenth century. / 147

Illustration 7.4: Church banner of the Church Militant. 1718. From the church of St. George (?) in Drohobych. Author: Ivan Medytsky (?). / 151

Illustration 7.5: Banner of the tailors' guild, Lviv. 1777. / 157

Illustration 7.6: Banner of the junior tailors' and tanners' guild. 1819. / 159

Illustration 7.7: Banner of the national guard of Yavoriv. 1848. / 162

Illustration 7.8: Ribbon for the banner of the Battalion of Ruthenian Mountain Riflemen. 1849. / 164

Illustration 7.9: Cartouche with date on the ribbon for the Battalion's banner. / 165

Illustration 7.10: Cartouche with coats of arms on the ribbon for the Battalion's banner. / 166

Illustration 7.11: Galicia side, banner of the Ukrainian Sokil-Father association of Lviv. 1911. / 167

Illustration 7.12: Kyiv land side, banner of Sokil-Father. / 168

Illustration 8.1: The cityscape of late eighteenth-century Lviv recently annexed by Austria. A print from 1772–1780. / 171

Illustration 8.2: The cityscape of mid-nineteenth century Lviv: new public buildings and housing envelop the old baroque town. Aquarelle by T. Czyszkowski, after 1840. / 171

Illustration 8.3: Edgar Kováts. Initial sketch of the Galician pavilion for the 1900 World Exhibition. 1899. / 173

Illustration 8.4: Kazimierz Mokłowski. Apartment buildings in a hybrid all-Galician style. / 174

Illustration 8.5: Ivan Levynsky and Julian Zachariewicz, the pavilion of the Ukrainian societies at the General Provincial Exhibition of 1894, and the precursor of all other buildings in the Ukrainian style (circled). / 175

Illustration 8.6: "View of the residence of the Ukrainian Pedagogical Society." Architect: Tadeusz Obmiński (his signature in Ukrainian is on the postcard), 1906. / 176

Illustration 8.7: "Dniester" insurance company building, 1905. Architects: Ivan Levynsky, Lev Levynsky, Tadeusz Obmiński, Oleksandr Lushpynsky. / 177

Illustration 8.8: Narodnyi Dim Residence, 1906-1907. Architect: Ivan Levynsky's firm. / 178

Illustration 8.9: Projected Polish academic home. Drawing by Alfred Zachariewicz and Józef Sosnowski, 1906. / 179

Illustration 8.10: Kazimierz Sołecki's sanatorium. An example of mixed Carpathian style. Architect: Oleksandr Lushpynsky, built in 1906-1908. / 180

Illustration 8.11: Invalidenhaus chapel. Source: Postcard (before 1906). Publisher: Jan Bromilski. / 181

Illustration 8.12: The original chapel, used as an Orthodox church, was replaced by St. George's church on present-day Korolenko Street. / 182

Illustration 8.13: St. George's church on Korolenko Street, designed in 1895, built in 1899. Architect: Gustav Sachs. / 183

Illustration 8.14: Havryshkevych's original design for the Transfiguration church. Frontal view. / 184

Illustration 8.15: The Transfiguration church's final appearance. Back view, a photograph by Teodozii Bahrynovych, 1910. / 185

Illustration 8.16: The ruins of the Trinitarian Monastery, ca.1850. / 187

Illustration 8.17: The Drum of the Transfiguration church with the sculptures of the apostles by Leonard Marconi. / 188

Illustration 8.18: The Lviv skyline. A photograph by Raskalov. / 189

Illustration 8.19: The Ascension church in Znesinnia. Built: 1897-1901. / 190

Illustrations 8.20 and 8.21: St. John's church before and after the "restoration." / 191

Illustration 8.22 and 8.23: St. Paraskevia church before and after the "restoration." / 192

Illustration 8.24: St. Nicholas church after reconstruction. / 193

Illustration 8.25: The "Hard Nut" project for the reconstruction of the Lviv City Hall by Kraków architect Roman Bandurski. / 194

Illustration 8.26: Franciszek Biesiadecki's villa. Architects: Alfred Zachariewicz and Józef Sosnowski. / 196

Illustration 8.27 and 8.28: The Heller Villa, Melnyk Street 7 and a fragment of the exterior ornament from the villa's exterior. / 197

Illustration 8.29: The Panchyshyn Villa. Karmeliuk Street 3 / 198

Illustration 8.30, 8.31, and 8.32. The Narodnyi Dim Residence. / 199

Illustration 8.33 and 8.34. The first (1899) and the second (1900) projects of the new main train terminal. Architect: Władysław Sadłowski. / 200

Illustration 8.35: The main train station terminal as completed in 1904. / 201

Illustration 8.36: The train station vestibule. / 202

Illustration 8.37: Tadeusz Obmiński's design. Waiting hall for third-class passengers. / 203

Illustration 8.38: St. Elizabeth church. / 204

Illustration 9.1: Modest Sosenko. / 207

Illustration 9.2: Painting in the sanctuary of the church of St. Michael in Pidberiztsi. / 212

Illustration 9.3: Painting in the dome of the church of the Dormition of the Mother of God in Slavske. / 218

Illustration 9.4: The iconostasis of the church of the Holy Trinity in Drohobych. / 220

Illustration 9.5: Painting in the dome of the church of the Holy Resurrection in Poliany (formerly Rykiv). / 225

Illustration 9.6: The Heart of Jesus. / 227

Illustration 9.7: Detail of the painting in the sanctuary of the church of St. Nicholas in Zolochiv. / 229

Illustration 9.8: Detail of St. Andrew the First-Called. / 231

Illustration 9.9: Detail of the painting in the sanctuary of the church of the Descent of the Holy Spirit in Polove. / 233

Illustration 9.10: Detail of the design for painting the church of the Dormition in Lviv. / 234

Illustration 10.1: Postcard showing the Ryznytsia building in Sambir (beginning of the twentieth century). / 244

Illustration 10.2: A cruciform cover. One of the liturgical coverings with which a priest covers the communion chalice. / 247

Illustration 10.3: An aer. The largest of the liturgical coverings for the Holy Gifts. / 248

Illustration 10.4: Decorative cloth. / 248

Illustration 10.5: Altar cloth for covering and decorating the main altar. / 249

Illustration 10.6–7: Phelonion. / 250

Illustration 10.8: Epitrachelion. / 251

Introduction

John-Paul Himka and Franz A. J. Szabo

The defining feature of the Habsburg Monarchy was its pluralism. The aspect of that pluralism that has received the most scholarly attention is the Monarchy's linguistic heterogeneity, with its nine official languages (ten if Croat and Serb are counted separately) and half a dozen lesser unofficial ones, and a plethora of ethnic intermarriages and consequent multilingualism that defied exact delineation. But the characteristics that made it, in Robert Evans' felicitous phrase, an "agglutination of bewilderingly heterogeneous elements,"[1] were not restricted to language. The Monarchy's various duchies and kingdoms had different historical, constitutional, and legal traditions, and even within linguistic groupings there was a broad range of cultural variation. Pluralism also characterized the confessional profile of the Monarchy. It often defined itself as a "Catholic Power," which reflected developments during the Counter-Reformation which ensured that to the last days of the Monarchy some 60 percent of its inhabitants were Roman Catholic. However, constitutional guarantees of Protestantism in some areas, the adoption of confessional toleration in the 1780s, and the expansion of the Monarchy to the east and south-east also made it the home of Lutherans of various stripes, Calvinists, Unitarians, Jews, Muslims, Old Catholics (after 1870), and above all of adherents to Eastern Rites – Greek and Armenian Catholics and Orthodox. The latter are the subjects of this volume.

In the past, Habsburg studies, long a flourishing scholarly discipline with its own journals and its own institutional centres scattered across Europe and North America, traditionally produced two kinds of study: those that examined the Monarchy as a whole from the vantage point of Vienna (or similarly the Hungarian part of the Monarchy from the vantage point of Budapest) and those that focused on a particular crown land or region of the Monarchy, such as Bohemia, Galicia, or Transylvania. The former frequently adopted an imperial view that oversimplified regional peculiarities, while the latter tended either to try to carve national

---

[1] R.J.W. Evans, *The Making of the Habsburg Monarchy, 1550-1700* (Oxford: Oxford University Press, 1987), 447.

narratives out of a multinational past or to ignore the larger context of local developments.

Recently, however, as Pieter M. Judson has put it, "among scholars of Europe, Habsburg history has become known as a laboratory for creative innovation in historical studies." Transnational and interdisciplinary perspectives have led to new approaches to local and regional phenomena within the context of their "common experiences of empire."[2] Neither a national narrative nor one framed within the context of a particular crown land can hope to do justice to historical realities that cannot be defined within either rubric. Thus, for example, one of the most noteworthy features of the ethno-linguistic complexity of the Monarchy was that in virtually no crown land did any language correspond with political/historical boundaries.[3] The same holds true for the religious pluralism of the Monarchy, where self-professed confessional identity could not be delimited either within a crown land or ethnic schema. The newer perspectives on the Habsburg Monarchy that marry local and transnational analyses and examine shared experiences across crown lands within the context of empire thus promise a more nuanced assessment of the complex historical reality that was the Habsburg Empire.

The studies in this volume explore just such shared practices and experiences encompassing a larger collection of territories within the Monarchy by focusing on those areas that contained large numbers of Christians whose faith and rituals derived from Byzantium rather than Rome, that is, Eastern Orthodox and Greek Catholics (Uniates). The Eastern Christians inhabited a large body of territory in the south and east of the Monarchy, starting from Bosnia in the west, through Slavonia, Transylvania, Bukovina, and Eastern Galicia in the east. These Eastern Christians were not of one nationality either; about half were Ukrainians and Rusyns, and the rest were mainly Romanians and Serbs, although there were also other nationalities represented in smaller numbers, such as Hungarians and Slovaks.

Following the newer perspectives on the Habsburg Monarchy, the intellectual intentions behind this volume, therefore, are to rectify some over-emphases and biases both in the fields of Habsburg studies and Eastern Christian studies, to stimulate the conception of a new field where those two fields meet, to bring together into that new field scholars from

---

[2] Pieter M. Judson, *The Habsburg Empire: A New History* (Cambridge MA: Harvard University Press, 2016), 10-12.

[3] Salzburg and Upper Austria came closest to this.

previously isolated national scholarly disciplines, and to call attention to the rich cultural legacy of Eastern Christianity in Central Europe. In looking at these populations situated in the south and east and differing in cultural tradition from the Roman Catholics and Protestants who constituted the majority of the Monarchy's inhabitants, the volume addresses a longstanding imbalance in the study of the Habsburg realm, in which studies of religious issues within the Austro-Bohemian-Hungarian triad of the Monarchy have been dominated by Catholic-Protestant confrontations and rivalries to the neglect of other aspects.

Eastern Christian studies constitutes a less cohesive field, with many journals and many centers, often confessionally based. It too has a focus in need of expansion, since Eastern Christian studies has largely been restricted to Byzantium and Russia. The whole Central European experience of Eastern Christianity is rarely considered. Yet it is an intellectually interesting experience, because, until the large wave of migration to the Americas at the end of the nineteenth century, the Eastern Christians of the Monarchy were the westernmost extension of the Byzantine religious heritage, the most exposed to the cultural trends of the West. Not accidentally, the vast majority of Uniates or Greek Catholics, that is, Eastern Christians in communion with Rome, lived in the Habsburg Monarchy. Many very original and inventive phenomena of sacral culture can be found here, truly unexplored treasures. Furthermore, the story of the Eastern Christians in Central Europe contains a strong narrative about the interface of religion and nationalism, or perhaps of the intertwining of religious and national conflict, in a way that the history of Byzantine or Russian Orthodoxy does not.

This volume is testing a new idea: that it makes sense to study the Eastern Christians of the Habsburg Monarchy, or of Central Europe, together. It is not that the study of Central Europe's Eastern Christians has been totally neglected, but such work as has been done has been done almost exclusively within a national paradigm – Serbian, Romanian, Ukrainian, Rusyn, or Hungarian. The benefit of an approach that sees these developments within a context of a shared experience of empire is that it demonstrates a way to think about history and culture that transcends the inward-looking national approach. This volume thus considers the Eastern Christian experiences within the broader, "imperial" context of the entire monarchy. Of course, nationality issues played an outsized role in the later Monarchy, but that does not mean that historiography has to be grounded in nationality as well. ·

The volume is divided into three parts. The first part is a survey of the history of Orthodox and Greek Catholics in the Monarchy from 1526, when the Habsburgs inherited Hungary and acquired their first Eastern Christians, until 1918, when the Dual Monarchy was dismembered. This sets the historical context for all the following studies. The editors have been fortunate in recruiting to this task Paul Robert Magocsi, who is well known as the author of many balanced and clear surveys of Central and East European history as well as reliable reference works in the same area. Since the editors were unable to find contributions relating to every corner of the Habsburgs' Eastern Christian world, Magocsi's substantive and thorough overview makes up in great measure for our unavoidable omissions.

In the second part of the volume are four historical studies of concrete moments in the life of the Eastern Christians. Two studies, by Sever Cristian Oancea and Ciprian Ghişa, concern eighteenth-century Transylvania and the confessional rivalry between Orthodox and Greek Catholic clergymen. Among other things, they discuss the impact of Habsburg toleration policies in creating religious tensions and look at the intellectual history of polemical texts. This is followed by Marija Petrović's study of Josephinism's impact on the Orthodox South Slavs of the Monarchy. She looks particularly at educational policies and the reduction of monasteries, clergy, and feast days. The final study, by Joel Brady, is written in the key of transnational history, moving back and forth between North America and the Monarchy. The study uses the framework of transnationalism very successfully for a period earlier than those to which transnational approaches have usually been applied. The time frame is 1890-1914, when conversions from Greek Catholicism to Orthodoxy increased tensions between the confessions within international and transnational contexts.

As Paul Robert Magocsi notes in his survey of the Eastern Christians, "there was one area in which both Greek Catholic and Orthodox churches did leave a lasting impact" - on the "cultural landscape." The third part of the volume focuses precisely on Eastern Christian sacral culture in the Monarchy, and this constitutes perhaps the most pioneering section, since so little has been written on the topic in English. In fact, four of the five studies here were translated from Ukrainian especially for this volume. These studies concern Ukrainian- and Rusyn-inhabited lands, particularly Galicia and northeastern Hungary (today Transcarpathia oblast in Ukraine and the Prešov region in Slovakia).

The first study, by Bernadett Puskás, looks at the sacral culture of a single eparchy in the eighteenth century, that of Mukachevo, an eparchy whose territory is now split among Hungary, Slovakia, and Ukraine. She examines as a single ensemble the iconography, carving, decoration, and other artistic production of the eparchy, revealing an interesting hybridity where the paths of East and West crossed. Roksolana Kosiv looks at a particular and neglected artistic genre: banners, both sacred and secular. These were church, municipal, guild, and military banners, often with characteristics specific to the region of their provenance, Galicia. Andriy Zayarnyuk's very rich text on Eastern Christian features of Lviv's public space at the turn of the twentieth century returns to themes of hybridity and confessional rivalry. It also begins a discussion of the invention of tradition, in this case the creative search for a distinct local architectural style. The contribution by Olesya Semchyshyn-Huzner examines in detail the pathbreaking work of the artist Modest Sosenko, who fused modernist and secessionist art with Ukrainian national traditions, creating a national revival style that remains prominent in Ukrainian sacral art to this day. Natalia Dmytryshyn also looks at the search for "our own style" in sacral needlework, i.e., in the sewing and embroidery of sacred cloths and vestments. As she points out, at the turn of the twentieth century women engaged in "a creative, constructive, and quite masterful folk reimagining of sacred handicraft." Her essay also brings to bear methodological insights from women's studies.

All in all, this is a unique collection that we, as the editors, hope will stimulate more interest and research in the historical and cultural legacy of the Habsburg Monarchy's Eastern Christians. The collection had its origins in a 2009 international conference on Eastern Christians in the Habsburg Monarchy jointly organized by the Wirth Institute for Austrian and Central European Studies and by the Research Program on Religion and Culture of the Canadian Institute of Ukrainian Studies of the University of Alberta in Edmonton, Canada. The editors wish to express their gratitude to the staff of these Institutes for their labors in helping to organize the original conference, and above all to the sponsors – the Wirth Endowment and the Research Program on Religion and Culture – who made this international collaborative venture possible.

Eastern Christians in the Habsburg Monarchy, 1526-1918

Paul Robert Magocsi

The goal of this study is to examine the evolution and structure of Greek Catholic and Orthodox communities in the Habsburg Monarchy from the sixteenth century until the demise of that state at the close of World War I in late 1918. The discussion, focusing for the most part on the distinct aspects of the Greek Catholic and Orthodox variants of Eastern Christianity, will describe the basic characteristics of these churches and their jurisdictional patterns within the Habsburg empire.

Territorial Growth and Religious Affiliation

The Habsburg Monarchy, which later was formally known as the Austrian Empire (1804) and then the Austro-Hungarian Empire (1867), began its modern evolution in 1526, the year in which Habsburgs inherited the throne of the kingdom of Bohemia and the kingdom of Hungary.[1] The addition of Hungarian lands changed the religious composition of the Habsburg realm, since the Hungarian kingdom included within its historic borders adherents of Eastern Christianity, specifically Orthodoxy. The Orthodox lived in the eastern part of Hungary, specifically in Subcarpathian Rus' and Transylvania, as well as farther south in an area known as Slavonia.

Whereas in theory the Habsburgs had inherited these lands in 1526, in practice they had little or no control over them. This is because most of the Hungarian kingdom at the time was ruled either directly by the Ottoman Empire or indirectly by that empire's vassal state, Transylvania, whose ruling Protestant princes challenged Habsburg claims to the Hungarian throne.

It was not until 1699 that the Habsburgs finally drove the Ottomans out of the Hungarian kingdom and by 1711 managed to subdue the last major uprising of Transylvania's rebellious princes and return that

---

[1] For further details on the Habsburg Monarchy and its relations with Hungary and the Ottoman Empire in the sixteenth and seventeenth centuries, see Robert A. Kann, *A History of the Habsburg Empire, 1526-1918* (Berkeley, CA: University of California Press, 1974), 18-101.

principality to the Habsburg realm. During the nearly century and a half before 1711, as Habsburg armies engaged and gradually drove out the Ottomans from Hungary, two developments occurred. First, the numbers of Eastern Christian Orthodox increased in Habsburg-ruled Hungary (in particular because of the re-acquisition of Transylvania and Slavonia); and secondly, a certain portion of the Orthodox faithful were brought into the fold of the Catholic church of Rome through the process of church union (*Unia*). Hence, initially most Eastern Christians, whether Orthodox, or those who joined the Catholic church - that is, Uniates or Greek Catholics - resided in the Hungarian kingdom.

At the end of the eighteenth century, the Habsburg Monarchy acquired new lands which were inhabited in part by Eastern Christians, although this time these new territories were annexed to the non-Hungarian, or "Austrian" half of the realm: Galicia (1772) with its Greek Catholics and Bukovina (1774) with its Orthodox. The last major Habsburg territorial acquisition came in 1908, when Bosnia-Herzegovina, which included Orthodox Serbs (as well as Catholic Croats and Muslim Bosniaks), was formally annexed to the Austro-Hungarian Empire.

At the outset of the twentieth century (1900), there were 39 million Christian inhabitants in Austria-Hungary. Over 8.5 million (18.7 percent of the empire's total population) were Eastern Christians, specifically 4.9 million Greek Catholics and 3.5 million Orthodox.[2] In terms of nationality, a factor of increasing importance in the nineteenth century, most of the Greek Catholics were primarily Ruthenians/Ukrainians (in Austrian Galicia), Romanians (in Hungarian Transylvania), and Carpatho-Rusyns, Slovaks, and Magyars (in northeastern Hungary). The Orthodox were primarily Serbs (in Hungarian Slavonia and neighboring Vojvodina and Banat, in Austrian Dalmatia, and in jointly ruled Bosnia-Herzegovina), Romanians (in Hungarian Transylvania), and Ruthenians/Ukrainians (in Austrian Bukovina).

Greek Catholics in the Habsburg Monarchy

Although this study uses the term *Greek Catholic*, it would be useful to note how adherents of that faith have been categorized within the larger framework of the Christian or, more particularly, the Eastern Christian world. The existing literature on the subject uses a variety of terms that range from the all-encompassing *Christian Church of the East* and *Eastern*

---

[2] The statistical data is taken from Paul Robert Magocsi, *Historical Atlas of Central Europe*, 2nd rev. ed. (Seattle: University of Washington Press, 2002), 111-14.

Rite Churches to the more specific *Uniate Eastern Churches*, and *Eastern-Rite Churches and Eastern-Rite Catholicism*.[3] Eastern Rite Churches may be categorized according to the liturgical rite they follow: the Syrian Rite of Antioch, the Coptic Rite of Alexandria, the Armenian Rite of Cilicia, and the Byzantine Rite of Constantinople. Most of the Eastern Christians — Greek Catholic and Orthodox — who are the subject of this chapter derive from the Byzantine Rite Church of Constantinople. The Greek Catholic phenomenon actually began beyond the Habsburg Monarchy and specifically in 1596, when some of the Orthodox hierarchs and clergy living in the eastern regions of the Polish-Lithuanian Commonwealth (modern-day Belarus and Ukraine) accepted the idea of church union - *Unia* with the Catholic church in Rome. Even earlier there had been attempts to implement church union in the wake of the schism that from 1054 increasingly separated the Christian world of Catholic Rome from that of Orthodox Constantinople.

A short-lived union was proclaimed at Lyons in 1274 and another at Florence in 1439.[4] Both these attempts, as well as subsequent efforts either to implement or undo church unions, were closely tied to political developments. In other words, secular politics as much as theological concerns were among the motivating factors behind Catholic-Orthodox reconciliation or separation. The Union of Florence came about in 1439, a time when the Byzantine Empire was about to be overtaken by the Ottoman Turks. At that time the political context was the following: Byzantium's Orthodox emperor was anxious to obtain military assistance from western European powers arrayed against the Islamic Ottomans, while for his part Pope Eugene IV (r. 1431-1447), by achieving union, hoped to appease those forces within the Roman Catholic church (several anti-popes) who were opposed to his rule.

Secular politics aside, Catholic and Orthodox churchmen had their own agendas. Four points of dogma were agreed on at the council of Florence: the doctrine of the *filioque*;[5] the existence of purgatory;

---

[3] See, for instance, Adrian Fortescue, *The Uniate Eastern Churches* (London: Burns Oates and Washburn, 1923); Donald Attwater, *The Christian Churches of the East,* 2 vols., 2nd ed. (Milwaukee: Bruce Publishing Co., 1948), the second volume of which carries the subtitle: *Churches in Communion with Rome*; Joan L. Roccasalvo, *The Eastern Catholic Churches* (Collegeville, Minn.: The Liturgical Press, 1992); and Robert F. Taft, *The Byzantine Rite: A Short History* (Collegeville, Minn.: The Liturgical Press, 1992).

[4] For details on the early efforts at Church Union, see Oscar Halecki, *From Florence to Brest, 1439-1596,* 2nd ed. revised (New York: Fordham University Press, 1968), 15-82.

[5] The *filioque* issue, which later was exaggerated to become a seemingly irreconcilable theological difference between Catholics and Orthodox, had to do with a clause in the

unleavened bread as a legitimate matter of the Holy Eucharist; and the primacy of the pope in Rome. (From today's perspective it seems incredible that Roman papal primacy did not figure more prominently.) At the same time, however, the council accepted the principle of theological diversity, so that both the Western and Eastern traditions, law, and liturgies could continue to be practiced, if specific conditions warranted and agreement was reached.

At Florence, the Orthodox metropolitan of Kyiv (Izydor) resident in Moscow agreed to promote the idea of union among the Orthodox of eastern Europe. In Muscovy, however, which was the leading Orthodox state at the time, the country's Orthodox hierarchy and secular ruler adamantly rejected the union. By contrast, in Constantinople, the very fount of the Orthodox world, the Florentine union was accepted in late 1452. The next year, however, what remained of the Byzantine Empire fell to the Ottoman Turks. While the Ottoman Empire subsequently permitted the existence of Orthodoxy on its territory, it did so on the condition that the ecumenical patriarch of Constantinople repudiate the Union of Florence.[6] And this he did.

Some aspects of the Florentine union managed to survive in the eastern lands of the Polish-Lithuanian commonwealth (present-day Belarus and much of Ukraine), where the Orthodox inhabitants were designated as Ruthenians (from *Ruteni*, the Latin word for the ethnically Rus' population). The hierarchy of the Ruthenian church - metropolitans and bishops - was according to Orthodox tradition still chosen by church councils and, intermittently, was recognized by both the pope in Rome and the ecumenical patriarch in Constantinople. Whereas for a few decades (1472 to 1501) unionist sentiment prevailed within the Ruthenian church,[7] the situation changed in the course of the sixteenth century. That

---

fourth-century Nicene Creed concerning the Holy Spirit and whether it proceeds only "from the Father" (as in the original creed used by the Orthodox), or "from the Father and the Son" -- *filioque* in Latin (from a later modification of the creed used by Catholics). This issue remains high on the agenda of church leaders as witnessed by a recent meeting of theologians: "The *Filioque*: A Church Dividing Issue?: An Agreed Statement of the North American Orthodox-Catholic Theological Consultation, St. Paul's College, Washington, D. C., October 25, 2003," *Eastern Churches Journal* 10, no. 3 (Fairfax, VA, 2003): 103-30.

[6] Anything related to Rome was anathema to the Ottomans, who at the time considered the Vatican their greatest enemy in Europe.

[7] For further details on the survival of the Florentine union, see Halecki, *From Florence to Brest, 1439-1596,* 83-140; and Josef Macha, *Ecclesiastical Unification: A Theoretical Framework together with Case Studies from the History of Latin-Byzantine Relations,* Orientalia Christiana

was a time when Orthodox hierarchs in Poland-Lithuania could be approved for consecration only with the prior approval of the Polish king. This effectively meant that the local Orthodox hierarchy was subjected to the secular ruler of a Roman Catholic state.

Considering the persistence of the Florentine unionist tradition in the Ruthenian church, it is not surprising that the next effort at church union took place in the eastern lands of Poland-Lithuania. In 1590, several Orthodox bishops met in the town of Brest in southwestern Lithuania (today Brest-Litovsk in Belarus), where they accepted the idea of church union.[8] The Orthodox prelates agreed to acknowledge the supremacy of the pope in Rome, and in return they expected the king of Poland to guarantee to the Ruthenian church the same privileges, prerogatives, and immunities enjoyed by the Roman Catholic church. The Ruthenians also assumed they would be allowed to preserve the liturgy, structure, and traditions of their church,[9] and they did not challenge the theological belief of Roman Catholics regarding use of the *filioque* in their version of the Nicene creed.

Efforts to achieve church union did not depend solely on the work of religious figures. It was almost inevitable that secular figures would become involved in church matters. For example, Poland-Lithuania's Orthodox hierarchs, in particular bishop Gedeon Balaban of Lviv (r. 1569-1607), were becoming increasingly dissatisfied with the ecumenical patriarch of Constantinople (to whom the Ruthenian church was jurisdictionally subordinate), who, they felt, was interfering in the internal affairs of their church. To assure the success of their unionist efforts, the

---

Analecta, 198 (Rome: Pont. Institutum Orientalium Studiorum, 1974).

[8] There is an extensive literature on the Union of Brest. Aside from the earlier work by Halecki, *From Florence to Brest, 1439-1596*, 199-419, the best modern analysis, which includes a comprehensive updated bibliography, is found in Borys A. Gudziak, *Crisis and Reform: The Kyivan Metropolitanate, the Patriarchate of Constantinople, and the Genesis of the Union of Brest* (Cambridge, MA: Harvard Ukrainian Research Institute, 1998). For a critical assessment that is not in keeping with most standard interpretations, see Sophia Senyk, "The Union of Brest: An Evaluation," in Bert Groen and Wil van den Bercken, eds., *Four Hundred Years of the Union of Brest* (Leuven: Peeters, 1998), 1-16.

[9] The specific conditions of great concern to the Orthodox included: use of the liturgy according to the Byzantine ("Greek") rite and celebrated in the Church Slavonic language; communion under two species -- leavened bread and wine; the possibility for married men to be priests; election of bishops by church councils; musical accompaniment through the use of the human voice only (no instruments) in worship; the absence of statuary in churches and the presence of an iconostasis (icon screen) that separates the altar from the sanctuary; and observance of the Julian calendar. Some of these concerns emerged only after the union was concluded.

Ruthenian church hierarchy needed the support of the most influential Orthodox political figure in Poland-Lithuania, the palatine of Kyiv, Prince Kostiantyn Ostrozky (1526-1608). Initially, the prince was himself a strong supporter of church union, although his understanding of union assumed the participation of the "whole Ecumenical church," that is, the entire Roman Catholic *and* Orthodox world, including the ecumenical patriarch of Constantinople and other eastern patriarchs (at the time under Ottoman rule), as well as the church in neighboring Muscovy and Moldavia.

When Ostrozky's grandiose scheme proved untenable, the pro-unionist Ruthenian bishops continued their efforts to achieve church union, even if it were only to apply to Poland-Lithuania. Both groups met, but separately, in the town of Brest in October 1596. The pro-union forces, soon to be known as Uniates, proclaimed the union of Brest, which subordinated the Ruthenian church to the pope in Rome. The opposition forces led by Prince Ostrozky rejected the church union and instead proclaimed their intention to protect the Orthodox faith against interference from Poland's secular authorities led by that country's king, its Roman Catholic church, and its Uniate allies. Hence, a process that began in 1590, when most of the Orthodox bishops in Poland-Lithuania had initially favored the idea of church union, ended in 1596 with the division of the Ruthenian church into two mutually antagonistic forces: Uniate and Orthodox.

Initially, the Polish secular authorities recognized only the Uniates and outlawed the Orthodox. The Orthodox church eventually was able to regain its legal status with the result that after 1632 two parallel church jurisdictions, Uniate and Orthodox, each with its own metropolitan and bishops, functioned in Poland-Lithuania until that state's demise in 1795.

Following the Union of Brest in 1596, which applied to Eastern-rite Christians in Poland-Lithuania, the idea of church union reached the Habsburg realm, specifically Hungary. The northeastern region of the Hungarian kingdom (the present-day Transcarpathian oblast in Ukraine and the Prešov region of northeastern Slovakia) was inhabited by Orthodox believers of primarily Carpatho-Rusyn and, to a lesser degree, Romanian, Magyar, and Slovak ethnicity.

In the seventeenth century, the political situation in Hungary was very complex. Most of the kingdom was ruled by the Ottoman Empire, while the far northern and eastern regions were under the authority of either the Austrian Habsburgs or Transylvanian princes. The Catholic Habsburgs and Protestant Transylvanians were engaged in a civil war over the right to rule the kingdom of Hungary. Caught in the middle were the Rusyn-inhabited Orthodox lands in northeastern Hungary, which in turn were divided between the warring Habsburgs and Transylvanians.

Beginning in 1614 two attempts were made to initiate a church union. Not surprisingly, those efforts were favored by the pro-Habsburg Catholic forces but opposed by Protestant Transylvania.[10] Finally, in April 1646, in the Habsburg-controlled city of Uzhhorod, sixty-three Orthodox priests accepted what came to be known as the Union of Uzhhorod. As with the earlier Union of Brest in Poland-Lithuania, the new Uniate church in the Hungarian kingdom would retain its Byzantine rite and married clergy, its bishops would continue to be elected by a council (*sobor*) of monks and clergy, and its priests would be guaranteed the same privileges accorded to the Roman Catholic clergy. The latter privileges, including exemption for the Uniate priests from serf duties owed to local landlords, did not come immediately, but only after a decree (the *Leopoldine Patent*) was issued in 1692 by the Habsburg ruler Leopold I (r. 1655-1705). Because at the time most of the Uniates in the Hungarian kingdom were ethnically Rusyn, the new body, as in neighboring Poland-Lithuania, was referred to as the Ruthenian church.

The Union of Uzhhorod initially applied only to those lands in the Hungarian kingdom owned by pro-Habsburg Roman Catholic landlords, in particular the Drugeth family, whose landed estates were located in present-day eastern Slovakia and the region around Uzhhorod in far western Ukraine. Somewhat later, in 1664, as Habsburg authority moved further eastward, the union spread to the central part of Subcarpathian Rus'/Transcarpathia (thanks to the pro-Catholic sympathies of the widow of the local Transylvanian prince) and finally to the eastern Maramorosh region in 1721.

The jurisdictional status of Hungary's Ruthenian Uniates was precarious, since its bishops were technically only "ritual vicars," that is, auxiliaries to the Latin-rite Catholic bishop of Eger.[11] This subordinate

[10] For further details on the church union in the Hungarian kingdom, see Antal Hodinka, *A munkácsi görög-katholikus püspökség története* (Budapest: Magyar Tudományos Akadémia, 1909), and Michael Lacko, *Unio Užhorodensis Ruthenorum Carpathicorum cum Ecclesia Catholica*, Orientalia Christiana Analecta, 143 (Rome: Pont. Institutum Orientalium Studiorum, 1955)—English edition: *The Union of Užhorod* (Cleveland and Rome: Slovak Institute, 1966).

[11] On the "struggle" against the Latin-rite diocese of Eger and the subsequent developments in the Ruthenian church of Hungary, see Koloman Žatkovič, *Jagerskoje vl'ijanije: bor'ba protiv toho v istorii mukačevskoje grečeskoho obrjada diocezii* (Homestead, Pa., 1933); and Athanasius B. Pekar, *The History of the Church in Carpathian Rus'* (New York: Columbia University Press/East European Monographs, 1992), 36-61.

status of the Uniates did not change until 1771, when, at the request of Austrian Empress Maria Theresa (r. 1740-80), the pope established a jurisdictionally independent eparchy of Mukachevo. About the same time, the term *Uniate* was changed to *Greek Catholic* and the episcopal seat of the Ruthenian eparchy of Mukachevo was transferred from Mukachevo to Uzhhorod, where a seminary to train priests was set up in 1778.

Under Habsburg rule the Ruthenian eparchy of Mukachevo functioned as a state-supported church. Its hierarchs, however, especially during the last decades of the nineteenth century, felt increasingly obliged to express their loyalty to the Hungarian state. Consequently, several bishops and many priests supported the state's policy of magyarization, whose goal was to assimilate the kingdom's non-Magyar inhabitants, including Carpatho-Rusyns. Not all clerics favored assimilation, however, so that in fact the Ruthenian Greek Catholic church came to be internally divided between clergy who supported magyarization and clergy (including the national awakener Aleksander Dukhnovych) who strove to preserve the cultural and national identity of the Carpatho-Rusyn people.[12] As we shall see, the eparchy of Mukachevo was reduced in territorial size in 1818 and again in 1912, with the result that by the eve of World War I it contained about 450,000 adherents mostly of Carpatho-Rusyn ethnicity with smaller percentages of Slovaks, Magyars, and Romanians.[13]

Yet another church union in the Habsburg Monarchy was to affect an even larger number of people, specifically in Hungary's eastern region of Transylvania.[14] Although in 1699 Habsburg Austria succeeded in driving the Ottoman Turks out of the kingdom of Hungary, it had not yet been able to eliminate rule by Protestant princes in Transylvania. Earlier the Transylvanians had issued an Edict of Toleration (1572) that provided for equal rights for the four "privileged" religions in the region: Catholic, Lutheran, Reformed Calvinist, and Unitarian. This edict did not, however, have any positive impact on the Romanians living in Transylvania, since

---

[12] On the nationalist struggle within the Greek Catholic eparchy of Mukachevo, see ibid., 84-100.

[13] The territorially reduced Mukachevo eparchy included the Hungarian counties of Bereg and Ung, most of Maramorosh and Ugocsa, and large parts of Zemplyn, that is, the present-day Transcarpathian oblast of Ukraine, far southeastern Slovakia, and small parts of far northeastern Hungary and north central Romania.

[14] On the broader context for the union movement in Transylvania, see Ovidiu Ghitta, "The Orthodox Church in Transylvania at the End of the Seventeenth Century: The Union with the Roman Church," in *The History of Transylvania*, ed. Ioan-Aurel Pop, Thomas Nägler, and András Magyari, vol. 2 (Cluj-Napoca: Roman Academy, Center for Transylvanian Studies, 2009), esp. 381-95.

almost all of them were adherents of Orthodoxy and, therefore, were not among the "chosen" religions. Their situation changed only after 1698, when Emperor Leopold I issued a decree promising the privileges of the royal edict to any person who joined one of Transylvania's recognized religions. That incentive, together with proselytizing work carried out by Jesuit missionaries, convinced the Orthodox metropolitan of Alba Iulia and his successor to convoke synods (councils) in 1697, 1698, and 1700 that agreed to church union with Rome. A year later the union of Alba Iulia was confirmed by the Habsburg authorities, who within a decade also finally succeeded in removing from Transylvania the last of its Protestant rulers opposed to church union. The Union of Alba Iulia accepted the dogmatic points of the earlier Florentine union. Moreover, the Romanian Uniates were permitted to elect their own bishops and metropolitans (as did the Romanian Orthodox) and to use Romanian instead of Church Slavonic in the liturgy. This was one of the earliest examples of the use of a vernacular language in the Catholic church.

Initially, most of Transylvania's Orthodox clergy accepted church union, hoping to enjoy the promised improved educational opportunities and socioeconomic status enjoyed by Catholics and members of the other four privileged religions. In fact, social equality was never realized among Transylvania's Romanians, and educational improvement was slow in coming. This led in the 1740s to a widespread movement for a return to Orthodoxy, followed by an anti-Habsburg uprising among the Orthodox between 1758 and 1762. Consequently, by the 1760s only one-sixth of Transylvania's Eastern-rite adherents were Uniate, while the remaining five-sixths were Orthodox.

Nevertheless, Transylvania's Uniate (Greek Catholic) church did survive, thanks to the dynamic leadership of bishops Ion Inochentie Micu-Klein (r. 1728-51) and Petru Pavel Aron (r. 1752-64). With the assistance of the Habsburg imperial authorities they transformed the eparchy of Făgăraş, in particular its seat at Blaj, into a cultural and educational center for prospective clerics as well as lay students. The schools that came into being in Blaj were the first to teach in the Romanian language, and their graduates helped spread education in that language throughout the rest of Transylvania.[15] In effect, by the nineteenth century, the Greek Catholic

---

[15] Cyril Korolevsky, *Living Languages in Catholic Worship* (London, New York, and Toronto: Longmans, Green and Co., 1957), 15-18; Keith Hitchins, "Religious Tradition and National Consciousness among the Romanians in Transylvania, 1730-1780," *Harvard Ukrainian Studies* 10, no. 3-4 (1986): 542-58.

church in Transylvania had become an instrument to promote the Romanian national awakening.[16] In 1855, the jurisdictionally independent Greek Catholic metropolis of Alba Iulia-Făgăraş was created, with its seat in Blaj and eparchies in Blaj, Gherla, Oradea, and Lugoj. By 1900, the metropolis had over 1.2 million adherents mostly of Romanian and a smaller number (18 percent) of Magyar ethnicity.

The size and status of the Greek Catholic church within the Habsburg Monarchy as a whole was to change radically as a result of political developments in the second half of the eighteenth century. Between 1772 and 1795 Prussia, Russia, and Habsburg Austria carried out three partitions that effectively removed Poland-Lithuania from the map of Europe. As early as 1772, the Habsburgs acquired territory north of the Carpathians which they formally designated the Kingdom of Galicia-Lodomeria, or Galicia for short. Galicia's eastern half was mostly inhabited by Rusyns (officially designated Ruthenians) who by the outset of the eighteenth century had become Uniate. In 1774, Habsburg Austria officially renamed the Uniate church *Greek Catholic* and provided a seminary for it (first in Vienna, then in Lviv) to train priests. This was followed by a series of reforms that guaranteed Greek Catholics full equality with Roman Catholics (1781) and the establishment of a jurisdictionally distinct metropolitan province of Halych and Rus' with its seat in the provincial capital of Lviv (1808). The Greek Catholic metropolis of Halych and Rus' was divided into the eparchies of Lviv, Przemyśl, and later Stanyslaviv, which together encompassed by 1900 a broad network of 1894 parishes serving 3.1 million Greek Catholic faithful throughout eastern Galicia and a small part of western Galicia (the Lemko Region west of the San River along the Carpathian foothills).[17]

Until the demise of Habsburg rule in 1918, the Greek Catholic church in Austrian Galicia functioned not only as a religious institution providing spiritual comfort to its adherents, it also engaged in civic and cultural

---

[16] For details, see James Niessen, "The Greek Catholic Church and the Romanian Nation in Transylvania," in *Religious Compromise, Political Salvation*, ed. James Niessen (Pittsburgh, PA: University of Pittsburgh Center for Russian and East European Studies, 1993), 47-68; and Radu Florescu, "The Uniate Church: Catalyst of Romanian National Consciousness," *Slavic and East European Review* 45 (1967): 324-42.

[17] The classic work on the Uniate/Greek Catholics in the Habsburg Empire, especially during the early period, remains Julian Pelesz, *Geschichte der Union der ruthenischen Kirche mit Rom von den ältesten Zeiten bis auf die Gegenwart*, 2 vols. (Würzburg and Vienna: Leo Woerl, 1878-81). See also Johannes Maday, *Kirche zwischen Ost und West: Beiträge zur Geschichte der Ukrainischen und Weissruthenischen Kirche* (Munich: Ukrainische Freie Universität, 1969), 114-28 and 147-99.

activity intended to preserve the national identity of its faithful.[18] For most of the century, the Greek Catholic metropolis of Galicia was associated with a somewhat vague Slavic oriented national identity known as Old Ruthenian (*starorusyny*), but after the ascent to office in 1900 of Metropolitan Andrei Sheptytsky (r. 1900-44) the church quickly became an instrument of the Ukrainian national cause.[19]

Galicia and neighboring regions of the Habsburg Monarchy were also home to another group of Eastern Christians. These were the Armenians, who already well before the Habsburg era began settling in a few cities and towns in Galicia (Lviv, Yazlovets, Kuty) in the mid-fourteenth century and in Transylvania (Gherla/Armenierstadt, Dumbrăveni/Elisabetstadt, Gheorhieni) in the sixteenth and seventeenth centuries. Initially, all Armenians were adherents of the Holy Armenian Apostolic (Gregorian or Orthodox) Church, a distinct ecclesiastical body that at the outset of the sixth century had broken communion with the imperial Church of Constantinople as well as Rome. The Armenian Church was headed by its own primate called the *katholikos* and followed its own rite.[20]

As early as 1363, Lviv became the seat of the Armenian Apostolic bishopric, but during the seventeenth century a significant portion of the community accepted the union with Rome, which was formalized in 1685.[21] The total number of Armenians in Austria-Hungary was never very large and was to decrease further as a result of assimilation (mostly

---

[18] John Paul Himka, *Religion and Nationality in Western Ukraine: The Greek Catholic Church and the Ruthenian National Movement in Galicia, 1867-1900* (Montreal and Kingston, ON: McGill-Queens University Press, 1999); Oleh Turii, "Hreko-Katolyts'ka Tserkva ta ukrains'ka natsional'na identychnist' u Halychyni," *Kovcheh* 4 (2003): 67-85.

[19] For details on Sheptytsky's relationship to the Ukrainian movement, see Paul Robert Magocsi, ed., *Morality and Reality: The Life and Times of Andrei Sheptyts'kyi* (Edmonton: University of Alberta, Canadian Institute of Ukrainian Studies, 1989).

[20] The Armenian liturgical rite, which uses the Armenian language, is followed by both the Armenian Apostolic and Armenian Catholic churches; while it diverges from both the Roman and Byzantine rites, it also has been influenced by both. See M. D. Findikyan, "Armenian Liturgy," *New Catholic Encyclopedia,* vol. 1, 2nd ed. (Detroit: Thomson Gale), 707-11. For the basic information on the community in the Habsburg Monarchy, see Bołoz Antoniewicz, "Die Armenier [in Galizien]," in *Die österreichisch-ungarische Monarchie in Wort und Bild,* vol. 12: *Galizien* (Vienna: KK. Hof- und Staatsdruckerei, 1898), 440-62.

[21] In 1635 an Armenian Catholic archdiocese replaced the Apostolic church seat in Lviv; in 1664 an Armenian Papal Academy was founded in the same city; in 1667 and in 1685 the union with Rome was publicly declared. On the complicated process leading to the Armenian church union in Galicia, see Gregorio Petrowicz, *L'unione degli armeni di Polonia con la Santa Sede (1626-1686),* Orientalia Christiana Analecta, 135 (Rome: Pontificum Orientalium Studiorum, 1950).

with Poles and Hungarians) during the second half of the nineteenth century, from about thirteen thousand in 1857 to five thousand in 1910. Armenian Catholics were always in the majority, accounting in 1880 for 80 percent of the group (evenly divided between those in Galicia and in Transylvania) as opposed to 20 percent Armenian Apostolic adherents (almost all in Bukovina).[22]

There were yet other Greek Catholic jurisdictions that came into being in the Habsburg Monarchy. As early as 1611, in Hungarian-ruled Croatia-Slavonia, the local Orthodox bishop accepted the union. He functioned initially from the monastery at Marča as an auxiliary to the Roman-rite bishop of Zagreb and was responsible mostly for Serb and Croat refugees who fled from the Ottoman invasions. In 1777 the pope in Rome established an eparchy with a seat in Križevci for all Greek Catholics living in Hungarian-ruled Croatia-Slavonia (mostly ethnic Croats and Serbs) and the Vojvodina (mostly Bačka Rusyns).[23] The eparchy of Križevci was at first subordinate to the Roman-rite archbishop of Esztergom, but after 1853 to the Roman-rite archbishop of Zagreb. The eparchy had always been small in numbers, with only twenty-five thousand adherents in 1900 of mostly Croat and Vojvodinian Rusyn ethnicity.

In the northern part of the Hungarian kingdom, Rome approved in 1818 the establishment of the Greek Catholic eparchy of Prešov. It was created by detaching 194 parishes from the western part of the eparchy of Mukachevo; that is, territory in what is today eastern Slovakia and northeastern Hungary.[24] The ethnic composition of the eparchy of Prešov was complex. When, after 1850, the Hungarian authorities conducted the first censuses and individuals were asked to indicate their national identity or their native language, the Greek Catholics who until then described themselves as Ruthenians (*rusnaký/rusnatsi*) in the sense of belonging to the Byzantine rite or Rus' faith (*rus'ka vira*), were now being

---

[22] Wolfdieter Bihl, "Die armenischen Kirche," in *Die Habsburgermonarchie, 1848-1918*, ed. Adam Wandruszka and Peter Urbanitsch, vol. 4: *Die Konfessionen* (Vienna: Österreichishe Akademie der Wissenschaften,1985), 479-88.

[23] Paul Robert Magocsi, "Greek Catholic Eparchy of Križevci," in *Encyclopedia of Rusyn History and Culture*, ed. Paul Robert Magocsi and Ivan Pop, 2nd rev. ed. (Toronto, Buffalo, and London: University of Toronto Press, 2005), 146-47.

[24] On the establishment of the eparchy and its development down to World War I, see Aleksander Vasil'evich Dukhnovich, *Istoriia Priashevskoi eparkhii* (St. Petersburg: Peterburgskii otdiel Slavianskago komiteta, 1877 -- English translation: Alexander Duchnovič, *The History of the Eparchy of Prjašev* (Rome: Juh, 1971); and Julius Kubinyi, *The History of [the] Prjašiv Eparchy* (Rome: Universitatis Catholicae S. Clementis Papae, 1970), esp. 27-130.

officially recorded as belonging to either the Rusyn, Slovak, or Magyar nationality. At least until World War I, the eparchial seat and its administration in Prešov either associated itself with the Carpatho-Rusyn nationality or, increasingly, favored the magyarizing (national assimilationist) policies of the Hungarian government. Of its 166,000 adherents in 1891, the Prešov eparchy was divided among Carpatho-Rusyns (59 percent), "Slovjaks"—a transitional identity between Rusyns and Slovaks (26 percent), Magyars (12 percent), and Slovaks (3 percent).[25]

It was the struggle over national identity, which was couched in terms of a debate about language, that led to the establishment in 1912 of another Greek Catholic jurisdiction in Hungary, the eparchy of Hajdúdorog.[26] Ever since the creation of the first Uniate/Greek Catholic churches following the Union of Brest in 1596, one of the hallmarks of the Eastern rite had been the use of Church Slavonic as a liturgical language. Although not the vernacular language of any one ethnic group, Church Slavonic was nonetheless understandable to many Slavic speakers. It was not easy, however, for native speakers of Hungarian to learn. Therefore, in the 1860s, Magyar nationalists and pro-Hungarian Greek Catholics of Rusyn ethnicity (the so-called magyarones) began a movement to convince Rome to allow them to use the Hungarian language instead of Church Slavonic in their liturgy. When, in 1896, Rome refused to allow the use of vernacular Hungarian, the movement switched tactics and demanded the creation of a distinct eparchy. Finally, in 1912, the pope approved the creation of the eparchy of Hajdúdorog by detaching 162 parishes (70 from Mukachevo, 8 from Prešov, 44 from Oradea, and 4 from Gherla). The new eparchy, with about 215,000 members who were mostly Magyars and magyarized Rusyns, had its seat in Nyíregyháza and comprised territory in what is today northeastern Hungary and far northwestern Romania.[27]

To get around Rome's proscriptions of the use of the Hungarian vernacular - yet at the same time not wanting to use Church Slavonic - it

---

[25] Paul Robert Magocsi, "Greek Catholic Eparchy of Prešov," in Magocsi and Pop, *Encyclopedia of Rusyn History and Culture*, 149.

[26] For background information, see Paul Robert Magocsi, "Greek Catholic Eparchy of Hajdúdorog," in Magocsi and Pop, *Encyclopedia of Rusyn History and Culture*, 144-46; and István Pirigyi, *A magyarországi görög-katholikus története* (Budapest: Görög Katolikus Hittudományi Főiskola, 1990), esp. Vol.2: 83-120.

[27] James Niessen, "Hungarians and Romanians in Habsburg and Vatican Diplomacy: The Creation of the Diocese of Hajdúdorog in 1912," *Catholic Historical Review* 80, no. 2 (1994): 238-57. For details on the new eparchy's ethnic composition, see Volodymyr Fenych, "Etnonatsional'na identychnist' hreko-katolykiv Mukachivs'koï ieparkhiï, in *Istorychna shkola profesora Volodymyra Zadorozhnoho – Naukovyi zbirnyk*, 2/*Carpatika* 30 (2004), esp. 53-55.

was agreed that the official language of the Hajdúdorog eparchy would be Greek. Although an approved liturgical language, Greek was as alien as Church Slavonic for Hungarian speakers. In the end, the eparchy continued to use Hungarian in direct violation of Rome's ban on "living languages."[28] As important for the supporters of Hungarian state policy during the last decades before World War I was the fact that the eparchy of Hajdúdorog (and before it the vicariate of Hajdúdorog created in 1873) became an instrument of magyarization that successfully helped transform the non-Magyar faithful (primarily Carpatho-Rusyns) into both Hungarian speakers and staunch Magyar patriots.[29]

The Orthodox in the Habsburg Monarchy

The Orthodox Eastern Christian church derives its structure from the ancient patriarchates in the Near East of which there were four - Alexandria, Antioch, Jerusalem, and Constantinople. In early Christian times all four were located in the Roman Empire, in particular its eastern "Byzantine" half. Centuries later, central and eastern Europe came under the jurisdiction of the so-called Great Church, or Patriarchate of Constantinople (the New Rome). The head of the Great Church of New Rome was known also as the ecumenical patriarch, who resided in Constantinople (modern-day Istanbul in Turkey), the imperial capital of the Eastern Roman, or Byzantine, Empire.

In contrast to the Catholic church, where the Pope in Rome is the supreme authority ("the vicar of Jesus Christ on earth"), the authority of the ecumenical patriarch is more symbolic in nature. Since Christianity spread throughout much of central and eastern Europe under the auspices of Constantinople (New Rome, Byzantium), the ecumenical patriarch is held in high regard as "the first among equals."[30] And who are his equals?

Again, in contrast to the Catholic church, which claims universality and is organized as a centralized institution, "national" churches

---

[28] Korolevsky, *Living Languages*, 23-45.

[29] Local Rusyns, especially members of the intellectual elite working in Hungary's capital, Budapest, were among the staunchest supporters of national assimilation and of introducing the Hungarian language into the liturgy. For details, see Mária Mayer, *Kárpátukrán (ruszin) politikai és társadalmi törekvések, 1860-1910* (Budapest: Akadémia kiadó, 1977), 136-68—English translation: *The Rusyns of Hungary: Political and Social Developments, 1860-1910* (New York: Columbia University Press/East European Monographs, 1997), 153-89.

[30] On the role of the ecumenical patriarch, see Deno Geanakoplos, *A Short History of the Ecumenical Patriarchate of Constantinople: "First among Equals" in the Eastern Orthodox Church* (New York: Holy Cross Press, 1983).

characterize the jurisdictional framework of Orthodox Christianity. This process began in the fifteenth century (first in Russia 1448/1589) and developed slowly until the nineteenth century, when several Orthodox "national" churches came into being. Hence, those countries - in particular, newly independent states - with significant Orthodox populations sought to establish self-governing churches within their respective borders.

Self-governing status is connected with the existence of an autocephalous church, a body that resolves all internal issues on its own authority, including the right to appoint its own bishops, who, acting through a council/synod, elect their own primate - a patriarch, metropolitan, or archbishop. Another criterion for autocephaly is recognition of that status by other autocephalous churches. Among the ways in which the ecumenical patriarch can play out his symbolic role as "first among equals" is by heading the process of recognizing a church's autocephaly.

In theory, the various Orthodox churches function together in a communion of faith symbolized by the sharing of common beliefs, liturgical practices, ecclesiastical canons, and traditions. Among those traditions is the convening of ecumenical councils. Since no council subsequently recognized by the Orthodox as ecumenical has occurred since the eighth century, debate and controversy continue in the Orthodox world as to who has the right to grant the status of autocephaly. Is it the "mother" church to which the autocephalous claimant belongs, or is it the ecumenical patriarch who has that right on a so-called interim basis until the convening of an ecumenical council? There have been times when the ecumenical patriarch has granted autocephaly, but one or more of the existing autocephalous Orthodox churches has not accepted his decision. There also have been times when a church declared itself autocephalous but the act was not recognized by either the ecumenical patriarch or other Orthodox churches. Usually, those in communion with the ecumenical patriarch consider such unrecognized autocephalous churches "uncanonical."

Quite often, autocephaly comes about according to the following scenario. Orthodox church hierarchs in a given country declare autocephaly, which, for the good of the "national interest," is quickly recognized by the state authorities. The new body then functions as an independent "national" church until such time as the jurisdiction to which it previously belonged and the ecumenical patriarch of Constantinople both recognize its new status. The period between self-declaration and canonical recognition may vary from a few years to several centuries.

Consequently, at any one time there may be several functioning - but for various reasons not canonically recognized - Orthodox churches.

The most extensive drive toward establishing independent Orthodox churches in central Europe occurred between the late eighteenth and late nineteenth centuries, with Greece, Serbia, Montenegro, Bulgaria, and Romania each creating its own distinct jurisdictional structure.[31] It is interesting to note that the Habsburg Monarchy did not try to create a single Austrian or Austro-Hungarian Orthodox church; rather, it recognized the existence of no fewer than four jurisdictionally independent Orthodox churches within its borders.[32]

The jurisdictional aspect of Orthodoxy in the Habsburg Monarchy was related for the most part to the Serbian Orthodox church. Already in the fourteenth century the Serbs had an autocephalous church headed by a patriarch with his seat in Peć. After Serbia came under Ottoman rule in the fifteenth century, the patriarchate at Peć was initially demoted, although its patriarchal status was eventually restored (1557). In its new incarnation, the Ottomans extended the authority of the Serbian church to other lands that it had conquered in the Balkans (Montenegro, Macedonia, Bosnia-Herzegovina) as well as to the Hungarian kingdom. Hence, it was because of Ottoman military conquests that the Serbian church was granted authority over Orthodox adherents in Hungary.

During the Austrian-Ottoman military struggle for control of the Hungarian kingdom, a large number of Serbs, discontent with Ottoman rule, were granted permission by the Habsburgs to settle within their realm. This was the origin of the "Great Exodus" of 1690, during which an estimated forty thousand families of Serbs - at the head of whom was Arsenius III, the Orthodox Patriarch of Peć - crossed the Sava River and settled in the recently regained Habsburg territories of southern Hungary, that is, Slavonia and its far eastern regions (Vojvodina and Banat) as well as an area north of Budapest. Within a year of their arrival, the Habsburg ruler Leopold I granted the Orthodox Serbs several privileges outlined in a decree (*Diploma Leopoldinum*, 1691) that assured the group toleration and internal autonomy and granted its patriarch several secular responsibilities (judgment in civil disputes, collecting of feudal dues, and

---

[31] For a brief overview of the creation of Orthodox "national" churches and their relationship to the ecumenical patriarchate of Constantinople, see Magocsi, *Historical Atlas*, 216-20.

[32] For an introduction to the Orthodox churches in the Habsburg Monarchy, see Emanuel Turczynski, "Orthodoxe und Unierte," in Wandruszka and Urbanitsch, *Die Habsburgermonarchie*, Vol. 4:399-478.

disposal of heirless properties).[33] In 1737, this new community of Serbs in Hungary established (with permission of the mother church in Peć) a metropolitan province with its seat in Sremski Karlovci (in the Srem region in present-day Croatia). In 1766, when the Ottomans abolished the Peć patriarchate in their realm,[34] the Karlovci province became a jurisdictionally independent body known as the Serbian Orthodox Slav Oriental Church. Its metropolitan seat was in Sremski Karlovci and it included six suffragan eparchies (Novi Sad, Timişoara, Vršac, Buda, Pakrac, and Karlovac); hence, it had authority over the entire Hungarian kingdom, including Croatia-Slavonia. In 1848, Sremski Karlovci was raised to the status of a jurisdictionally independent patriarchate.

The Orthodox Romanians in Hungarian-ruled Transylvania, who were themselves experiencing a national awakening during the second half of the nineteenth century, were growing increasingly discontent with the Serbian-dominated patriarchate of Sremski Karlovci. Therefore, in 1864 they petitioned the Habsburg government, which granted permission (as did the Serbian patriarch at Sremski Karlovci) to create an autonomous church with its seat at Sibiu and two suffragan bishops (at Arad and Caransebeş). Thus, the Romanians of Transylvania in the eastern part of the Hungarian kingdom had their own jurisdictionally independent Orthodox church.

The last split from the Serbian Orthodox church of Sremski Karlovci occurred in 1873. The Habsburg authorities seemed anxious to have ecclesiastical jurisdictions respond to the change in the political relationship brought about in 1868 between the Hungarian kingdom and the Austrian provinces of the empire. Thus, for the first time the "Austrian half" of the empire acquired its own Orthodox jurisdiction, which encompassed the Eastern Christian faithful in two geographically dispersed Austrian provinces: Bukovina in the northern Carpathians (comprised mostly of Ruthenians/Ukrainians and Romanians) and Dalmatia along the Adriatic coast (comprised mostly of Serbs). The new

---

[33] Since privileges were granted to the Serbian Orthodox church as a body and to individual church members (not to any specific territory), Leopold I's decree was an early example of personal "national" autonomy in the Habsburg realm. On the "Great Exodus" and settlement of Serbs in Habsburg-ruled Hungary, see Robert A. Kann and Zdeněk V. David, *The Peoples of the Eastern Habsburg Lands, 1526-1918* (Seattle and London: University of Washington Press, 1984), 181-84; and Paul Pavlovich, *The History of the Serbian Orthodox Church* (Toronto: Serbian Heritage Books, 1989), 96-110.

[34] At its request, the Serbian Orthodox church in Ottoman lands was returned to the jurisdiction of the ecumenical patriarchate.

Orthodox metropolitan province of Bukovina had its seat in that region's capital of Chernivtsi as well as eparchial seats at Kotor and Zadar in more distant Dalmatia along the Adriatic coast.

The fourth Orthodox church within the Habsburg realm was connected with the empire's most recent - and effectively last - territorial acquisition. Ever since 1878 the Habsburg Monarchy maintained a dominant political influence in the Ottoman region of Bosnia-Herzegovina. Three decades later (1908) it formally annexed the region and placed it under a joint Austro-Hungarian administration. Until that time the local Orthodox inhabitants were, as in the rest of the Ottoman Empire, under the jurisdiction of the ecumenical patriarch of Constantinople. Within the new political constellation under the Habsburgs, the Orthodox church of Bosnia-Herzegovina became fully autonomous, headed by a metropolitan resident in Sarajevo and three suffragan bishops (at Mostar, Tuzla, and Banja Luka).

The Habsburg Monarchy also became a refuge for a small group of Russian Orthodox "dissidents," the Old Believers or Old Ritualists, popularly known as Lipovans (Lipovany). They are Orthodox traditionalists who refuse to accept the liturgical reforms introduced in the seventeenth century by the Russian Orthodox church. The Muscovite and later imperial Russian civil and religious authorities condemned what they referred to as schismatics (*raskol'niki*), and they persecuted and banished them to peripheral areas of the tsarist realm or abroad, including the region of Bessarabia in Moldavia. About the same time that the northern part of Moldavia, that is, Bukovina, became part of the Habsburg realm (1774), a small group of Old Believers/Lipovans were allowed to settle in northern Bukovina. There they established a monastery at Bila Krynytsia, a remote settlement just on the Ukrainian side of that country's present-day border with Romania. Although their numbers in Austria-Hungary remained small (3200 in 1900, almost all in Bukovina), Bila Krynytsia became in 1846 the ecclesiastic center for a hierarchy that exercised oversight over similar Old Believer communities in several countries.[35]

---

[35] Some Old Believers (the *bezpopovtsy*) not only rejected the seventeenth-century reformed liturgy; they faced another problem. Once their clergy died they ended up without priests and the celebration of the sacraments, owing to the fact that they did not recognize the episcopate appointed by the official church. The community in Austria-Hungary were *popovtsy;* that is, priestly Old Believers, who set up a hierarchical structure based in Bila Krynytsia. Wolfdieter Bihl, "Lippowaner," in Wandruszka and Urbanitsch, *Die Habsburgermonarchie,* vol. 3: *Die Völker des Reiches* (Vienna: Österreichishe Akademie der Wissenschaften, 1980), 968-70.

There was still another aspect of Orthodoxy that played itself out in the Habsburg Monarchy, in particular during the last few decades of its existence. I have in mind the so-called return-to-Orthodoxy movement. The movement first took form in the 1870s and 1880s in the Austrian province of Galicia, where some East Slavic (Ruthenian) clerical and secular intelligentsia, who became concerned with linking their national identity to the Rus' lands in the East, began to argue that their people should abandon the Greek Catholic church and return to the "faith of their fathers" - Orthodoxy.[36] Neighboring tsarist-ruled Russia became for these activists a symbol of Holy Rus' and what they believed was the "true," or Orthodox, Christian faith. The Austrian Habsburg authorities got wind of these activities and in 1882 held a trial of several Russophile and Old Ruthenian intellectuals. Although accused of treason against Austro-Hungarian state interests, the defendants, led by the Greek Catholic priest and prominent civic activist Ivan Naumovych, were acquitted. Soon after, most emigrated to the Russian Empire.

Another aspect of the return-to-Orthodoxy movement - and one that was much more complex and difficult for Austro-Hungarian authorities to contain - was related to the phenomenon of massive emigration between the 1880s and 1914 of East Slavic Greek Catholics from Austrian Galicia (Ruthenians) and northeastern Hungary (Carpatho-Rusyns) to the industrial regions of the northeastern United States. In the New World, Galicia's Ruthenian (later Ukrainian) and Hungary's Uhro-Rusyn Greek Catholics were met with suspicion and often outright scorn from the American Roman Catholic hierarchy (mostly of Irish origin), who found unacceptable, even sacrilegious, Greek Catholic practices which allowed for a married priesthood, a liturgy in Church Slavonic instead of Latin, and the celebration of holy days according to a different calendar.[37]

In reaction to such mistreatment by the American Roman Catholic establishment, a few Greek Catholic priests (led by Alexis Toth, now St. Alexei) and faithful broke with Rome and joined the Russian Orthodox church in North America. These immigrants - Ruthenians/Rusyns from Galicia and Subcarpathian Rus' - identified themselves not only as Orthodox, but also as Russians. Their new Orthodox communities,

---

[36] An excellent introduction to the early stages of the return to Orthodoxy movement in Galicia is found in Himka, *Religion and Nationality in Western Ukraine*, 73-78.

[37] For an introduction to the Orthodox revival among Greek Catholics in the United States before World War I, see Paul Robert Magocsi, *Our People: Carpatho-Rusyns and their Descendants in North America*, 4th rev. ed. (Wauconda, IL.: Bolchazy-Carducci Publishers, 2005), 22-27.

churches, and seminaries in North America began to receive financial assistance from the Russian imperial government, including funds directly from Tsar Nicholas II himself. Some of these new immigrant "converts" to Orthodoxy returned to their Carpathian homeland in Europe, where they convinced their fellow villagers to drive out the local Greek Catholic priest and accept instead Orthodoxy. Among the first inhabitants to return to Orthodoxy were in northeastern Hungary: Romanians in the village of Săcel (1900) and Carpatho-Rusyns in the villages of Becherov (1902), Velyki Luchky (1903), and Iza (1903).[38]

At a time when international tensions were on the rise between Austria-Hungary and the Russian Empire, the Habsburg authorities tried to nip the Orthodox revival before it developed into a widespread movement. With the assistance of the Greek Catholic clergy and secular pro-Hungarian (magyarone) activists who were opposed to identifying Carpatho-Rusyns as Russians or with anything in the East, the Hungarian government organized several trials (1901, 1904-06, 1906) at which Greek Catholic villagers from Săcel, Iza, and Velyki Luchky and a few priests were accused of treason against the state for having "converted" to Orthodoxy. The most sensational of these "treason trials" took place in the county seat of Maramorosh-Sighet in northeastern Hungary, between December 1913 and March 1914, at which 94 defendants were sentenced to varying prison terms totaling thirty-seven years.[39] As the court proceedings in Sighet were coming to an end, in neighboring Austrian Galicia another treason trial was opened in Lviv (March-June 1914), at which two Orthodox priests active in the Lemko Region as well as a student and prominent Galician Russophile journalist were accused (although eventually acquitted) of spying for Russia.

The Habsburg government's campaign against the Orthodox threat in its northeastern territories continued and even intensified after the outbreak of World War I in August 1914. Within a month, as tsarist Russian troops moved rapidly into eastern Galicia, retreating Habsburg forces killed several real or suspected Orthodox Rusyns,[40] the imperial

---

[38] On the impact of returning immigrants and the spread of Orthodoxy in the Carpathian homeland, see Mayer, *Rusyns of Hungary*, 124-52.

[39] There is an extensive literature on the Orthodox "treason" trials, especially that of 1913-14. See ibid., 139-42, and Ivan Pop, "Maramorosh Sighet trial," in Magocsi and Pop, *Encyclopedia of Rusyn History and Culture*, 321. In 2001, the main defendant at the Sighet trial, Archpriest Aleksei Kabaliuk, was canonized by the Ukrainian Orthodox church (Moscow Patriarchate) and is considered to be the first Subcarpathian Rusyn Orthodox saint.

[40] Among the victims killed in September 1914 was the Orthodox priest Maksym Sandovych,

authorities organized in Vienna two more well publicized treason trials (1915, 1916-17) and authorized the arrest in Galicia of several thousand Ruthenians (especially of the Old Ruthenian and Russophile orientation), who were deported to Europe's first concentration camps set up at places like Thalerhof in the western part of the Habsburg lands.[41] The treason trials in Hungary and the wartime arrests in Galicia did, indeed, succeed in containing the return-to-Orthodoxy movement. It did not die, however, and was to take on even greater intensity in central Europe's new political configuration that came into being after the disappearance of Austria-Hungary in late 1918.[42]

Concluding Remarks

Despite comprising nearly 19 percent of the population of the Habsburg Monarchy (1900), Eastern Christians (whether Greek Catholics or Orthodox) generally did not have a high profile or play an influential role in Austria-Hungary. One reason for this had to do with the socioeconomic status of both Greek Catholics and Orthodox, the vast majority of whom were peasant-serfs until as late as 1848. Another reason had to do with the fact that the Habsburg imperial family were staunch defenders of Roman Catholicism, which remained the religion that governed the official, social, and cultural order of Austria-Hungary until its very demise in 1918. Other religions may have been tolerated, whether Protestantism, Judaism, Islam, and other Catholic rites (Armenian and Byzantine Greek), but any serious advance within society, whether on an individual or corporate level, was generally reserved to those who were (or who became through conversion) Roman Catholic.

---

acquitted only a few months before at the Lviv treason trial, who as a result of his martyrdom for the faith was proclaimed St. Maksym by the Polish Autocephalous Orthodox church in 1994. On the wartime persecution of the Orthodox, most especially among the Lemko Rusyns of Galicia, where the Habsburg-tsarist Russian conflict was at its most intense, see the entries by Bogdan Horbal, "'Talerhof' and 'Vienna trials'," in Magocsi and Pop, *Encyclopedia of Rusyn History and Culture*, 488-89 and 530; for the larger context of these developments, see Mark von Hagen, *War in a European Borderland: Occupations and Occupation Plans in Galicia and Ukraine, 1914-1918* (Seattle and London: University of Washington Press, 2007).

[41] At the two Vienna trials, all thirty-one defendants (Galician Russophile political and cultural activists) were found guilty and twenty-four sentenced to death (later commuted by the emperor).

[42] During the 1920s in Czechoslovak-ruled Subcarpathian Rus' and the Prešov Region, and in the Polish-ruled Lemko Region, no less than one-third of the Greek Catholic Carpatho-Rusyn inhabitants converted ("returned") to Orthodoxy.

It is true that after the 1860s the archbishops of all churches were appointed *ex officio* to the upper chamber (House of Lords) of the Austrian and Hungarian parliaments. Nevertheless, those Greek Catholic and Orthodox prelates generally played no particular role in the empire's civic life and its governmental decision-making process. Somewhat of an exception was the Greek Catholic bishop (1899) and long-term metropolitan (1900-44) of Galicia, Andrei Sheptytsky, who was able to move about easily and have some influence within the highest levels of Habsburg governmental and secular society. It is no coincidence that this was possible not only because Sheptytsky held the aristocratic title of count, but also because he was born and raised a Roman Catholic who only later in life changed to the Byzantine (Greek) Catholic rite.

There was one area in which both Greek Catholic and Orthodox churches did leave a lasting impact. What I have in mind is the Austro-Hungarian cultural landscape enriched by church architecture, interior design, and religious paintings. Many of the Greek Catholic and Orthodox cathedral churches were built or reconstructed with Eastern Christian elements, whether on the eve of or during Habsburg rule. To this day they make a distinct and often aesthetically pleasing impact on the urban landscape. Among such structures that immediately come to mind are the Greek Catholic cathedrals in Lviv (St. George), Uzhhorod, Prešov, and the monumental Orthodox cathedral church and episcopal palace in Chernivtsi (since 1945 the seat of the University of Chernivsti). Although all these structures contain iconostases covered with images done in traditional two-dimensional style, the Eastern Christian prelates also engaged artists to decorate other parts of the interiors (including Tiepolo-like Baroque ceilings) with frescoes and portraits of religious figures in the figurative style of late nineteenth century central Europe.[43]

Aside from monumental structures based in large urban centers, the Habsburg authorities were also concerned with rural religious edifices in the countryside. Empress Maria Theresa commissioned architects to create standardized designs for the construction of masonry churches that came to dominate many villages inhabited primarily by Greek Catholic adherents. Less appreciated at the time were Eastern Christian Carpathian village structures built entirely in wood. In the late twentieth century, these

---

[43] Post-Communist central and eastern Europe has seen extensive restoration efforts of Greek Catholic cathedral churches, as depicted recently in several lavishly illustrated publications, such as Szilvester Terdik, *Görögkatolikus püspöki központok Magarországon a 18. században: művészet és reprezentáció* (Nyíregyháza: Szent Atanáz Görögkatolikus Hittudományi Főiskola, 2014); Andrej Pribula et al., *Prešovské biskupstvo* (Prešov: DINO, 2008).

rustic gems were "discovered" by foreign and domestic connoisseurs who now rank them among the greatest achievements of European religious architecture.[44] In post-Communist times many of these urban and rural Eastern Christian structures (exteriors and interiors) have been restored in such a way that today they probably exceed their original aesthetic glory.

Hence, whereas the Austro-Hungarian Habsburg Monarchy is long gone, the Eastern Christian world that it welcomed and supported from the sixteenth through early twentieth centuries continues to live through the witness of an increasing number of faithful and through the visible presence of architectural monuments that in some places dominate the cultural landscape of the empire's successor states.

---

[44] There is an extensive literature on wooden church architecture in the Carpathians, most of which came into being during Habsburg times. For a useful introduction that compares Carpathian churches with those in other parts of Europe, see David Buxton, *The Wooden Churches of Eastern Europe* (Cambridge: University of Cambridge Press, 1981).

Politics, Religion, and Confessional Identity among the Romanians of Bistriţa: A Case Study

Sever Cristian Oancea

After proving successful in the Hereditary Lands, the Habsburg Counter-Reformation gradually gained ground in Hungary,[1] and by the end of the seventeenth century, it reached multiethnic and multireligious Transylvania.[2] With the new political context, the Romanians became part of the Habsburg catholicization strategy.[3] Thus, following Vienna's proposals, the Romanian church held several synods, and at the end of the seventeenth century, the Transylvanian Orthodox clergy united with the

---

[1] A concise presentation of this process is in Robert J.W. Evans, "Die Grenzen der Konfessionalisierung: Die Folgen der Gegenreformation für die Habsburgerländer (1650-1781)," in *Konfessionalisierung in Ostmitteleuropa: Wirkungen des religiösen Wandels im 16. und 17. Jahrhundert in Staat, Gesellschaft und Kultur*, ed. Joachim Balcke and Arno Strohmayer (Stuttgart: Franz Steiner Verlag, 1999), 395-413. See also the volume edited by Rudolf Leeb et al., *Geheimprotestantismus und evangelische Kirchen in der Habsburgermonarchie und im Erzstift Salzburg (17/18. Jahrhundert)* (Vienna: Böhlau, 2009).

[2] Transylvania was annexed by the Habsburgs at the end of the seventeenth century. Political and religious privileges were granted through the *Diploma Leopoldinum* (1691). The political estates were represented by the nobles, Saxons, and Szeklers. The four "accepted" religions were Catholicism (Hungarians and Szeklers), Lutheranism (Saxons), Calvinism (Hungarians and Szeklers), and Unitarianism (Hungarians and a few Saxons from Cluj). The Romanians were not part of the political estates, and Orthodoxy was only "tolerated." However, Catholics had only a vicar, while the Orthodox church was placed under the jurisdiction of a metropolitan bishop in Alba Iulia (Gyulafehérvár/Karlsburg).

[3] The Habsburg Counter-Reformation in Transylvania relied on the reestablishment of the Catholic bishopric in Alba Iulia, the Catholic "party," the mission of the Catholic orders, and the implementation of the union of the Orthodox church with Rome, which the historiography has perceived as an *instrumentum regni*. The Viennese policy also aimed at weakening the power base of the Protestants through the conversion of all Romanians to Catholicism. For a general study of the Counter-Reformation in Transylvania, see: Zsolt Trócsanyi, "Az ellenreformáció Erdélyben 1711-től a felvilágosult abszolutizmus kezdeteig," *Theológiai Szemle* 22 (1979): 219-26. For the religious policy on the *Königsboden* and conversion to Catholicism, see Sever Cristian Oancea, "Catholic Seduction or Habsburg Clientele? Denominational Change in the Eighteenth-Century Transylvanian Saxon Society," *Colloquia Journal of Central European History* 15 (2008): 5-30. For the specific Romanian case, see Mathias Bernath, *Habsburg und die Anfänge der Rumänischen Nationsbildung* (Leiden: E.J. Brill, 1972), 69-135, and more recently, Greta Monica Miron, *"...poruncește, scoală-te, du-te, propoveduește..." Biserica greco-catolică din Transilvania. Cler și enoriași* (Cluj-Napoca: Presa Universitară Clujeană, 2005), 31-61.

church of Rome (1697-1701).[4] The union with Rome was encouraged by Vienna, the Jesuits, and the Transylvanian Romanian ecclesiastical hierarchy, but it also engendered heated Orthodox anti-Uniate propaganda. The period 1744-61 was marred by religious disputes, many communities being "conquered" by the Orthodox message. The first serious challenge occurred in 1744, when the Orthodox monk Visarion Sarai[5] promoted a virulent anti-Uniate discourse in Southern Transylvania.[6] Even though the Uniate counter-action aimed at both reconquering "lost ground" and building an identity discourse,[7] the Orthodox movement continued to spread into the northern regions of the principality. In this regard, Sofronie of Cioara's movement (1759-61)[8] represented the strongest attack ever encountered by the Uniate church in Transylvania. Addressing a less educated rural clergy[9] and an insufficiently catechized population,[10] its message reached even the

---

[4] For the entire context of the union with Rome, see Bernath, *Habsburg und die Anfänge der Rumänischen Nationsbildung*, 69-135.

[5] For a detailed description of Visarion Sarai's action against the union with Rome, see Greta Monica Miron, "Acţiune ortodoxă -- acţiune catolică. Efectele mişcării lui Visarion Sarai în Hunedoara, Haţeg, Zarand şi Alba," *Studia Universitis Babeş-Bolyai Historia* 50 (2005): 1-36.

[6] In this discourse Uniate priests were "non-priests," their sacraments invalid, and the believers were advised not to accept the religious services of the Uniate clergy because this was a mistake that would lead them to hell. Miron, "Acţiune ortodoxă," 1.

[7] For a detailed analysis of the identity discourse, see Ciprian Ghişa, *Biserica Greco-Catolică din Transilvania (1700-1850). Elaborarea discursului identitar* (Cluj-Napoca: Presa Universitară Clujeană, 2006); idem., "Aspects of Confessional Alterity in Transylvania: The Uniate -- Non-Uniate Polemic in the Eighteenth Century" in this collection; and Pompiliu Teodor, "The Confessional Identity of the Transylvanian Greek Catholic Church," in *Confessional Identity in East-Central Europe*, ed. Maria Crăciun, Ovidiu Ghitta, and Graeme Murdock (Aldershot: Ashgate, 2002): 167-80.

[8] Sofronie of Cioara was an Orthodox monk from Transylvania. After entering a monastery in Wallachia, he returned to Transylvania. Apparently, he had contacts with the metropolitan bishop of Karlowitz, and starting in 1759, he began his struggle for Orthodoxy in Transylvania.

[9] In his report of 1761, Bishop Petru Pavel Aron remarked that not only the believers, but also many priests did not know the significance of the union with the church of Rome: Florin Valeriu Mureşan, *Satul românesc din Nord-Estul Transilvaniei la mijlocul secolului al XVIII-lea* (Cluj-Napoca: Institutul Cultural Român, 2005), 262.

[10] In a letter to the Transylvanian treasury, the vicar Atanasie Rednic explained that the Romanians could not be won over through dogma, but only with the help of visible examples. In his letter to the Austrian Central Treasury (*Hofkammer*), Count Bornemisza remarked "that this people can be attracted towards and maintained within the only blessed Roman church and doctrine only through visible practices and not through profound secrets, which in most cases they do not understand...." Helmut Klima, "Die Union der Siebenbürger Rumänen und der Wiener Staatsrat im theresianischen Zeitalter," *Südostdeutsche Forschungen* 6 (1941): 250-53.

remote and officially Uniate north of the principality, managed to "reconvert" entire villages to Orthodoxy, and remodeled the religious behavior of many communities. The religious strategy of the Habsburgs and the Uniate church was to reconquer the "lost ground." It proved the least successful in southern Transylvania, partially successful in the center, and "successful" in the remote northern Bistrița district in the context of the militarization of the Rodna Valley.

This article discusses the manner in which the political, social, and religious context of the eighteenth century shaped the religious affiliation of the Romanian community living in northeastern Transylvania, more precisely the Bistrița district during the anti-Union movement in Transylvania. The focus is on the events surrounding the movement of Sofronie, the census undertaken by the Habsburgs under General Adolf Nikolaus Buccow,[11] and the incorporation of the Rodna Valley into the Habsburg Military Frontier (1761-63). Based on research on eighteenth-century religious communities in Transylvania and especially on Saxon or royal land, the so-called *Königsboden* (*Fundus Regius*), I look at the question of how confessional affiliation was determined during the Union crisis of 1761-63. I argue that religious labeling constituted a politically established process, which depended heavily on the clash between Vienna's religious policies and the local political, religious, and social contexts. In this sense, religious labeling overpowered to a certain extent the *self*-perception linked to denominational affiliation. Starting from the case study of Bistrița (Bistritz/Besterce), I argue that, unlike the southern regions of the principality, the union with Rome in Bistrița was severely challenged for the first time only in 1761. According to the sources, until that year, the challenges and disputes within the Romanian community had been political, economic, and social. It was only when Sofronie's movement emerged that the confessional factor started to represent a challenge within the Romanian communities. The denomination of the Romanians living in northeast Transylvania was officially "Uniate" (Greek Catholic), even if Orthodoxy survived in many forms. Thus, in my view, the Orthodox revolt in Bistrița (1761) had no local roots; it was imported from outside, but afterward enjoyed support from certain local leaders. Nevertheless, Buccow's census proved that Romanian society was not sufficiently catechized to understand the significance of the union with

---

[11] Adolf Nicholas von Buccow (1712-64) was a general named military commander in Transylvania. In 1761 he headed the commission whose task was the resolution of the Romanian religious issue.

Rome. It could not assess its own "dogmatic" denomination, and therefore the religious identity could be easily "interpreted" and, to a certain extent, arbitrarily determined by political actors. In these circumstances, Bistrița became a disputed territory, since the court strove to achieve the complete reinstatement of Greek Catholicism in northeast Transylvania, which had initially succeeded only in theory. The real conversion to Greek Catholicism was determined by the political and ecclesiastical actors and achieved in the context of military support and over the course of several decades.

The Local Political, Social, and Denominational Context before 1761

The Romanians living in northeast Transylvania were situated in a borderland of the principality, in the proximity of Maramureș (Máramaros) county (Hungary, later Transylvania) and Orthodox Moldavia (a Romanian principality under Ottoman suzerainty). They lived in the district of Bistrița, an administrative entity that was part of the *Königsboden*[12] and Rodna.[13] It was therefore under Saxon political jurisdiction. The district's administration pertained to the *Magistrat* (town council) in Bistrița and had two components: Bistrița (the Saxon district) and Rodna (the Romanian district). In Rodna, the Romanians formed the majority population and enjoyed extensive rights, such as their own village judges and tax collectors. In addition, similarly to other Romanians living in the noble counties (*comitates*), they had their own churches. In Bistrița, the Romanians were in a minority. Here, they lived in a territory with a special political and juridical status, inhabited by a Lutheran Saxon majority. In this territory, which included the town of Bistrița, the Romanians (but also the Hungarians and Szeklers) had no right to own land (*Landrecht*) and consequently had only a few churches. This situation underwent a gradual change in the new Habsburg context.

The Habsburg Counter-Reformation extended over the Orthodox population of Transylvania, and by the end of the seventeenth century, the Orthodox church in Bistrița had undergone an institutional transformation as well, namely the union with the church of Rome. Here,

---

[12] *Königsboden* [Lat. *Fundus Regius*, Ro. *Pământul Crăiesc*, Hu. *Királyföld*] is a territory of Transylvania also known as the Saxon Land. For details about its special organization and status, see Zsuszanna Cziráki, *Az erdélyi szászok története Erdélyi szász irodolomtérténet*, (Kozálmisleny: Imedias Kiadó, 2006), 20-24.

[13] The Rodna Valley was given to the people of Bistrița by King Mathias of Hungary in the fifteenth century (1469, renewed in 1475, and reconfirmed by King Vladislas II in 1498). The town lost this territory in 1763, in the context of the extension of the Habsburg Military Frontier.

the church union was institutionalized from the very beginning,[14] and starting in 1715, Năsăud (Naszód/Nassod/Nußdorf) became the final residence of the Uniate archdeacons or archpriests. The archdeacons became an elite clergy; their allegiance to the church of Rome was constant during the eighteenth century, and they openly expressed it.[15]

As for the lower clergy, the statistics of 1733[16] and 1750[17] reveal a Uniate majority. However, only a small number of priests from Bistriţa attended the local Catholic grammar school (*gymnasium*).[18] Moreover, during the first two decades after the church union, a large part of the clergy accepted it only after having been ordained by Orthodox bishops in Maramureş and Moldavia. This trend continued during the sixth decade as well, but officially it was no longer so widely spread in Bistriţa.[19] This raises the question of how genuine or sincere the Uniate priests were about the Union, and hence whether they were capable of effectively propagating the union among their communities. In the absence of sources describing their profession of faith, level of catechization, and even clerical formation, we can only suppose that their religious behavior was either determined by their wish to gain legitimacy or by the privileges

---

[14] The archdeacon Costel of Şieuţ was among the signatories of the 1698 church union manifesto. Moreover, in 1700, he and twenty other priests from this region accepted the union with Rome. Ştefan Buzilă, "Protopopii şi vicarii Năsăudului," *Arhiva Someşană* 27 (1940): 302.

[15] For instance, in 1745, the archdeacon Atanasie Anton signed a declaration of commitment to the church union, and in 1762, the newly elected archdeacon of Năsăud, Dumitru Naszodi, expressed his allegiance to the church of Rome. Miron, *"...porunceşte, scoală-te, du-te, propovedueşte....,"* 476, 477.

[16] According to Inochenţie Micu's statistics, out of the eighty-two priests in Bistriţa, only ten were Orthodox: Virgil Şotropa, "Două tablouri istoricǫ statistice din anii 1714-1733 privitoare la preoţii români din Valea Someşului," *Anuarul Institutului de Istorie Naţională Cluj* 2 (1923): 383-89.

[17] According to the statistics of Petru Pavel Aron, in Rodna the district there were only eight non-Uniate priests, but subsequently they were mentioned as "schismatic under the protection of the archdeacon." Mureşan, *Satul românesc*, chapter 9, endnote 107.

[18] Romanians coming from the district of Bistriţa are quite rarely encountered in the list published by Virgil Şotropa. For a list of all the Romanians who studied at the Piarist gymnasium, see Virgil Şotropa, "Români la gimnaziul latino-catolic din Bistriţa 1729-1779," *Transilvania* (1901): 3-17. A complete list of all the students can be found in the Archive of the Roman Catholic Church of Gherla.

[19] The protocol from Blaj (Blasendorf, Balázsfalva, the seat of the Uniate bishop) includes a list of priests who embraced the church union in 1755. Here I could find only one priest from this district who had been ordained in Moldavia. Biblioteca Academiei, Filiala Cluj-Napoca [henceforth BAFCN], Fond Manuscrise Latine 279, f. 6.

entailed by the Uniate priestly status.[20] However, their allegiance to the church of Rome determined denominational stabilization and herewith the weakening of local Orthodoxy. Thus, sources referring to religious tension in northeast Transylvania before 1761 are quite rare and rather contradictory.[21] Moreover, due to the geographic remoteness from the south, the anti-Uniate propaganda promoted by Visarion Sarai did not reach this region.[22] During the first decades of the eighteenth century, Orthodoxy arrived here from the other side of the Carpathians. Furthermore, the sources that I examined do not mention any aggressive Orthodox stance towards Greek Catholicism.[23] Quite to the contrary, sources from the epoch give the impression of peaceful coexistence and even cooperation.[24]

As Remus Câmpeanu argues in his book, the denominational stability enabled the crystallization of a "model" Uniate church.[25] Throughout the eighteenth century, the archdeacons of Năsăud claimed privileges and exemptions for their Uniate clergy (and also their families) based on the Diploma of Leopold.[26] In addition, they pressed - with constant Habsburg support - for extensive rights for the Uniate church on the *Königsboden*, such as the building of churches and *portio canonica* for the clergy.[27] Their politics generated a situation that was not atypical of the other regions of

---

[20] Conversely, my colleague Ciprian Ghişa maintains that the Uniate clergy had a genuine Uniate identity. His argument is based on the fact that, despite not having always been granted privileges, the priests remained faithful to the Uniate church.

[21] Sever Cristian Oancea, "Înainte de Sofronie. Românii din Bistriţa la răspântia dintre unire şi ortodoxie," *Şcoala Ardeleană* 4 (2010): 240-47.

[22] The information concerning Orthodox agitation in Bistriţa is quite contradictory. In 1745, Count Haller wrote to the *magistrat* in Bistriţa warning about the Orthodox propaganda. Only two years later the magistrate was accused by the Transylvanian Government [Gubernium] of having supported Orthodox priests against Uniate ones. However, according to the archdeacon, there was no anti-Union propaganda in the district. Virgil Sotropa, Al. Ciplea, "Documente bisericeşti," *Arhiva Someşană* 1 (1924): 25-28.

[23] Oancea, "Înainte de Sofronie," 242.

[24] I refer here to the consecration of the Sângeorz monastery in the presence of the archdeacon and "hinländige Vicarius." It was founded by a former Orthodox Bishop from Moldavia, Mihail. Oancea, "Înainte de Sofronie," 245.

[25] This is an expression that Remus Câmpeanu used to describe the evolution of the Năsăud vicariate in the eighteenth century. Remus Câmpeanu, *Elitele româneşti din Transilvania în veacul al XVIII-lea* (Cluj-Napoca: Presa Universitară Clujeană, 2000), chapter "Un vicariat etalon," 218-33.

[26] Ibid., 219.

[27] For a detailed account, see Virgil Şotropa, "Lupta românilor bistriţeni pentru biserică," *Arhiva Someşană* (1937): 31-39; and idem, "Soarta românilor din satele săseşti," *Arhiva Someşană* 18 (1936): 275-345.

the principality. On the one hand, the union and the Uniate clergy encountered the opposition of the town administration or local council (*Magistrat*), which hardly complied with the Uniate church and Viennese policy. Many eighteenth-century conflicts and complaints reveal this tension in the district. On the other hand, the politics of the Năsăud archdeacons and Uniate clergy met with some resistance within the local Romanian community, especially from certain village judges and tax collectors. Many sources from the epoch refer to such episodes.[28] The tension increased during the revolt of the Rodna district against the *Magistrat* in Bistrița (1755-62), when the Uniate clergy allied with the rebels and supported Ştefan Cute (the leader of the revolt) against the *Magistrat* and also against the Romanian judges and tax collectors (who were the traditional allies of the *Magistrat*). In the course of these events, even the archdeacon had to flee to Moldavia for a short period in order to avoid being accused of instigation by the town council. These events proved that the Romanian community was far from being socially uniform and was in fact divided by different group interests. Sofronie's uprising reached Bistrița in this tense context.

The Church Union Crisis: Sofronie's Uprising in Bistrița

In 1759, the Habsburgs finally acknowledged that the conversion of all Romanians to Greek Catholicism did not have the expected outcome. On account of this, the Viennese court adopted a new religious strategy and issued an edict of toleration (*Toleranzpatent*), which reestablished the Orthodox church in Transylvania (13 July 1759). The objective of this patent was to control Orthodoxy within a well-defined framework.[29] Nevertheless, the Viennese strategy failed and the Orthodox movement continued to "conquer" entire Romanian-inhabited regions.

Sofronie's movement began in 1759 through the dissemination of a false imperial order, according to which the Romanians were allowed to choose their denomination freely. In reality, the imperial order stipulated that all those who had declared themselves Uniate before 13 July 1759

---

[28] Most of the conflicts between the clergy and the tax collectors pertained to the taxation of priests or members of their families. Very often, the priests threatened to excommunicate the collectors. In the archives in Cluj, I found accounts of many such cases, some of them being presented by Virgil Şotropa in his study of the Romanians' revolt against the *magistrat*: Virgil Şotropa, "Revolta districtului năsăudean 1755-1762," *Arhiva Someşană* 22, 23 (1937, 1938).

[29] Pompiliu Teodor, "Die Konfessionspolitik der Habsburger in Siebenbürgen (1692-1759): Der rumänische Fall," *Colloquia Journal of Central European History* 1 (1994): 147-48.

could no longer change their denomination. However, Sofronie recommended that the Romanians assemble and choose "the Greek law and rite, under the leadership of the church of Jerusalem." Moreover, he ordered that the keys of churches be confiscated from Uniate priests.[30] The activity was supported by emissaries who read the famous Sofronian letters. Sofronie's message successfully expanded from the southern part of the principality[31] to the central and northern parts, more precisely to the counties of Cluj (Kolozs),[32] Dăbâca (Szolnok-Doboka),[33] and the Bistriţa district. Even the remote county of Szatmár (Sathmar/Satu-Mare) could not withstand the Orthodox revolt.[34]

The religious uprising in Bistriţa began in this context, when the Sofronian message reached northeast Transylvania. Greek Catholic historians have argued that the advent of the Orthodox emissaries in Bistriţa was the direct result of a plot of Lutheran Saxons against the union with Rome[35] and in complicity with the local Romanian judges and tax collectors. However, the sources mention no direct involvement of the Saxons or the town administrations in the anti-Uniate movement. The active complicity of the Romanian local leaders in the revolt against the Uniate clergy is indeed mentioned by several sources. Thus, the final report of a royal commission under Buccow states: "The commission understood with indignation that the servants, soldiers, as well as the town and district tax collectors, who were mostly Romanians, not only left the union, but also instigated the people against it."[36] In another article, Virgil Şotropa mentions that the tax collector Lazăr from Năsăud urged the locals as well as the inhabitants of the district in general to lock the churches; he lied to them that the local Saxons promised that there would be no punishment for their actions.[37] I could not confirm this in the

---

[30] Greta-Monica Miron, *Biserica greco-catolică din Comitatul Cluj în secolul al XVIII-lea* (Cluj-Napoca: Presa Universitară Clujeană, 2007), 73-74.

[31] For a general view of Sofronie's uprising in Transylvania, see: Augustin Bunea, *Episcopii Petru Pavel Aron şi Dionisiu Novacovici sau Istoria Românilor transilvăneni de la 1751 până la 1764* (Blaş, 1902); and Silviu Dragomir, *Istoria desrobirei religioase a românilor din Ardeal în secolul al XVIII-lea*, vol. 2 (Sibiu, 1930).

[32] Miron, *Biserica greco-catolică*, 73-147.

[33] Greta-Monica Miron, "Viaţă parohială şi diversitate confesională în Transilvania secolului al XVIII-lea," in *Studiu de caz: uniţi şi ortodoşi din comitatul Dăbâca* (Cluj-Napoca: Argonaut, 2016), 85-118.

[34] Ovidiu Ghitta, *Naşterea unei biserici. Biserica greco-catolică din Sătmar în primul ei secol de existenţă 1667-1761* (Cluj-Napoca: Presa Universitară Clujeană, 2001), 302-38.

[35] Buzilă, "Protopopii şi vicarii Năsăudului," 350.

[36] Şotropa, "Lupta românilor bistriţeni," 475.

[37] Virgil Şotropa, "Mănăstiri şi călugări în Valea Rodnei," *Arhiva Someşană* 27 (1940): 373.

sources, but the statement that the plot was organized by the tax collectors "who were mostly Romanians" allows us to question who the others were and speculate that they were perhaps Saxons. The involvement of the Romanian tax collectors is confirmed by another important source: the Uniate archdeacon Anton Naszodi's account of the revolt. In it he mentioned certain judges and tax collectors who acted against the union. In addition, he argued that the main instigator was Maxim Gallan of Năsăud,[38] an allegation also confirmed by the town council. Maxim Gallan converted to the "schism" as a result of Sofronie's appeal.[39]

Other sources mention that Ştefan Cute, a direct collaborator of the Uniate clergy and especially of archdeacon Anton Naszodi during the revolt against the town council, had contacts with the Sofronian emissaries as well as certain Uniate priests.[40] This means that just as in the other regions of the principality, the Sofronian emissaries looked for support among the local leaders, and their presence in the region must be associated with the gradual spread of the revolt to the Uniate territories in the north. In my view, the revolt was not simply the result of a local plot against the Uniate church. This may be confirmed by the fact that the anti-Uniate ideas reached this area only six months after the Romanians in Bistriţa had "found out" from Sofronie's message that their priests had changed their denomination.[41] Nevertheless, the revolt was mainly backed by certain local leaders who had been in conflict with the clergy in the past. It is thus fair to ask how anti-Uniate the revolt was, and whether it was a religious uprising or merely a revolt against the Uniate clergy, but as Greta-Monica Miron has suggested to me, a confessional conflict should not be excluded. While an unequivocal answer cannot be found because of a lack of sources, it can be argued that just as in other regions of the principality, the success of the Sofronian movement in Bistriţa depended on the effectiveness of the Orthodox emissaries, on how well they promoted Sofronie's viewpoint, and especially on how local communities perceived and evaluated what they had to say. Certainly, the impact was similar to the other regions: churches were locked and priests were prevented from serving at the altar or lost their parishioners.

---

[38] Oancea, "Înainte de Sofronie."

[39] Şotropa, "Mănăstirişi," 351.

[40] When Ştefan Cute was arrested, they found on him not only Sofronie's message but also several letters from Uniate priests advising him not to follow Sofronie. Şotropa, "Mănăstirişi," 399-400.

[41] Most Romanians answered during the census organized by the *magistrat* that they had found out about the church union during the Sân' Petru rebellion in July 1760.

According to the testimonies taken during the census ordered by General Adolf von Buccow in Transylvania soon after he arrived to Sibiu (Hermannstadt/Nagyszeben) in 1761, Sofronie's revolt first reached Sigmir (Schönbrik/Szépnyer) in the Bistrița district in December 1760, and within three months it extended over almost all the villages of the Rodna Valley.[42] As in other regions of the principality, Sofronie's action rested on the circulation of the "imperial" letters from village to village. The letter containing three - most likely fake - imperial seals was read out loud before the assembled population. They were told that the empress had decreed that Romanians should return to the "old Greek law" and thus banish the Uniate priests from their churches. The text of the Sofronian message read out in Bistrița can be found in the *magistrat*'s description of the Orthodox revolt in Năsăud (March 1761, collected from the judge Kapro Szimion). It was presented as having been sent by the vicar Sofronie of Zlatna and had the following content:

> God and the magnanimous Queen took mercy on you, to show you the path to the old Greek law so that you turn towards the Orient. Her Highness dispatched a commission to Hermannstadt, which shall visit the entire country, being empowered to banish all the Uniate priests from the churches. For this reason, you must banish all your Uniate priests immediately; otherwise, you will have to build your own churches.[43]

The message was backed by intense missionary activity and, sometimes, violent actions against the Uniate clergy. In his account of the Orthodox revolt, the archdeacon Anton Naszodi mentions that the Sofronian emissaries went everywhere. Moreover, they enjoyed the support of certain Romanian leaders in the region. They established contacts with apostate priests and brought communion from the Orthodox priests in the

---

[42] Sources on the chronology of the Sofronian revolt in Bistrița are quite rare. With a few exceptions, we can only reconstruct it on the basis of the declarations collected by the Saxon senators during the census. However, in certain cases the information seems to contradict other sources. Thus, according to the peasants' testimony, the Orthodox message arrived at Sigmir in December 1760. The attack against the union in the district started in January 1761 and continued until March.

[43] Arhivele Naționale, Direcția Județeană Cluj (henceforth ANDJC), Fond Primăria Orașului Bistrița, Seria II a, Fasc 253, f. 9.

neighboring Dăbâca county,[44] a region where Orthodoxy had remarkable success.[45] As a result, similarly to the counties of Cluj and Dăbâca, almost all churches in the region were locked and the Uniate priests were no longer allowed to celebrate the liturgy. Uniate communion was presented to the peasants as cursed, and in certain cases priests were attacked. Thus, the priests at Sântioana (Szászszentiván/Johannisdorf) were attacked in their homes; in Mocod (Mácod/Makendorf), the priests were named "impure" [spurkatz],[46] and even in Năsăud - the center of the Uniate church in the region - the Orthodox movement was victorious. Here, the church was locked by force as well.[47] In another case, the peasants accepted the service of the Orthodox priests who came from Moldavia. Nevertheless, the lack of any mention in the documents suggests that the villages in the Saxon district were not affected by the movement.[48]

Apparently, the Sofronian message received no support from the local clergy. A report of the *magistrat* addressing the issue of the Orthodox revolt reveals that the Sofronian letter had to circulate from village to village and had to be read out only by non-Uniate deacons. In addition, we are told that only Năsăud did not have a single non-Uniate deacon.[49] This implies

---

[44] Magyar Országos Levéltár (henceforth MOL), B2, Erdélyi Kancelláriai Levéltár, Acta Generalia, microfilm, 30379, 405.

[45] See also Greta-Monica Miron, "Confessional Coexistence and Conflict in Eighteenth-Century Transylvania. Case Study: The Movement Led by Sofronie in Dăbâca County," *Studia* 58 (2013): 95-123.

[46] MOL, 406.

[47] The report of the *magistrat* describing the violence against Popa [Father] Mitru according to the testimony of Kapro Szimion: "As soon as they found out about this, the entire village went to the church, Father Mitru was also there, they told him about the order, but he had the keys in his hands and he showed them to them and protested by saying: 'Here are [the keys], I do not want to give them to you voluntarily. Whoever wants to have them [should] come and take them.' The village had him stopped in order to take the keys away, but he did not want to do this voluntarily, and five jurors went to him and locked the church. When the keys were handed over, [Father Mitru] protested once again. They sent this edict on the day when they received it from Salva." Kapro Szimion also mentions that the churches of the entire Romanian district were locked. ANDJC, Fond Primăria Oraşului Bistriţa, Seria II a, Fasc. 253, f. 9.

[48] In my view, there are several explanations for this. First, the Sofronian emissaries either were not present there, or they did not find any support from the local leaders, because here the only Romanian authority was the priest. Secondly, the Romanians living in these villages received and claimed certain rights on account of their religious status as Greek Catholics (Uniates). Consequently, the abnegation of this status would have triggered the loss of these rights. Finally, not all the Romanians had churches and priests in their villages, and therefore the typical Sofronian revolt, characterized by attacks against the clergy and the closure of churches, could not take place there.

[49] ANDJC, Fond Primăria Oraşului Bistriţa, Seria II a, Fasc. 253, f. 9.

that, unlike in Dăbâca, the clergy involved in the anti-Uniate movement was not local, since officially there were only a few Orthodox priests in the district and the involvement of the Uniates is not registered in the sources. Nevertheless, the critical question for scholars researching the other regions of the principality is why the communities suddenly repudiated their priests and gave more credit to foreign missionaries. Were they indeed convinced that the Uniate communion was cursed or that the priests changed or betrayed "the old Greek Romanian Law"? If we consider the low level of catechization, we can assume that fear of religious change could have influenced the behavior of the peasants. However, there was also deliberate manipulation. The letter, sent by a high-ranking cleric, the vicar Sofronie of Zlatna, was presented on behalf of the empress and was supported by a social group that had had conflicts with the local Uniate clergy in the past. These conflicts turned into an open revolt during the religious uprising. Considering this, we can question whether the religious conflict was not exploited by the judges in order to take revenge on an old social rival, i.e. the Uniate clergy. We know that Ştefan Cute not only had the Sofronian message on him, but the Uniate clergy also advised him not to give credit to Sofronie. This shows that there were also cases when the Sofronian message lacked success. Nevertheless, Ştefan Cute was a traditional ally of the Uniate archdeacon, and his support should be understood in this context as well. Nevertheless, the religious factors must not be neglected: another traditional enemy of the *magistrat*, Marcu a Bariţii, converted to Orthodoxy "following Sofronie's orders," as was mentioned in the *magistrat* report when he was arrested. This may prove that he was indeed convinced by the Orthodox missionaries, which implies that religious factors did play a role in the revolt.

The Religion of the Romanians: A Controversial Issue

The statistics issued by the *magistrat*[50] and the Buccow commission[51] for the Bistriţa district in 1761 have engendered heated historiographical debates between the two Romanian churches in Transylvania, where

---

[50] According to data submitted by the town's senators, there were only 242 Uniate families, but 110 Uniate priests in this district. Arhivele Naţionale, Direcţia Judeţeană Cluj, Fond Primăria Oraşului Bistriţa, Fascicola, 189, 2 r-v.

[51] The commission headed by General Buccow counted 4508 Uniate families for Bistriţa, and only 42 Orthodox families. Virgil Ciobanu, "Statistica românilor ardeleni din anii 1760-1762," *Anuarul Institutului de Istorie Naţională* 3 (1926): 692-93.

traditional Orthodox and Greek Catholic polemics resurfaced after 1990.[52] Orthodox authors indignantly mention the "injustice" that General Buccow inflicted, and argue that despite the commission's decision, most of the Romanians living in Transylvania and Bistriţa wanted to be Orthodox. They support their arguments with the *magistrat*'s census as well as a narrative of Orthodox martyrdom in Bistriţa.[53] This view enjoyed support among certain Saxon and Hungarian historians as well.[54] Greek Catholic authors on the other hand insist on the accuracy of the Buccow commission's statistics and uphold the thesis of the Lutheran Saxons' plot against the Greek Catholic church.[55] Though they are highly subjective and poorly argued, both historiographical positions emphasize the involvement of the political authorities in determining the religious affiliation of the Romanians in this period. However, they overlook the entire historical and geographical context in which these numbers were arrived at. It was a clash between several political actors and the local Romanian reality.

On 9 April 1761, General Buccow issued a proclamation to all Transylvanian Romanians. They were informed about the creation of a commission charged with investigating their religious situation. Moreover, their representatives were invited to Hermannstadt to present their complaints in front of him on 26 April.[56] In addition, Buccow ordered a census of all Transylvanian Romanians. The census had to be carried out concurrently by both the political authorities and Uniate archdeacons.

---

[52] I refer to the traditional polemics on the authenticity of the church union documents. On this, see Silviu Dragomir, *Românii din Transilvania şi unirea cu biserica Romei. Documente apocrife privitoare la începuturile unirii cu catolicismul roman, 1697-1701* (Cluj-Napoca: Editura Arhiepiscopiei Ortodoxe Române, 1990).

[53] The most prominent supporter of these views was Silviu Dragomir. His arguments inform numerous Orthodox theologians to the present day. See Silviu Dragomir, *Istoria desrobirei religioase a românilor din Ardeal în secolul XVIII*, vol. 2 (Sibiu: Editura şi tiparul Tipografiei arhidiecezane, 1939), 283-84. For the martyiological approach, see *Mărturie şi martiriu în Transilvania secolului al XVIII-lea*, ed. Dorel Man and Flore Pop (Cluj-Napoca: Editura Renaşterea, 2004).

[54] E.g., Gottfried Poschner, "Gegenreformatorische Bestrebungen in Bistritz im 18. Jahrhundert," *Programm des evangelischen Gymnasiums Bistritz* (1883-84): 3-51; and Zoltán I. Tóth, *Az erdélyi román naciolalizmus első százada* (Csíkszereda: Pro-Print Könyvkiadó, 1998), 207-08.

[55] This opinion was primarily maintained by two local Greek Catholic historians: Virgil Şotropa, "Contribuţii la istoria bisericească," *Arhiva Someşană* 21 (1937): 273-78; and Ştefan Buzilă, "Protopopii şi vicarii Năsăudului," *Arhiva Someşană* 27 (1940): 351-52.

[56] The entire text of the proclamation was published in Augustin Bunea, *Episcopii Petru Pavel Aron şi Dionisie Novacovici sau Istoria Românilor Transilvăneni de la 1751 până la 1764* (Blaş: Tipografia Seminarului Arhidiecesan, 1902), 207-08 n. 2.

Each census taker had a list of nine questions, and priests and peasants had to answer only the last one individually.[57]

Buccow's summoning of the Romanian representatives to Hermannstadt represented an important step for the Uniate church in Bistriţa in counterbalancing the Orthodox offensive in northeast Transylvania. Thus, a delegation of ten Romanians from this region went to the Austrian general and declared that the Romanians from the Bistriţa district wanted to continue to remain forever part of the Uniate church and that they would not be "infested" by anyone for their decision. Consequently, they received Buccow's protection.[58] The nature of the "delegation" has been strongly contested by the Romanian Orthodox literature. According to it, the delegation was the result of corruption on the part of the Uniate clergy.[59] I could not find any further reference to this issue, but certainly this action influenced the future Catholicizing attitude of the Habsburgs towards the Romanians living in this district.

The census began in May 1761. Unfortunately, we have only found the detailed documents pertaining to the census conducted by the Saxon senators; those of the archdeacons (the nine questions) have thus far been untraceable. The majority of the priests declared themselves Uniate. There were only five non-Uniate priests in the entire district.[60] However, we do not know whether the Greek Catholic priests understood the significance of the church union, given that in certain cases, they adopted a confusing attitude or did not answer individually. Thus, all fifteen priests at Zagra declared "through the voice of Popa [Priest] Flore" that they were registered with the Uniate archdeacon.[61] In Mititei, the four priests declared that they wanted to remain what they were and preserve the faith in which they grew up. Moreover, they added that they did not know the difference between union and schism because nobody had told them anything about the union when they were ordained. Even the parish priest of the town suburb, Dumitru, declared himself Uniate, although he was "schismatic at heart."[62] All these confusing cases were interpreted by the *magistrat* as Uniate.

The commitment of the clergy to the union can be seen in several ways. The more educated priests assumed a Uniate identity, as was

[57] Şotropa, "Lupta românilor bistriţeni," 454.

[58] Bunea, *Episcopii Petru Pavel Aron,* 101.

[59] Virgil Şotropa, "Înfiinţarea regimentelor de graniţă," *Arhiva Someşană* (1938): 64.

[60] ANDJC, Fond Primăria Oraşului Bistriţa, Seria II a, Fasc. 253, f. 9.

[61] Şotropa, "Lupta românilor bistriţeni," 462.

[62] Ibid., 460.

certainly the case of the archdeacon of Năsăud, Anton Naszodi. Others most probably remained loyal to the church of Rome due to the authority of the archdeacon or on account of their clerical privileges, as certain scholars have argued.[63] Here, unlike in other regions of the principality, we found only one "apostate" priest. The priest in Ilva declared that though he had been Uniate, his wish was to be like the villagers, and he did not want to "know" about the church union.[64] This situation can be interpreted as a desire to be accepted by the peasants, so as not to lose his community.

For peasants themselves, the situation was different. Most of the Romanians living in the Saxon district and having a Uniate priest declared themselves loyal to the Uniate church. Therefore, they were deemed Uniate by the Saxon senators. Nevertheless, in many cases, they acknowledged that they did not know the significance of the church union. Their allegiance must have been directly connected not only to the authority of the Uniate priest in Romanian society, but also to the fact that they had been granted or demanded certain rights in the Saxon villages on account of their religious status as Uniate. Thus, the peasants in Tonci declared themselves Uniate and loyal to the priest who was celebrating the liturgy for them in Vermeş (Krassóvermes). In this village, they declared that they had a church by the grace of Her Majesty.[65] The other Romanians living in the Saxon district, most of them isolated and without priests, declared either that they wanted to be non-Uniate or that they wished to preserve the old Greek law. The uncertainty or perhaps intentional ambiguity, which also occurred in the counties, was interpreted by the town councilors to signify non-Uniate.

The situation of the Romanians living in the suburb of the town remained confusing as well. In most cases, they did not know what to answer; they did not know whether they were Uniate or non-Uniate: "they have no knowledge about either the union, or non-union, [they know] only what their priest taught them."[66] This was confirmed in several cases when the inhabitants of the suburb wanted to preserve the old Greek law. In certain other cases, though they admitted they did not know the difference, they declared themselves non-Uniate. However, despite the senators' acknowledgment that it was a confusing situation, the Romanians were

---

[63] Mureşan, *Satul românesc*, 268.
[64] Şotropa, "Lupta românilor bistriţeni," 464.
[65] Ibid., 470-72.
[66] Ibid., 467.

eventually deemed non-Uniate.[67] This may suggest that as a Protestant institution, the local town council indeed supported Orthodoxy.

More radical were the majority of Romanians living in the district of Rodna. They declared that they had heard of the union with Rome for the first time either during the rebellion at Sân' Petru (Barcaszentpéter/Petersberg) in the summer of 1760 or when they received the first order sent by Sofronie. However, sources from the era contradict this. A petition from the Romanians of Bistrița sent to Count Bethlen in 1755 was signed by "humble Wallachians of the Greek Catholic rite."[68] Moreover, during an investigation of the Orthodox monks coming to Transylvania (1752), the peasants in Feldru declared: "No non-Uniate priest can occupy our church, because we summoned the monk to convert to the union."[69] This seems to indicate that they accepted Orthodox priests, if they first converted to the Union with the Church of Rome.

In most cases, the answers were not individual, but given by some local leaders. They advocated the "old Greek law." Thus, in Mititei, Istrate Oproaie declared on behalf of the village that they wanted to preserve the old Greek law. Similar situations occurred in Zagra, Runc, and Găureni. It is difficult for us to grasp the significance of the "old Greek law" after more than three centuries. Certainly, as in Rodna, the peasants understood the union as a change. For instance, the peasants in Runc perceived this change in terms of ritual: "for six years, we have not been read the list of dead persons [pomelnice]."[70] In most cases, the old Greek law was interpreted as Orthodoxy. Consequently, the magistrat considered most Romanians living in the Rodna Valley as non-Uniate.[71] However, the final Buccow verdict presented Uniates as the religious majority in the Rodna Valley. This conclusion was drawn after comparing the senatorial investigation with that carried out by the archdeacon.

In fact, religious determination was the outcome of a political clash and uncertain confessional identity. Buccow's commission was not satisfied with the magistrat's census. As a result, five Saxon senators were arrested under the pretext of having plotted against the union with Rome. Indeed, a negative attitude towards the church union was suspected throughout the Saxon Königsboden. Consequently, the commission had to examine the situation, and the final data for Bistrița was presented only

[67] ANDJC, Fond Primăria Orașului Bistrița, Seria II a, Fasc. 189, f.2.
[68] Mureșan, Satul românesc din Nord-Estul Transilvaniei, 268.
[69] Șotropa, "Mănăstirîși," 119-27.
[70] Șotropa, "Lupta românilor bistrițeni," 460-61.
[71] ANDJC, Fond Primăria Orașului Bistrița, Seria II a, Fasc. 189, f. 2.

after the controversies had been eliminated.[72] We can assume that the controversies were "eliminated" by taking into account the attitude of the archdeacon Anton Naszodi who requested the improvement of the situation as early as 27 April.[73] Moreover, a letter to General Johann Jakob Möringer of 30 June mentions that the archdeacon expressed his confidence in the zeal and objectivity of the Austrian general.[74] The final statistics confirmed the "help" given by the general, while religious affiliation was determined in accordance with the Viennese policy in the field. The Romanians were finally deemed Uniate, although the census proved that in many cases, the Union was definitely rejected. Thus, the reality was certainly different from the one presented on paper.

The Final Habsburg Achievement: Conversion through Militarization

The statistics did not correspond to the reality. Even after the Romanians received "protection" from General Möringer, anti-Uniate polemics persisted. A general state of revolt and threat of emigration was present among the Romanians, but it was also linked to the future military status of the region, as contemporary reports confirm. Furthermore, isolated conflicts continued to occur,[75] and the protest in Maior proved that Orthodoxy still represented a challenge to the church union. Thus, on Trinity Sunday in 1761 a new conflict between two so-called apostates and the Uniate priest occurred in Maior. On this occasion, two Romanian peasants, Demian Farkas and Josif Schorobetie, who had declared themselves non-Uniate, did not allow the Uniate priest into their homes. They were arrested and later released on bail, guaranteed by twelve Romanians. In 1762, they sent a petition to Möringer and requested on behalf of most Romanians living in the Bistriţa district, who "professed their non-Uniate faith," that their women and children be allowed to preserve the faith in which they grew up and knew from their youth. However, Möringer recommended they stay calm.[76] The Habsburg strategy was to implement the union with Rome in this region, a plan that was finally to be accomplished through the extension of the Military Frontier into the Rodna Valley.

---

[72] BAFCN, Ms. Lat., 279, f. 11.

[73] MOL, 300379, 405.

[74] BAFCN, Ms. Lat., 279, f. 13.

[75] For instance, in September 1761 the Uniate priest in Dumitriţa complained that his church had been locked by two "apostate" Romanians; therefore, he requested military assistance. The two Romanians were arrested and later released. ANDJC, F 189, 223.

[76] ANDJC, F 235, 236.

Historians have long debated the reasons behind the militarization and unanimously agreed that this represented a strategy to convert the Romanians to Greek Catholicism.[77] The court's aim to attract the Romanians towards the church union was clearly expressed by General Josef Siskowics.[78] Indeed, the final imperial resolution on the militarization stipulated that only Uniates could be drafted into the border regiments, whereas "schismatics" could be drafted only into imperial infantry regiments.[79]

The events that occurred in Salva (Szálva) during the blessing of the military flags in 1763 reveal the persistence of religious tensions. On 10 May, the flags of the regiments had to be consecrated in the presence of General Buccow and the Uniate bishop, Petru Pavel Aron. During the event, Tănase Todoran of Bichiş complained about the situation of the Romanians in the army. The Romanians rebelled, and even the general and the bishop had to flee. After this revolt, a delegation went to the Orthodox Bishop Dionisie Novacovici and complained that Uniate priests exerted pressure on them to embrace the church union. They complained about the aggressive military action and threatened emigration. Moreover, they demanded a non-Uniate priest. The Orthodox Bishop could not legally interfere, and the delegation went to the Catholic bishop, Baron Anton Bajtay, who urged them to stay calm and return to Bistriţa. Under these circumstances, they appealed to the president of the Transylvanian Estates, János Lázár.[80] The Austrian Colonel Stefan Lutsch von Luchstenstein had to investigate the situation. The Catholic bishop from Alba (Anton Bajtay) suggested that religion was only a pretext for evading military service and therefore he recommended that the rebels be punished as an example to others. In case they emigrated, the bishop suggested that they could be replaced. Luchstenstein's final report

---

[77] Eudoxiu Hurmuzaki, *Fragmente din Istoria Românilor* (Bucureşti: Socecŭ, 1900), Volume 2; Eugen von Friedenfels, *Joseph Bedeus von Scharberg, Beiträge zur Zeitgeschichte Siebenbürgens im 19. Jahrhundert. Erster Theil, 1783-1847* (Vienna: Carl Graeser, 1885) 360; Virgil Şotropa, "Înfiinţarea graniţei militare năsăudene," *Arhiva Someşană* 24 (1938): 1; Mathias Bernath, *Habsburgii şi începuturile formării naţiunii române* (Cluj-Napoca: Ed. Dacia, 1994) [Romanian translation of *Habsburg und die Anfänge der rumänischen Nationsbildung*], 173; Carl Göllner, *Regimentele grănicereşti din Transilvania, 1764-1851* (Bucharest: Editura militară, 1973), 20-21, Valeriu Şotropa, *Districtul grăniceresc năsăudean şi locul său în lupta pentru progres social şi libertate naţională a românilor din Transilvania* (Cluj-Napoca: Ed. Dacia, 1975), 62.

[78] Friedenfels, *Joseph Bedeus von Scharberg*, 360-61, Nota 2.

[79] Bernath, *Habsburgii şi începuturile formării naţiunii române*, 177.

[80] Hurmuzaki, *Fragmente din Istoria Românilor*, 227.

confirmed not only that the fears were military in nature, but also that the whole district "inclines towards the schism." Nevertheless, he reported that the Romanians "embraced" the union everywhere with the exception of Mocod.[81] The leaders of the revolt were eventually sentenced to death.

The militarization represented an important step in converting the Romanians to Greek Catholicism, and religious stabilization could be achieved by means of military discipline. However, Orthodoxy still represented a threat that had not disappeared. Because of this, and certainly also to gain better control over the situation, the Viennese court intended to create a Greek Catholic episcopate in Bistriţa.[82] Moreover, the later episcopate and military investigations also proved that the situation had not changed significantly since 1761.[83] However, in 1948 the communist regime encountered a Greek Catholic population here, which means that the Viennese strategy ultimately proved successful. Sofronie's endeavors had no lasting effects on northeast Transylvania. Sofronie's revolt of 1761 only raised the question of religious affiliation, the Romanians now being told that there were two denominations.

Conclusions

Northeast Transylvania represented an exception on the *Königsboden*. Unlike in the southern parts of the principality, the Greek Catholic (Uniate) church developed there in a peaceful religious milieu until 1761, when the Sofronian emissaries reached this remote Romanian-inhabited territory. Sofronie's uprising proved that the Uniate church in the Bistriţa district was also vulnerable in the face of Orthodoxy. As in other regions, religious peace disappeared within a few months here. Also, as in other regions of the principality, the clergy was repudiated, churches were locked, and the peasants resorted to the religious services of Orthodox priests. Thus, the "old Romanian Greek law" resurfaced. It succeeded because it was a well-coordinated movement within a Romanian society which reacted as in the counties: church occupation by the Orthodox

---

[81] Lajos Szádecki, *Halmágyi István naplói, 1752-53. 1762-69. és iratai 1669-1785* (Budapest: Magyar Tudományos Akad. Kőnyvkiadó-Hivatala 1906), 79.

[82] Helmut Klima, "Bistritz als geplanter Sitz eines griechisch-katholischen Bistums," *Kirchenblätter* 63 (1940): 245-46.

[83] For instance, in 1776 an Austrian lieutenant colonel investigated the attitude of Romanians from Bistriţa towards the church and the norms imposed by it. He realized that the level of catechization was in many cases very low, and even the priests did not always behave properly. As for the allegiance towards the church union, it was dubious in several villages. Miron, *Biserica greco-catolică din Transilvania*, 240-41.

adherents, the banning of Uniate services and priests, and a confessional identity "crisis". The political, military, and church actors proved to be decisive for the course of events: the local town council exploited the situation and favored Orthodoxy, and the Uniate archdeacon "converted" the whole district on paper, so that military intervention became justified, punishing the disobedient and persuading by force.

The census of Buccow proved that confessional identity was imbued with confusion and misunderstanding. Priests, even in many cases Uniate priests, did not understand the significance of the union with Rome. The peasants perceived religion in terms of rite and not dogma. Many did not know who they really were, because they were not able to understand the difference between being Orthodox and Uniate. Under these circumstances, their religious identity was questionable. The local authorities and the Saxon Lutheran senators took advantage of the situation and interpreted the "old Greek law" as Orthodoxy. Confusing cases, such as those in the suburb of Bistrița, were labeled as Orthodox. The archdeacon's census acted as a counterweight. We still do not know what the findings of his census were, but the Buccow commission declared a Uniate majority in Bistrița by comparing the statistics. Legislation placed obstacles in the way of apostasy. Moreover, through the extension of the Military Frontier, religious behavior was disciplined and the church union gained adherents.

Although no severe threats occurred again after 1763, the Uniate bishop's visitations or military investigations revealed how unrealistic the numbers were. Even eighty years later, the situation was not significantly different from that of the 1761 census. The Orthodox alternative did not disappear, as the discussions in Vienna on the creation of a Uniate episcopate for the district of Bistrița clearly reveal. Nevertheless, the peaceful period that followed after 1763, as well as the military discipline that was imposed, guaranteed the success of the Uniate church until the advent of communism in Romania. In 1948, the Romanians in the town and region of Bistrița "reconverted" to Orthodoxy, and in 1990, after the collapse of the communist regime, few returned to the Uniate church. Considering today's attitude - "it's the same God" - we are entitled to understand Romanian denomination building in the eighteenth century as not only a matter of doctrine, but of politics.

Aspects of Confessional Alterity in Transylvania: The Uniate - Non-Uniate Polemic in the Eighteenth Century
Ciprian Ghişa

Historical Context

The union of the church of the Transylvanian Romanian people with the church of Rome was achieved as a result of the three synods of union in Alba Iulia (1697, 1698, and 1700), during the reigns of the metropolitans Teofil and Atanasie Anghel. The union was achieved by following the model provided by the council of Florence. The union statement posited the acceptance of the Catholic faith (four points in particular: the acknowledgement of papal primacy, the *filioque* clause of the creed, the existence of purgatory, and the Latins' use of unleavened bread), but retained certain aspects of Orthodoxy (the oriental rite, the Julian calendar, the law (*Pravila*), and its own hierarchical structure). But after the union agreement a tumultuous period followed in which the bishops laid too little stress on promoting the union among the faithful and on instructing them on the great change that had occurred. But what was the danger of the lack of a specific identity discourse centered on the above-mentioned issues of faith, practice, and discipline? The result could have been a significant loss of believers, fluctuations and instability within the church, and a blow to the very foundation upon which the union was built. The believers would have found themselves losing trust in their pastors, might have considered them false prophets, and consequently feared being exposed to the dangers of hell. Under the circumstances, the safest recourse would have been a return to Orthodoxy. This, in fact, was precisely the experience of the Uniate church of the Romanian Transylvanians in the middle of the eighteenth century, affected by the anti-union activity of the Orthodox monks Visarion Sarai (born Nicolae Sarai) and Sofronie of Cioara between 1744 and 1761.

The first episode opened on 11 March 1744, with the arrival of the Serbian monk Visarion Sarai in Transylvania. As his subsequent trial showed, he had little knowledge of the dogmatic teaching of the church, but due to his ascetic lifestyle and the visions of the Virgin Mary that he claimed to have had, the Romanian population welcomed him as an authentic holy man. His message was direct and had a powerful impact on the people that were listening to him. He denied that he preached against the church union as such, but it is obvious that he portrayed it ambivalently in his sermons, and his main message was that only those who persevered in the faith into which they were born could hope for eternal salvation.[1] In addition, Sarai contested the validity of ordinations and baptisms performed by the Uniate church.[2] At the trial of 27 April 1744 he argued that it was not possible for someone to be saved by belonging to two religions at the same time, asserted that the union was actually a combination of the Latin and the Orthodox faiths, and claimed that the oriental law was lost through the union with Catholics.[3] This created a serious identity problem for many of the faithful: What is the union? Who are the Uniate people? Sarai thus not only created confusion but sparked unrest. It emerged that in several cases peasants said that they had heard for the first time from "a man sent by God" that their priests had accepted the union and that they themselves were now considered Uniate. Sarai suggested that the sacraments bestowed by the Uniate priests lacked validity, thus threatening the ones that received them with damnation.[4] The message was explosive and resulted in a violent reaction against Uniate priests, who were denounced as papists, as alien and dangerous, and as "devils from hell."[5] What weight could the attachment towards the bishop of Blaj be given against the potential of losing one's soul? It was revealing indeed that almost fifty years after the celebration of the union, there existed a considerable number of people who had not even heard about it. Clearly, not having been instructed on what it meant to be Uniate, many simply continued with their old beliefs and practices. Thus we see that in 1744 many people clung to their old Orthodoxy, understood as the sum of the ritual practices inherited from their ancestors. But this also entailed an ethnic dimension. Eastern-rite Christianity was a distinguishing characteristic of the Romanian

---

[1] Keith Hitchins, "Religia şi conştiinţa naţională românească în Transilvania în secolul XVIII," in *Conştiinţa naţională şi acţiune politică la românii din Transilvania 1700-1868* (Cluj-Napoca: Ed. Dacia, 1987), 45.

[2] Octavian Bârlea, "Biserica Română Unită şi ecumenismul Corifeilor renaşterii culturale," *Perspective*, no. 3-4 (1983): 70-72.

[3] G. Bogdan-Duică, *Călugărul Visarion Sarai. Studui istoric din istoria Transilvaniei* (Caransebeş: Tiparul Tipografiei Diecezane, 1896), 19.

[4] Hitchins, "Religia şi conştiinţa naţională românească," 48; Mihai Săsăujan, *Politica bisericească a Curţii din Viena în Transilvania (1740-1761)* (Cluj-Napoca: Presa Universitară Clujeană, 2002), 149-50.

[5] Hitchins, "Religia şi conştiinţa naţională românească," 49.

population of Transylvania, and in the words of the Hungarian historian Zoltán Tóth, "Orthodoxy, envisioned as tradition, was the essence of the Romanian community."[6] Romanian people therefore identified with it in part because it distinguished them from the other Transylvanian "nations," i.e., the Hungarians, Saxons, and Székelys. Hence, in accusing Uniate priests of being papists, it was suggested that they not only belonged to a different law, but also to a different people. The Sarai case was thus the first serious confrontation between Uniate and Orthodox positions, leading to both a spiritual crisis and a real crisis of identity, religious and national in nature.[7]

The union experienced a second blow with the arrival in Transylvania in the second half of 1759 of the monk Sofronie of Cioara. As a member of the privileged Serbian Orthodox church in Karlowitz (Sremski Karlovci/Karlóca), he took a much more aggressive approach than Sarai and soon found himself leading a real rebellion against the union.[8] As a virulent opponent of the union, he denounced Uniate priests ordained by a bishop that was consecrated by the pope. He openly urged the people to abandon their Uniate clergy and to receive only priests ordained according to the Oriental rite in Karlowitz. The central theme of his discourse was again connected to the issue of law. He reiterated the argument of Visarion Sarai that Uniates adhered to two laws, Latin and Orthodox, so that as a consequence neither baptism nor any other sacraments performed by Uniate clergy had any sacramental value.[9] The Uniates were actually "German-like papist people," so that if the faithful became Uniates, they would transform themselves into "papists" and all their pieties would be to no effect.[10] As the historian Ovidiu Ghitta has suggested, the faithful were confronted with a choice between "tradition and innovation; more

---

[6] I. Zoltán Tóth, *Primul secol al naționalismului românesc ardelean 1697-1792* (Bucharest: Ed. Pythagora, 2001), 72.

[7] Ibid., 71-72, 143.

[8] For further information regarding the activity of Sofronie of Cioara, see also: Silviu Dragomir, *Istoria dezrobirii religioase a românilor din Ardeal în secolul XVIII*, vol. 2 (Sibiu: Tipografia arhidiecezană, 1920), 154-93; D. Prodan, *Supplex Libellus Valachorum* (Bucharest: Ed. Științifică și Enciclopedică, 1984), 205-15 [original edition: *Supplex Libellus Valachorum, Or, The Political Struggle of the Romanians in Transylvania During the XVIIIth Century*, Volume 8 of *Bibliotheca Historica Romaniae* (Bucharest, 1971)]; Ovidiu Ghitta, *Nașterea unei biserici* (Cluj-Napoca: Presa Universitară Clujeană, 2001), 302-38; Săsăujan, *Politica bisericească*, 230-35; Gheorghe Gorun, *Reformismul austriac și violențele sociale din Europa centrală, 1750-1800* (Oradea, Ed. Muzeului Țării Crișurilor, 1998), 162-79.

[9] Dragomir, *Istoria dezrobirii religioase*, 2:160; Bârlea, "Biserica Română Unită," 123-24.

[10] Samuil Micu, *Istoria românilor*, 4 vols. (Bucharest: Ed. Viitorul Românesc, 1995), 2:339; Dragomir, *Istoria dezrobirii religioase*, 2:160.

precisely, between being loyal to a very clearly portrayed thing in their mind at that time [the old Greek rite] or being stigmatized as carrier of novelty [the recent union]," and since no one had explained to them what the union actually meant (i.e., precisely the preservation of the Eastern ecclesiastical tradition), the choice between the two was easily made in favor of the first.[11] Sofronie's impact was dramatic: the union lost four fifths of its believers.[12] In the census taken by the bishop Petru Pavel Aron in 1750 there were 550,097 Uniate and only 25,065 Orthodox believers recorded; in 1761 the Austrian general, Adolf Buccow, counted only 25,164 Uniate families, compared to 126,652 Orthodox families.[13]

Since the laity among the Romanians was largely illiterate, it is reasonable to conclude that the responsibility for this dramatic reversal lay with the Uniate hierarchy and its clergy. A "break in the solidarity between Uniate priests and believers" and "a credibility crisis" of the Uniate clergy were obvious, and the cause was undoubtedly "a pastoral failure at the local level."[14] It is interesting to note, however, that during this time the clergy itself remained faithful to the union, still outnumbering their Orthodox confreres 2238 to 1380 in 1761.[15] In part their loyalty was no doubt due to the privileges that they enjoyed under the Leopoldine Diplomas of 1699 and 1701, which constituted the legal basis for the Uniate church in Transylvania, but this cannot be the only explanation.

In order to better understand the failure of the Uniate response to this Orthodox initiative, it is necessary to analyze the extent to which the Uniate hierarchy was able to elaborate and consolidate a specific Uniate identity discourse in the first half of the eighteenth century in conjunction with the need to assess their vision of the ecclesiastical union in general. Atanasie Anghel, in his fifteen years as metropolitan, could not achieve anything memorable in terms of transmitting the message of the union to his parishioners. His own occasional hesitation, including a short desertion in the year 1711, could certainly not improve the situation. At this point a new clerical elite was still lacking, and Atanasie's agenda was dominated by material considerations and by issues concerning the

[11] Ghitta, Naşterea unei biserici, 307.
[12] Bârlea, "Biserica Română Unită," 126-27, 130-31.
[13] Zenobius Pâclişanu, "Istoria Bisericii Române Unite, 1752-1783," Perspective 14-16, no. 53-60 (1991-93): 38.
[14] G. M. Miron, "Adevăraţii uniţi sau preoţii români din Transilvania secolului al XVIII-lea între unire şi ortodoxie," in Tentaţia istoriei în memoria profesorului Pompiliu Teodor, ed. Nicolae Bocşan et al. (Cluj: Presa Universitară Clujeană, 2003), 569-71.
[15] Pâclişanu, "Istoria Bisericii Române Unite," 38.

acknowledgement of his rights. He was followed by Bishop Ioan Pataki, chosen after four electoral synods held between October 1713 and December 1714 and after the intervention of the Transylvanian chancellery and the governor, Sigismund Kornis. He did not enjoy the trust of his protopopes (deans) from the very beginning, in part due to his preference for the Latin rite and his refusal to accept the Eastern teaching on the epiclesis. This led him into conflict with the clergy from Făgăraş (Fogaras/Fogarasch) and Ţara Bârsei (Barcaság/Burzenland), which immediately dissociated itself from him and submitted itself to the jurisdiction of the Orthodox bishop from Râmnic in Little Wallachia, which was briefly part of the Habsburg Monarchy during 1718-39. Another revealing aspect of Pataki's attitude towards the Oriental rite was the fact that, in 1716, the intervention of the Pope was necessary in order to force him to cease celebrating mass in the Latin rite and to do so in the Oriental. By the bull *Rationi congruit* he was officially made bishop of Făgăraş in 1721, finally settling there in 1723 when the old metropolitan church in Alba Iulia was demolished. Suspicion of Pataki never abated, and he could lead his archeparchial see only with difficulty. After his death in 1727 the see remained vacant until 28 September 1732, when Inochentie Micu-Klein was consecrated as bishop in Făgăraş. His battle for the rights of the Uniate clergy as well as his political activity are well known. Under him the episcopal seat was moved to Blaj, where he was much preoccupied with material endowment of the church. He was also the bishop who understood the need of the Uniate church to create an ecclesiastical elite for itself, and he therefore supported sending young monks to study abroad (Petru Pavel Aron, Silvestru Caliani, Grigore Maior, Gherontie Cotore, and Atanasie Rednic) in Trnava, Rome, Vienna, but also at the Jesuit school in Cluj. In this way he laid the foundation of the Blaj schools and monasteries. On the political side he was active in the Transylvanian diet and in lobbying the Vienna court, but he is best known for the 1743 petition *Supplex Libellus Valachorum*, which demanded the application of the rights granted by the diplomas of Leopold I.[16]

The biggest problem with the Uniate church of Transylvania in the first half of the eighteenth century was the fact that its priests made little or

---

[16] For the evolution of the Greek Catholic church in Transylvania under Atanasie Anghel, Ioan Pataki, and Inochentie Micu Klein, see: Pâclişanu, "Istoria Bisericii Române Unite," 271-343; Bârlea, "Biserica Română Unită," passim; Prodan, *Supplex Libellus Valachorum*, 151-99; Mathias Bernath, *Habsburgii şi începuturile formării naţiunii române* (Cluj-Napoca: Ed. Dacia, 1994) [Romanian translation of *Habsburg und die Anfänge der rumänischen Nationsbildung* (Leiden: Brill, 1972)], passim.

no effort to make clear to the great mass of believers precisely what union with Rome meant. Zenobius Pâclişanu has suggested that there was little difference for a believer between belonging to the Oriental rite in 1680 and a Uniate one in 1730. As he put it: "the union did not produce any change in daily practice, they [the faithful] believed the full extent of what they had believed before, they prayed and fasted as they did before, the church sermons were the same, as were their superstitions and the customs, without any connection to dogma, whether union or non-union."[17]

The most important mistake of the Uniate hierarchy was to believe that the vow of Atanasie and his protopopes taken in 1700 would also implicitly bind the mass of believers, but this was hardly the case because the union was not complete. Micu-Klein considered all villages and all priests to be Uniate, and thus under his authority, if they did not explicitly declare themselves against the union.[18] He conceived his jurisdiction primarily in geographical terms, without focusing on an identity discourse and without clarifying the issues connected to aspects of the Catholic faith. Micu-Klein pretty much insisted that he was summoned to take care of all the Romanian people in the Habsburg Monarchy, considering his jurisdiction to include Maramureş (Maramarós/Maramuresch), Partium, Banat, and even Oltenia in Little Wallachia. He also always considered Romanians living in Braşov (Kronstadt/Brassó) to be Uniate, even if they were largely still Orthodox. In short, Uniate identity was focused on his person.[19] The notion that his authority represented the basis of the union proved to be a great error and made the union vulnerable. The moment believers began to fear that through the union they renounced the ancient law, their loyalty to the bishop was undermined and with it the basis of the union itself.

Inochentie Micu-Klein left Transylvania in 1744 and never returned from his exile in Rome. The church that he left behind was in a state of great confusion, which was aggravated once Sofronie entered the principality. Within fifteen years the Uniate church ceased being the church of all Romanians in Transylvania and became a minority confession. At the same time, the position of Orthodoxy was strengthened when an imperial decree in July 1759 recognized freedom of worship for Orthodox people in the province. Thus, the Uniate church ceased to be the

---

[17] Pâclişanu, "Istoria Bisericii Române Unite," 317.

[18] Ibid., 317; Bârlea, "Biserica Română Unită," 49-51; Hitchins, "Religia şi conştiinţa naţională românească," 41-42.

[19] Bârlea, "Biserica Română Unită," 47-49.

single official church of the Transylvanian Romanians. The change was radical: from majority to minority, from monopoly to plurality. The response had to come rapidly in order to consolidate what remained and to be able to counterattack. In order to achieve these goals, however, it was necessary to work hard to disabuse the faithful of the notion that union automatically meant a modification of the rite. As Greta Monica Miron noted: "It can be said that the Uniate priests were the victims of their own inability to explain the significance of the union to the believers. Their ignorance and lack of education was also reflected by the faithful who, having no coherent and convincing explanations about the meanings of the union with the church of Rome, were easily convinced by the Orthodox propaganda built around the false idea that the union meant giving up the Oriental rite."[20]

In response to the Viennese court's demand, the Greek Catholic bishop of Munkács (Mukachevo), Mykhail Olshavsky, made a pastoral visit to the regions affected by the activity of Visarion Sarai at the end of 1745 and the beginning of 1746. He was convinced that the cause of the decay could be found in the failure of both the Uniate and Roman Catholic leaders in explaining to parish priests and to people in general the true meanings of the union with Rome. He asked for an immediate mobilization of the clergy to present the main aspects of the union to the peasants and to ensure them that their spiritual life had not been put in danger.[21] This required in the first instance the creation of an educated clergy, and in the second a clear strategy on the articulation and creation of a Uniate ecclesiastical identity, what Wolfgang Reinhard called "confession formation (*Konfessionsbildung*)." It involved identification and clarification of the concrete principles that would form the basis of a whole identity discourse; the diffusion and promotion of the new norms of faith; the effective use of propaganda and interdiction of counter-propaganda; the gradual assimilation of the new principles through education; ongoing training of the elite; adjustments of the rituals; and changes at the level of language, mostly of the liturgical language. For such a program to succeed, the support of the state authorities was imperative.[22] The Uniate bishops Petru Pavel Aron (1751-64), Atanasie Rednic (1764-72), and

---

[20] Miron, "Adevărații uniți," 570.
[21] Hitchins, "Religia și conştiinţa naţională românească," 47.
[22] Wolfgang Reinhard, "Disciplinamento sociale, confessionalizzazione, modernizzazione: Un discorso storiografico," in *Disciplina dell' anima, disciplina del corpo e disciplina della società tra medioevo ed età moderna*, ed. Paolo Prodi, = volume 40 of *Annali dell'Istituto storico italo-germanico* (Bologna: Società editrice il Mulino, 1994), 111.

Grigore Maior (1772-82) quickly understood the need for determined action and for the application of real missionary zeal. The real union could be developed only after the clergy successfully assimilated the elements of Catholic dogma and began to present it to the people of their communities.[23] The subsequent construction of a mass Greek Catholic identity needed a lot of energy, diplomacy, and determination in order to overcome people's innate conservatism. The bishops themselves had to undertake many pastoral visits, organize district and provincial synods, create scholarships for a significant number of future clergymen to study abroad, establish new schools, and launch an ambitious publication program both to promote the union with Rome and to publish new liturgical books to replace the Orthodox ones existing in the parishes. This was not only an internal reform of the Greek Catholic church, it was a program of revival in the spirit of the Tridentine Catholic reformation.

Aspects of the Polemical Literature of the Mid-Eighteenth Century

Thus, by the middle of the eighteenth century, the Greek Catholic hierarchy understood that it was time to carry out major and coherent action to form and to strengthen the confessional identity of its own believers. The members of the Greek Catholic elite formulated two types of discourses. The first was meant to convince the faithful of the truthfulness of Catholic doctrine and of the fact that the union *in fide* did not bring any changes to the Greek rite. They focused on the presentation of the four Florentine points,[24] describing them not as novelties but as a part of the whole teaching based on Scripture, confirmed by the councils and preached by the Holy Fathers of the church. The second type of discourse was complementary to the first one and consisted of providing responses to the accusations brought by non-Uniates. This discourse was essentially defensive and apologetic in tone and lacked cohesion because it referred only to ad hoc questions raised by the non-Uniates. The two types of discourses were sustained by a large number of printed books, including catechisms and prayer books and theological discourses. Among these was the first book published in the new printing house in Blaj, which opened in 1747, *Floarea adevărului* (*Flocusculus veritatis*) (1750);

---

[23] Pompiliu Teodor, "The Confessional Identity of the Transylvanian Greek Catholic Church," in *Confessional Identity in East-Central Europe*, ed. Maria Crăciun, Ovidiu Ghitta, and Graeme Murdock (Aldershot: Ashgate, 2002), 170.

[24] The Council of Florence of 1439 had successfully negotiated the reunification of several Eastern churches on the basis of the acceptance of the *filioque* in the creed, the definition and number of sacraments, the doctrine of purgatory, and the principle of papal supremacy.

Învăţărură creştinească (*Doctrina Christiana*), which saw editions between 1755 and 1763; *Dialog ucenicul cu dascălul* (Dialogue between Master and Disciple) (1756); Petru Pavel Aron's, *Păstoriceasca datorie* (Duties of Pastoral Life, 1759) and his *Pastoriceasca poslanie* (Pastoral Letter, 1760); and Niceta Horvat's *Poslanie* (Epistle) (1780).

The union faced a sustained polemic from its Orthodox rivals on two fronts: through the monks or other clergymen who came to Transylvania from Serbia or Wallachia; and through books and manuscripts of all types that had a strong anti-union message and that had been spread throughout Transylvanian parishes (despite several imperial decrees of 1746, 1765, and 1768 forbidding their entry and diffusion).[25] The latter were a part of the larger polemic between Catholics and Orthodox that was very lively in the seventeenth and eighteenth centuries. They are a local reflection, adapted to the specific context of Transylvania, of an increasing tension between the two confessions. The reaction from the broader Orthodox world was sustained and encouraged by Dositheos, the patriarch of Jerusalem, mostly after 1672. Many of the books written in Greek against Calvinism and Catholicism were printed in Wallachia and Moldavia, where the local prince was a fervent supporter of such activities.[26] For example, the work of Nektarios, former patriarch of Jerusalem, *Against the Pope's Primacy*, published in Iaşi in 1682, was dedicated to Gheorghe Duca, the prince of Moldavia. In 1683, two fifteenth-century works were republished: *Against the Heresies*, by Simeon, archbishop of Thessalonica; and *Explanation of the Canons of the Church*, by Mark Eugenikos, the metropolitan of Ephesus. In 1690 Maxim of Peloponnese's *Book against the Schism of the Papists* was published in Bucharest, as was a book by Meletios Sirigos against Catholic doctrine and the positions of patriarch Cyril Lukaris. Iaşi was a particularly active publication center: the *Tome of Reconciliation*, which contained several writings against Catholicism, was printed there in 1692; John Eugenikos' *Sermon for Combating the Outlaw and False Decision Composed in Florence at the Synod Held by the Latins* was published in 1692; *Tome of Love against the Latins*, containing twenty-five writings from different periods against the Latins, appeared in 1698, followed in 1705 by the *Tome of Joy*, a collection of texts containing, among others, the letter of Photius against Pope

---

[25] Pâclişanu, "Istoria Bisericii Române Unite," 122.

[26] B. Murgescu, "Confessional Polemics and Political Imperatives in the Romanian Principalities (Late 17th – Early 18th Centuries)," in Crăciun and Ghitta, *Church and Society*, 174-75.

Nicolas I, letters of Gennadios Scholarios against the Florentine union, writings of Nicolaos Kerameus against the pope's primacy, as well as works of Meletios Pigas and Dositheos Notaras.[27]

Some of these works were also translated into Romanian. This included the book of Maxim of Peloponnese, printed in Snagov by Antim Ivireanu, the metropolitan of Wallachia, under the title *Carte sau lumină cu drepte dovediri din dogmele Bisericii Răsăritului asupra dejghinării papistaşilor* (Book or Light with True Proofs from the Dogmas of the Eastern Church on the Schism of the Papists).[28] It had wide circulation in Transylvania and was one of the central works of the anti-union polemical literature. It was structured in chapters referring to each of the Florentine points, with the express purpose of combating them in turn. The main focus, of course, was on the pope's primacy, which takes up 164 of the 210 pages of the book. The Florentine points were considered heretical and "novelties," and the Latins were blamed for being responsible for the schism of the church (*"dejghinarea Bisericii"*). The message was direct, without ambiguity, and blunt. It was not the only such book that circulated in Transylvania. In 1760 the work of Nil, archbishop of Thessalonica, *Carte sau lumină cu drepte dovediri pentru Vavilonul cel tăinuit care iaste la râmleni* (Book or Light with True Proofs for the Secret Babylon that is in Rome), was published in Râmnic.[29] It had the same combative character, arguing that "they (the Latins) estranged themselves from the Orthodox church of the East," that the beast seen by prophet Daniel (Daniel 7: 3-10) was in fact "the rule of the pope," Rome being considered the Great Babylon, the "mother of whores and of all the ugliness of the world." The book also referred to the words of St. Andrew of Neocaesarea, who explained that the seven heads of the beast were like seven mountains. That was the home of the whore, meaning Rome itself.[30]

In addition to printed books, various manuscripts also circulated in Transylvania during the eighteenth century. *Întrebări şi răspunsuri despre legea a treia ce s-a izvodit adică Uniia în Ţara Ardealului* (Questions and

---

[27] For all these aspects, see: Murgescu, "Confessional Polemics," 175-76; M. Păcurariu, *Legăturile Bisericii Ortodoxe din Transilvania cu Ţara Românească şi Moldova în secolele XVII-XVIII* (Sibiu, 1968), 41; N. Şerbănescu, "Antim Ivireanu tipograf," *Biserica Ortodoxă Română* 74, no. 8-9 (1956): 727-28.

[28] Păcurariu, *Legăturile Bisericii Ortodoxe*, 42; I. Mateiu, "O carte din 1699 contra desbinării religioase," *Revista Teologică* 28, no. 7-8 (1938): 299-302.

[29] A. Sacerdoţeanu, "Tipografia episcopiei Râmnicului, 1705-1825," *Mitropolia Olteniei* 12, no. 5-6 (1960): 328-29.

[30] Nil, Archbishop of Thessalonica, *Carte sau lumină* (Râmnic,1760).

Answers on the Third Law that Appeared, Meaning the Union, in the Land of Transylvania) by Visarion of Upper Sâmbăta was a 1746 transcription of a public debate between him and the Uniate archpriest of Făgăraş, Vasile Baran, in which he had emerged victorious.[31] Another manuscript that circulated widely was a response to *Floarea adevărului*. Dated between 1750 and 1755 but unsigned, it originated in Wallachia, probably in Râmnic, and was likely written by someone in the circle of Bishop Grigore or even by him.[32] The library of Blaj also contains an *Apology of the Eastern Church*, by a certain teacher named Cristea, dating from 1771. It contained several texts, among which were four referring to the Florentine points analyzed from the perspective of Greek Orthodoxy. They might have been inspired by a work of Maxim of Peloponnese: *On the Procession of the Holy Ghost Only from the Father*; *Against the Rule of the Pope over the Whole World*; *For the Unleavened Bread*; *For the Third Place Called by Them as Purgatory Meaning Purifying*.[33] Finally, one could add a number of popular texts such as the rhymed chronicle *Plângerea sfintei mănăstiri a Silvaşului din eparhia Haţegului din Prislop* (The Cry of the Silvaş Monastery from the District of Haţeg from Prislop) with its strong anti-union message.[34]

The manuscript texts are of particular interest. Both the 1746 manuscript and the one composed as a reply to *Floarea adevărului* have several points in common: they are strongly polemical, they address the four Florentine points with a particular emphasis on papal primacy, and they use the same literary sources. Implicit in the attack on the four points, of course, was the accusation of heresy, which was a recurring theme in the old disputes between Latins and Greeks. Indeed, Orthodox writers stressed that the church of Rome was guilty of seventy-two heretical doctrines identified by Constantine Panagiotes, a number that appears in both texts mentioned above.[35] The 1746 manuscript posits the notion that entering the union, having previously been in the possession of the whole

---

[31] The text was published by Ghenadie Enăceanu in the journal *Biserica Orthodoxă Română*. For analysis of this text, see: Ghenadie Enăceanu, "Uniaţia seu legea a treia," *Biserica Orthodoxă Română* 8, no. 8 (1883): 496-97; Teodor Bodogae, *Despre cunoştinţele teologice ale preoţilor români de acum 200 de ani. Semnificaţia unui manuscris* (Sibiu: Tipografia Archidiecesană, 1944), lviii; Păcurariu, *Legăturile Bisericii Ortodoxe*, 76.

[32] The text was published by Teodor Bodogae. About this text, see Teodor Bodogae, *Despre cunoştinţele teologice*, xiii-lxvii; Pâclişanu, "Istoria Bisericii Române Unite," 386.

[33] Nicolae Comşa, *Manuscrisele româneşti din Biblioteca Centrală de la Blaj* (Blaj: Tipografia "Lumina" Miron Roşu, 1944), 157-58.

[34] See the text in Ioan Lupaş, *Cronicari şi istorici români din Transilvania. Şcoala Ardeleană*, 2 vols. (Craiova: Ed. Scrisul românesc, 1941), 1: 58-78.

[35] *Întrebări şi răspunsuri pentru legea a treia*, 511; Bodogae, *Despre cunoştinţele*, 12.

arsenal of the true teaching of Christ, was in fact a "betrayal" of their own ancestors who had died before 1700. If the union's position were correct, it would mean that all one's Orthodox ancestors had suffered eternal damnation. In fact, however, it was the Uniates that had left the "law of the fathers."[36]

In addition, these authors formulated the theory of the "union as a third way." The 1746 text called the Uniate church "the third church" and admonished its adherents with the words: "Uniates, you are not in the law of the pope nor in ours"; rather they were "threefold in law," unlike the Orthodox, "who did not accept a third law."[37] What this meant was articulated even more pointedly by the 1750-55 text. It characterized the church as our mother, who was nursing us "with both her sweet breasts of the old and new laws," whereas the Uniates "devised a new mother with three breasts." The author added: "of course, a woman with three breasts is impossible to find." Uniates, in short, fell between two stools: "as you are right now, you are not on the side of the Easterners, nor on the one of the Westerners, you are neither warm nor cold."[38] The "union" was, in fact, not a real one because it did not reflect in any way the union that had once existed between the church of the East and the church of the West. In any case, the guilt for the separation belonged to the Westerners, and to the popes in particular: "The church of the East did not separate itself from the church of Rome; it remained in the state in which the holy apostles and the holy councils had left it. The pope separated from it as a putrid limb that was worthy to be thrown away because of his fabrications and impious acts." Rome was the great Babylon, the home of the devils, as predicted in Revelations 18:2.[39] Another bone of contention in both texts was the issue of fasting. As the fasts had been modified by the Latins, it meant that the Uniates were guilty of this error as well: "When you are truly united with the Westerners, then you will not respect the four great fasts of the year nor the Wednesdays and Fridays, but the Saturdays as the Jews and the Westerners do. And you will celebrate the Liturgy with unleavened bread...." Such accusations touched on cherished practices, and Visarion Sarai and Sofronie of Cioara turned people against the union insisting precisely on arguments like these. The manuscript authors thus concluded that maintaining the Oriental rite was impossible through the

[36] *Întrebări şi răspunsuri pentru legea a treia*, 503.
[37] Ibid., 497-504.
[38] Bodogae, *Despre cunoştinţele*, 2-3, 12.
[39] *Întrebări şi răspunsuri pentru legea a treia*, 503-04, 511.

union, and that, eventually, union would mean the adoption of the Latin ritual norms. That is why the Orthodox texts use the expression "the new law" for the union.[40]

The dispute between the representatives of the two Romanian churches in Transylvania was unequal from the very beginning. The Uniate discourse was intricate, defensive, and more difficult to understand, obsessively repeating the same arguments, offering easy openings for rebuttal. It attempted to remain diplomatic and avoid harsh language. In comparison, the Orthodox priest made strong arguments, his discourse was longer and more elaborate, and the tone condescending, incriminating, and offensive and sometimes ironic. "If you had not been an archpriest," the author inveighed, "I would have taken you for a fool; why do you love vanity and speak lies?"[41] In the 1746 text the Uniates were called "the lost ones," "the deceived ones," and "unfortunates," who uttered lies and used words that appeared beautiful on the surface but were meaningless. The same attitude can be found in the text from 1750-55. Its author wondered: why did the Uniates call the book "The Flower of Truth" - *Floarea adevărului*, when he could only find lies in its pages. The Uniates "vomited gossip," were "abducting wolves," and "disturbers and destroyers of Christ's clothing," and the reason they left the Eastern church was "haughtiness of the mind." All of this was a sure sign of madness.[42] Such comments show what a strong reaction the union provoked in the Orthodox milieu. Its representatives considered it necessary to counterattack with vigor, especially after the scholar Gherontie Cotore wrote his polemic manuscript in 1746 and the group of monks around bishop Petru Pavel Aron published *Floarea adevărului*, the book meant to define and strengthen the Greek Catholic confessional identity. Certainly, the author of the Râmnic manuscript of the early 1750s singled out these two Greek Catholic authors: "If there had not been Atanasie, the metropolitan of Bălgrad in Transylvania, neither the union nor Aron, the bishop from Blaj, nor Gherontie Cotorea would ever have been; we see them printing books with diligence and at great expense just to reinforce the union."[43]

The Orthodox polemicists found arguments from Scripture, from Greek liturgical books, and from different Eastern Fathers of the church,

---

[40] Ibid., 498-99; Bodogae, *Despre cunoștințele*, 12.
[41] *Întrebări și răspunsuri pentru legea a treia*, 504.
[42] Bodogae, *Despre cunoștințele*, 1-7.
[43] Ibid., 10.

such as St. John Chrysostom, St. Basil the Great, St. Athanasius the Great, St. Gregory of Nazianzus, St. Cyril, St. John the Theologian, and Theophylact of Ohrid. To the complaints of the Uniates about the anti-union activity of Visarion Sarai, they responded that Sarai had been the servant of Christ, sent by God as Jonah to the people of Nineveh.[44] These public disputes between Uniate and Orthodox clergymen, as well as the dialogue between the Râmnic circle around bishop Grigorie and the Blaj circle around bishop Petru Pavel Aron, showed how polarized and irreconcilable their respective positions were. The Rhymed Chronicle of Prislop Monastery illustrates this state of maximum confessional tension well, and reflects the whole Orthodox frustration in facing the advance of the union, sustained as it was by the state authorities. The Prislop Chronicle begins with a presentation of the "golden age" of the pre-union period, of the connections with Wallachia, of the patronage of the great Romanian Orthodox monastery of Tismana, and of the organization of Transylvanian Orthodoxy sustained by the Wallachian princes. This happy period ended suddenly the moment the "terrible tyranny of the popes," whose purpose was to destroy Orthodoxy in the entire world, reached Transylvania. The disaster took place at the time of Metropolitan Atanasie, a hierarch "too easy to deceive." Accepting the union, Atanasie and his clergymen received a series of privileges, but it was all for naught because the promises remained unfulfilled, and the metropolitan seat in Alba Iulia was destroyed. Indeed, everything was in danger until the coming of Visarion Sarai, a man sent by God. The chronicle concludes with a presentation of Sarai's activity and his subsequent persecution, and a detailing of the "heresies" of the *Floarea adevărului*.[45]

The Uniate Response

The introduction of *Floarea adevărului* referred to the tense confessional situation in mid-eighteenth century Transylvania and noted that the arrival of Visarion Sarai was the moment when peace and love among the brothers and the sons of the same church were broken.[46] *Păstoriceasca poslanie* also noted with regret that the church of Christ - that is the Greek Catholic church - had to face many disorders and separations, because of "certain innovators," and was forced to pass through a very difficult time. Bishop Petru Pavel Aron laid the responsibility entirely on

---

[44] *Întrebări şi răspunsuri pentru legea a treia*, 497-98, 500-01.
[45] *Plângerea Sfintei Mănăstiri*, 59-76.
[46] *Floarea adevărului*, 10.

the Orthodox camp, arguing that they were the ones who "broke the love."[47] In the *Dialogul ucenicul cu dascălul* the word "disunion" was put in direct relation with "dejghinare" (separation) and "întunecare" (dullness).[48] Textually, connections were also made to the brief ninth-century schism of Photius, ecumenical patriarch of Constantinople, but the message was addressed to the contemporary situation as the modern non-Uniates extracted their arguments from the writings of Photius and other anti-papal polemicists, such as Michael Cerularius (c. 1000-1059) or Mark of Ephesus (1392-1444). The Uniate texts referred largely to the persons considered responsible for the Great Schism, who were characterized as "sporitorii dejghinării" (those who deepened the separation),[49] "înnoitorii" (innovators),[50] "hulitorii" (blasphemers),[51] or "înșelatorii" (deceivers)[52] that hated the truth and loved the darkness more than the light.[53] The first accusation referred to the breach caused inside the Uniate church after 1744 by Visarion Sarai. The others referred to the overall message of the Orthodox: it was their message that was a novelty, an invention, non conformable to tradition, a lie that threw the ones who believed it into damnation. Moreover, "înnoitorii" were also associated with "the heretics"[54] and "the Pharisees,"[55] and were accused of being the ones that had sowed cockles.[56] As Petru Pavel Aron wrote: "Their blasphemies and opinions were fabricated by them in order to hold believers back from the true faith and confession and to lead them towards heresies and separation, just as the Pharisees used to do."[57] Generally Uniate polemicists agreed that, as the *Dialogul ucenicul cu dascălul* had it, "the initiator of this non-union was Photius."[58] The theme was also taken up in the works of Aron[59] and Niceta Horvat, the latter calling the

---

[47] Aron, *Păstoriceasca poslanie*, 4, 11.
[48] *Dialog ucenicul cu dascălul*, 19, 26.
[49] Aron, *Păstoriceasca poslanie*, 40.
[50] Ibid., 4, 22, 29, 54.
[51] Niceta Horvat, *Poslanie sau dreapta oglindă a păcii, dragostei și unimii. Prin carele cu drepte dovediri cei uniți să mântuiesc de hulele carele lor li să aruncă. Iară neuniții nici iritici a fi nici schismatici mai ales în neamul românesc a nu să putea aeve a zice să arată* (Vienna, 1787), 54.
[52] *Dialog ucenicul cu dascălul*, 45.
[53] Ibid., 46.
[54] Aron, *Păstoriceasca poslanie*, 49.
[55] *Dialog ucenicul cu dascălul*, 29; Aron, *Păstoriceasca poslanie*, 56.
[56] Aron, *Păstoriceasca poslanie*, 63. Cockle is a poisonous weed mentioned in Job 31:40: "Let thistles grow instead of wheat, and cockle instead of barley."
[57] Ibid., 56.
[58] *Dialog ucenicul cu dascălul*, 16.
[59] Aron, *Păstoriceasca poslanie*, 8.

followers of Photius's teachings "fotiani" and "Photiens."[60] Both Aron and Horvat considered Maxim of Peloponnese as the most representative follower of Photius in the modern period, with Horvat constructing a significant part of his theological discourse as a response to the arguments made by the Greek polemicist.[61]

Aron's list of the "innovators" also included Nicephorus Xanthopoulos, author of the *Synaxarion* found in the *Triodion* of Bucharest, and the metropolitan of Kyiv, Peter Mohyla, whose work, Orthodox Confession of the Catholic and Apostolic Eastern Church (1645), was republished in 1691 in Buzău.[62] This shows how embedded the Transylvanian Greek Catholic discourse was within the broader European polemics between the Greeks and the Latins. Aron's primary objective was to combat the position of Transylvanian Orthodoxy and to protect his own besieged ecclesiastical edifice. By rebutting Orthodox theories and "proving" their "falseness," he was hoping to offer his clergy (and through it, the believers) credible answers to Orthodox accusations. Identifying the "innovators" also had the purpose of pinpointing those works that circulated throughout the rural communities that were considered misleading, for which purpose Aron created a sort of local Index. The Uniate authors repeatedly asserted that the grounds of all non-union arguments were very shallow and that the "innovators" fabricated everything "with their minds," finding their arguments not in Scripture but in "tâlcuiri" (human interpretations).[63] Niceta Horvat's denunciation of Maxim of Peloponnese was symptomatic of the general tone: Maxim wrote his work out of madness, ignorance, unrestrained envy, blindness, and drunkenness; and his arguments were inspired by the devil, the father of all lies.[64] At the same time, the Orthodox authors were accused of perverting the books of the church fathers and interpreting them in the wrong way. Aron wrote: "They read the books, but they do not believe them, do not confess them, and do not respect them as they teach." From the earliest centuries of the church, the innovators had modified and perverted patristic writings and changed some of the teachings regarding the union in order to deceive ignorant people.[65] Despite the fact that the

---

[60] Horvat, *Poslanie*, 56, 64.

[61] Ibid.,14-19, 26, 41, 48, 49, 53, 54, 56, 64, 66, 88.

[62] Aron, *Păstoriceasca datorie*, 47, 61; Aron, *Păstoriceasca poslanie*, 8, 38, 40, 43, 48.

[63] *Dialog ucenicul cu dascălul*, 28, 34; Aron, *Păstoriceasca poslanie*, 24.

[64] Horvat, *Poslanie*, 14, 19, 41, 43, 48, 65, 66, and passim.

[65] Aron, *Păstoriceasca poslanie*, 53-54.

Greeks, the Serbs, and the Wallachians had all these books at their disposal, they did not teach true doctrine.[66]

In light of the fact that before the union, Catholicism and Calvinism were considered to be the two main threats to the church of the Transylvanian Romanians, Uniates now had to eliminate all the suspicions of Roman Catholicism that were sustained not only by the Orthodox discourse at the ideological and polemic levels but at that of popular beliefs as well. Now that the union accepted the church of Rome as the true church of Christ whose faith and rite were legitimate and in conformity with the tradition of the holy fathers, Uniates had to stress that Orthodoxy was responsible for the great schism and that the Latins could not be blamed or accused of anything. In his manuscript of 1746, Gherontie Cotore, one of the most important Uniate ecclesiastical leaders of the time, made a long list of all the accusations brought by the Greeks against the Latins (including those on ecumenical councils, ritual practices, celibacy of the priesthood, indissolubility of matrimony, and fasts), commented on them in turn, and rejected them all as lies and calumnies.[67] Some of these arguments found their way into books published shortly thereafter. *Floarea adevărului* and *Păstoriceasca poslanie* both addressed the issue of fasts from a Uniate perspective, upholding the notion that differences in rite were legitimate.[68]

A Discourse of Reconciliation

All Uniate authors argued that the restoration of Christian unity was desired by God and taught by Scripture, but posited no concrete steps for a real reconciliation with the Orthodox, who were considered heretics and schismatics. A notable exception, however, was the work of Niceta Horvat, which was published in Vienna in the general atmosphere of confessional toleration that followed Joseph II's toleration edicts. His purpose was quite different from that of the other Uniate authors, for he was intent on opening a dialogue and finding a formula acceptable to both sides. Of course, he did not renounce the elements of the faith he considered to be true, but he addressed his message directly to non-Uniates, trying to convince them of the grounds of his arguments. He was certainly very hard on Maxim of Peloponnese, but only because he

---

[66] *Dialog ucenicul cu dascălul*, 15.

[67] Gherontie Cotore, *Despre Articuluşurile ceale de Price*, ed. Laura Stanciu (Alba Iulia: Bibliotheca Universitatis Apulensis, 2000), 77-83.

[68] *Floarea adevărului*, 13; Aron, *Păstoriceasca poslanie*, 58.

considered the Greek author as an impediment to a real consensus. The major difference between Horvat's book and the work of Gherontie Cotore or the *Floarea adevărului*, which analyzed the same matters, is that the latter addressed first of all the Uniate believers, warning them about the dangers of not knowing the truth and of the significance of the union with the church of Rome. Horvat, on the other hand, seems to have wanted to address non-Uniates as well as Uniates and to be a mediator between the two sides. He insisted that the quarrelling among Transylvanian Romanians, filled as it was with hatred and disunion between believers, was extremely harmful to the church of Christ, and he preferred to call both Uniates and non-Uniates "sons of the Eastern church."[69] In his discussion of the Florentine points he underscored the fact that the Eastern church had never condemned the Latins for their faith and customs. "Neither the Western church nor the Eastern church," he argued, "has ever been discovered as being heretical or schismatic by any council." He enumerated all the Greek emperors and Eastern holy fathers that individually or during the eight ecumenical councils of the first millennium collaborated "like brothers" with the Latin side and underlined the reciprocal respect that the Latins showed the Greeks.[70] Horvat urged reconciliation, speaking from the point of view of the Uniate church; and though he made no concessions in matters of doctrine, he always sought to use language and arguments that would palliate a discourse that had been very intolerant and intransigent in the texts published before his. In trying to solve the dogmatic and ritual divergences of the two sides, Horvat can be said to have followed in the footsteps of the clergymen who tried to find a basis of reconciliation between East and West at the Council of Florence in 1439 and to be among the pioneers who fought for the reunification of the two Romanian churches of Transylvania at the end of the eighteenth and in the first half of the nineteenth centuries.

Conclusions

The polemical discourse between Uniate and Orthodox Romanians of the Habsburg Monarchy during the second half of the eighteenth century reflects the tense and confused confessional situation prevalent within the Transylvanian Romanian space at the time. Its initiators were Gherontie Cotore and especially bishop Petru Pavel Aron, the Uniate leader during

---

[69] Horvat, *Poslanie*, 1, 5.
[70] Ibid., 111-22.

this time of confrontation. The two sides seemed to have held irreconcilable positions, and as a consequence it was a dialogue from a distance, harsh and totally without diplomacy. Of course, this was not unusual, considering the tone of the general polemic between the Greeks and the Latins. Indeed, many arguments regarding doctrines and rites in these Transylvanian exchanges were extracted from this larger polemic. On the other hand, some of them came out of local confessional realities, of the evolution of events after 1700 and, above all, after 1744, the year when Visarion Sarai provoked the entire explosion of attacks and counterattacks bitterly sustained by both sides. Ironically, the polemicists of both sides availed themselves of the same vocabulary of abuse: innovators, blasphemies, separation, deceivers, lies, damnation, and the like. And both proceeded from the assumption that they had the totality of the truth on their side. Each one's church was the real Eastern church, catholic and orthodox. The Uniate discourse was also partially defensive. This was explicable because its message was elaborated only after the Orthodox accusations had been formulated and spread among the believers. But once it was, the discourse became inflamed and tensions increased due to the major breach created among ordinary people from the same village or the same family. "Through the union, the sons of the same people become, suddenly, mortal enemies, hating each other and persecuting each other with fury."[71]

---

[71] Toth, 285.

Josephinist Reforms in the Metropolis of Karlovci and the Orthodox Hierarchy

Marija Petrović

In the period between the 1740s and the 1790s, the Habsburg lands went through a period of substantial state-imposed reforms. Many of these affected the role and the position of the Catholic church and church-state relations. At the beginning of the 1740s the position of the Orthodox in the Habsburg lands was still determined by the imperial privileges that had been granted by Leopold I in the late seventeenth century and subsequently confirmed by other Habsburg rulers. These privileges granted the Orthodox wide autonomy in matters of church organization, worship, and religious rites and customs. The clergy were exempt from taxation, while the metropolitan had rights that made him more than just a religious leader.[1] This applied only to the Orthodox (both Serbs and Romanians) living under the jurisdiction of the metropolitan of Karlovci - that is to say on the territories of the Military Frontier, southern Hungary, and the Banat and did not extend to the Orthodox living in Transylvania, and later in Galicia and Bukovina.[2]

Although not always strictly observed, the privileges gave the metropolis a large degree of autonomy. However, as there were almost no written regulations that determined the everyday running of the metropolis and the eparchies within it, everything from the collection of church fees to the election of abbots and bishops was left to the whims of

---

[1] The privileges were issued by Leopold I on 21 August 1690, and confirmed in December of the same year. A year later they were extended to give the Serbian church hierarchy authority in political matters. Leopold I confirmed both sets of privileges on 4 March 1695. All the documents were published in *Srpske privilegije od 1690-1782*, ed. Jovan Radonić and Mita Kostić (Belgrade: Naučna knjiga, 1954). The English translation of the document from 1691 was published as "The 'Serb Privilege' of 1691," in *The Habsburg and Hohenzollern Dynasties*, ed. C.A. Macartney (London: Macmillan, 1970), 78-82.

[2] In order to avoid repetition, unless otherwise specified, I use Orthodox to mean the Orthodox population of the metropolis of Karlovci. I also use the terms Orthodox and Serbs interchangeably, because the metropolis was an institution of the Serbian Orthodox church and the hierarchy was exclusively Serbian, although the actual population included a fair number of Romanians, especially in the Banat.

the bishops and metropolitans.[3] At a period when the Habsburg rulers were embarking on extensive reform of the Catholic church, it is hardly possible to imagine that they would have continued to accept such a degree of independence for one small religious group, which after all was just a "tolerated" religion. On the other hand, if we take it that the aim of the Josephinist reforms was to introduce a simpler and more practical type of piety into the church while making it more useful to the state, the Orthodox metropolis of Karlovci was open to criticism and in need of reform on both of these accounts.

Maria Theresa and Joseph II's reforms of the Catholic Church aimed to create a church that would provide better pastoral care and be more cost effective therefore less burdensome for the general population, and more useful for and supportive of the state. This was achieved over the years by reorganization and an increase in the number of eparchies, parishes, and secular parish priests, as well as better education for the latter. Many of the changes were supposed to be introduced at the expense of the monasteries, whose numbers were significantly reduced and the monks made to engage in useful activities such as care for the sick, education, or pastoral work.

Most of these reforms were started in some form during Maria Theresa's reign, though it was Joseph's accession in 1780 that marked the beginning of the period of energetic activity on this front. By 1790 the Catholic Church of the Habsburg lands was noticeably reshaped. The organization of the eparchies was altered, and new bishoprics founded in both the Hereditary Lands and Hungary. About six hundred new parishes were established, while the number of secular clergy was increased by about twenty-five percent. The education of the clergy as well as popular education were now closely supervised by the state. At the same time, the Jesuits disappeared from the scene (abolished by the pope in 1773), while more than one third of the monasteries were closed. The state firmly established its right to interfere in the temporal affairs of the church, leaving only matters of dogma under its jurisdiction.[4]

---

[3] A rare instance of a modern history of the metropolis of Karlovci acknowledging this is Radoslav M. Grujić, *Pravoslavna srpska crkva* (Belgrade-Kragujevac: Kalenić, 1995), 121-22.

[4] Derek Beales, *Joseph II*, 2 vols. (Cambridge: Cambridge University Press, 1987-2009); Franz A.J. Szabo, *Kaunitz and Enlightened Absolutism 1753-1780* (Cambridge: Cambridge University Press, 1994); Hanns L. Mikoletzky, *Österreich, das grosse 18. Jahrhundert: Von Leopold I. bis Leopold II.* (Vienna-Munich: Österreichischer Bundesverlag, 1967). For the reforms of the Catholic church in Hungary see Joachim Bahlcke, *Ungarischer Episkopat und österreichische Monarchie: Von einer Partnerschaft zur Konfrontation (1686-1790)*

Due, however, to the obviously different position and importance of the metropolis, some aspects of the general reforms never arose in dealings with the Orthodox (papal supremacy or various problems associated with the power of the Jesuits, to name just two). Several of the main issues, regarding in the first place the reorganization of the administrative structure of the church, reform of education (of both clergy and laymen), and matters of popular customs and worship were equally important for the Orthodox. Although it may seem surprising, the issue of religious toleration can be left out of this narrative. It brought great change to Orthodox individuals and to Orthodox people living outside the metropolis, but on the metropolis of Karlovci as a whole it had very little impact. Thus, in terms of the issues addressed one can argue that in content, the reforms among the Orthodox fitted perfectly within the general Josephinist church reforms. What I propose to do in this paper is to look more closely at each of the three main spheres of reform, and then turn to examine the role the church hierarchy played in this process. Only when examined in detail do the Josephinist reforms of the metropolis reveal their interesting and puzzling side.

Church Organization

The systematic reforms of the Orthodox church started relatively late, in 1769, when the imperial commissary at the Sabor[5] (gathered to elect a new metropolitan) raised the question of the administrative reorganization of the metropolis.[6] Once more the main issues look very familiar: organization of the eparchies, regulation of parishes and parish clergy on the one hand and of the monasteries on the other. The main aims of the reforms were to make the metropolis economically viable but also to strengthen its institutions on both the central and local level. In contrast to the Catholic Church, it transpired very early that the biggest problem in the metropolis was that the secular clergy were too numerous and the population too poor to support the whole extensive church structure. Thus, its reorganization inevitably concentrated on various reductions.

The biggest single change in the reorganization of the metropolis was the abolition of one of its eparchies, the eparchy of Kostajnica, whose

---

(Stuttgart: Franz Steiner, 2005), and Robert J.W. Evans, "Maria Theresa and Hungary," in *Austria, Hungary and the Habsburgs: Essays on Central Europe c. 1683-1867* (Oxford: Oxford University Press, 2006), 17-35.

[5] A church council.

[6] The minutes of the Sabor were published in Djordje Rajković, "Srpski narodni sabor 1769. u Karlovcima," *Letopis Matice Srpske*, 114 (1872): 151-202.

territory was divided between the two neighbouring eparchies - Karlstadt and Pakrac. This was done partly in order to comply with the original imperial privileges, which recognised only seven Orthodox eparchies within the metropolis.[7] However, the main reason for this change was that none of the three eparchies could comfortably support their bishops, because not only were they fairly small, but they were almost exclusively on the territory of the Military Frontier, by far the poorest area inhabited by the Serbs. In 1781 Joseph contemplated abolishing another Orthodox eparchy - that of Buda, as it was found too small and poor to support a bishop.[8] However, at the demand of the synod he decided that the eparchial leadership was simply to be left vacant for a couple of years, in order for its funds to recover. After five years, in 1786, a bishop of Buda was again elected.[9]

But what had a much larger and more lasting impact on religious life in the metropolis was the reorganization of parishes that followed. However, before anything could be accomplished, it was necessary to establish the current state of the metropolis. Thus, the first step was a census of population, with separate lists of parish priests. The population and clergy numbers that emerged from the census of 1771-73 (see Table 1) showed that there were far too many parish priests. Although the data is not complete, it clarifies why some reductions were necessary. On average there was one priest for every forty to seventy families.[10] These ratios were significantly different from the situation in the Catholic church in the

---

[7] This number was exceeded with the acquisition of the Banat (1718), and at the time of the Sabor of 1769 there were eight eparchies (Arad, Bačka (Novi Sad), Buda, Karlstadt (Gornji Karlovac), Kostajnica, Pakrac, Temeswar, and Vršac) plus the archeparchy, the territory under the direct jurisdiction of the metropolitan. "Leopold I to Patriarch Arsenije Čarnojević, 4 March 1695," in Srpske privilegije, 54-56; Vienna, Austrian State Archives: Hofkammer Archiv [henceforth HKA], Banater Akten, box 142/1778.

[8] At that time the eparchy of Buda had fewer than three thousand families. See Table 2.

[9] Johann H. Schwicker, Politische Geschichte der Serben in Ungarn (Budapest: Ludwig Aigner, 1880), 348-49.

[10] Dickson gives five as the average number of people per household in the eighteenth-century Habsburg lands. One arrives at the same number by comparing the total number of men and women and the number of households from the general census of 1783-84. Peter G. M. Dickson, Finance and Government under Maria Theresia, 1740-1780, 2 vols. (Cambridge: Cambridge University Press, 1987), 1:442-43; Gusztav A. Thirring, Magyarország népessége II. József korában (Budapest: Magyar Tudományos Akadémia, 1938), 46-47, 91-110. The average household in the Military Frontier was, as could be expected, larger and had approximately ten people. Nada Alaica, "A Mixing of Identities: Orthodox and Catholic Peasants in the First Banal Regiment" (DPhil. thesis, Oxford University, 2004), Appendix 1.

Habsburg lands, where in 1780 there was about one secular priest per 820 persons in Upper Austria, 620 in Lower Austria, and as many as 900 in Bohemia (though there were exceptions like Trieste, where the ratio was one per 370).[11]

Table 1: Population Census 1771-73[12]

Eparchy	Number of households	Number of priests	Households per priest
Archeparchy	NA	322	
Arad	33,741	673	50
Bačka	10,168	247	41
Buda	3450	76	45
Kostajnica	NA	186	
Karlstadt	NA	106	
Pakrac	NA		
Temeswar	46379	652	71
Vršac	35472	455	77
Total	129210	2717	47

Although the large number of priests was in theory beneficial for the care of souls, it had to be balanced against the economic burden the priests presented to the local communities. In this respect the number of Orthodox priests was significantly too large, especially as the people were fairly poor. The other disadvantage of such a large number of priests was

---

[11] Peter G. M. Dickson, "Joseph II's Reshaping of the Austrian Church," *The Historical Journal* 36 (1993): 103.

[12] Data from Mitropolijsko-patrijaršijski arhiv, Archives of the Serbian Academy of Sciences and Arts, Sremski Karlovci [hereafter MPA], Collection 'A,' 375/1773. It is possible to get an approximate picture of the situation in the eparchies for which the data is not available from the conscription undertaken in order to elect delegates for the Sabor of 1769. According to this census, the archeparchy had 15,310 households and 381 priests (approximately forty households per priest), Pakrac eparchy had 6153 homes and 125 priests (approximately fifty households per priest), and Kostajnica eparchy had 7427 households and 162 priests (forty-six households per priest). Data for Karlstadt eparchy is not given. Ilarion Zeremski, "Popis sveštenstva i naroda u Mitropoliji Karlovačkoj iz 1769," *Glasnik Istoriskog Društva u Novom Sadu*, 4 (1931): 55-58.

that not only priests, but also all who lived under the same roof with them were exempt from paying taxes.[13] The new regulations therefore specified that the number of priests was to be fixed at one for villages with fewer than 130 households, and two for those with fewer than 250 (150 and 200 respectively in the Military Frontier). This did not affect all the eparchies in the same way, but in some as many as half of the priests were made supernumerary. The regulations were easier to accept as the new ratios were not meant to be achieved immediately. The supernumerary priests were allowed to keep their homes and privileges and were only banned from serving in parishes. It was expected that numbers would be gradually reduced as some of the priests died.[14]

In contrast to all the attempts to tax Catholic clergy, Maria Theresa did not try to impose taxes on the Orthodox clergy at all, though she regulated strictly and in great detail both the fees that the priests were to pay to the bishops and the fees the parishioners had to pay to their priests.[15]

Joseph II had very little to add to the reorganization of the metropolis initiated by his mother. He ordered another census, which was carried out in 1781, but then did not act on it, except to issue several warnings to various bishops that they really must not ordain new priests before all of the superfluous ones had died.[16] Joseph's behaviour can to a certain extent be explained by the numbers from the census (see Table 2). Although there were noticeable regional differences, the average was about 120 families (about six hundred people) per parish. This fitted very nicely with Joseph's aim not to have more than seven hundred people in a parish, and was probably one of the reasons why he did not further intervene with the parish organization of the metropolis.[17]

---

[13] This was especially problematic in the Military Frontier, where a priest's household was exempt not only from taxes but from military service as well. As most families lived in *zadruge* (extended families), several priests from a few different families could mean that a large part of the male population of a village was exempt from military service.

[14] MPA, Collection 'A,' 253/1774; §37, *Regulament* (Vienna, 1777) and §37, "Rescriptum Declaratorium Illyricae Nationis" [hereafter "Declaratorium"].

[15] The extensive fees for various church services were published as appendices B and C, *Regulament*, 1777. The same appendices were included in the "Declaratorium" in 1779 but have been lost.

[16] MPA, Collection 'A,' 122/1782; 164, 300 and 301/1783 (although the letter is actually dated 25 January 1784).

[17] Derek Beales, *Prosperity and Plunder: European Catholic Monasteries in the Age of Revolution, 1650-1815* (Cambridge: Cambridge University Press, 2003), 193.

Table 2: Population census 1781[18]

Eparchy	Number of households	Number of parishes	Households per parish
Archeparchy	17,598	175	100
Arad	38,045	481	79
Bačka	11,335	61	185
Buda	2995	48	62
Karlstadt	12,495	118	105
Pakrac	9974	100	100
Temeswar	47,801	287	166
Vršac	42,599	239	178
Total	182,842	1509	121

Contrary to the situation in the Catholic Church, the reorganization of the parishes did not immediately raise the issues of the secular clergy and the monasteries. This was partly because the number of monks was not very great, but more because there was no widespread tradition of having monasteries in towns/villages and using monks as parish priests. The question of the regulation of the monasteries, however, was raised in 1770. As with the reform of parishes, it was impossible to plan anything without conducting a survey first. Thus, the first survey, to establish the numbers of monks and their revenue, was conducted early in 1771. During the following several years another two surveys were carried out in order to establish a more detailed picture of life in the monasteries (monks' occupations and education, internal discipline, state of the libraries, etc.).[19]

---

[18] Based on the summary of the census from Vienna, Austrian State Archives: Haus-, Hof- und Staatsarchiv [henceforth HHStA], Illyrico-Serbica, box 6.

[19] The surveys have not been fully preserved. Ruvarac published the 1771 survey of the monasteries of the archeparchy, while Grujić published the results of the same census for the Banat monasteries. Miklošić published the second survey of the monasteries of the archeparchy. Most of the original documents have been lost. Dimitrije Ruvarac, "Opis Fruškogorskih manastira od 1771. godine," Arhiv za istoriju srpske pravoslavne karlovačke mitropolije [hereafter Arhiv] 3 (1913): 98; Radoslav M. Grujić, Prilošci istoriji srp. Banatskih manastira u drugoj polovini 18. veka (Sremski Karlovci: Srpska manastirska štamparija, 1906), 24-51; Fr. Miklošić, "Izvještaj od god. 1772 o manastirih na Fruškoj Gori u Sriemu," Starine, 8 (1876): 1-19.

According to the survey of 1771, there were thirty-six Orthodox monasteries (and six small "daughter" houses) in the metropolis. The proportion of monasteries to the overall population in Austria was similar to that in Hungary and well below the number of Catholic houses in the Hereditary Lands even after the dissolution of the Jesuits.[20] Compared with the Catholic houses in the central lands, the Orthodox monasteries of the metropolis were smaller and poorer. Even the monasteries of the archeparchy, which were the biggest and the richest, had, with only one exception, fewer than twenty monks. The average number of monks across the metropolis was ten, though there were houses in the Banat with as few as two monks. Only the five richest monasteries had annual incomes above 2000 fl.[21]

Once the results of the surveys were known, Maria Theresa decided that the smallest monasteries were to be abolished. As a result, six small "daughter" houses were merged with their main houses, and three small monasteries in the Banat and two small monasteries in the Pakrac eparchy were merged with bigger neighbouring ones. Only one monastery, Ráckeve/Srpski Kovin in Buda eparchy, was abolished.[22] The second round of the abolition of the Orthodox monasteries, planned for 1777, was in the end abandoned due to the bishops' protests and general unrest that followed the introduction of various reforms of popular religious customs.[23]

Thus, Maria Theresa's policies towards the Orthodox monasteries differed significantly from her actions regarding the Catholic houses in the central Habsburg lands. This has often been quoted as obvious evidence of her anti-Orthodox sentiments.[24] However, they were not completely without parallels. The reorganization of the Orthodox monasteries mirrored

---

[20] Before Joseph's reduction of the monasteries in the Hereditary Lands there were approximately seven hundred houses to eight million people, and in Hungary two hundred houses to a similar number of people. Beales, *Prosperity and Plunder*, 180-93.

[21] The average size of a house in Lower and Upper Austria and Hungary was about thirty brethren. The average annual revenue for Lower Austrian houses was more than 10,000 fl. Dickson, *Finance and Government*, 1:73.

[22] MPA, synodal documents, 209/1774, and the translation of the same document in Dimitrije Ruvarac, "Izvod iz sinodske rasprave odnoseći se na regulisanje pravoslavnih manastira 23. septembar 1774," *Srpski Sion*, 15 (1905): 49-50.

[23] MPA, synodal documents, 209/1774; MPA, Collection 'A,' 194/1778; §§ 46 and 47, "Beschwerde des Illyrischen Cleri und Nation über das neue Regulament de a. 1777," HHStA, Illyrico-Serbica, box 6, published in Dimitrije Ruvarac, "Žalba mitropolita Vićentija Jovanovića Vidaka protiv regulamenta od 2. januara 1777," *Arhiv* 1 (1911): 71-184.

[24] For the clearest examples of this, see Djoko M. Slijepčević, *Istorija Srpske crkve*, vol. 2 (Munich, 1966), 28-29; Mita Kostić, *Dositej Obradović u istorijskoj perspektivi 18. veka* (Belgrade: Naučna knjiga, 1952), 41-43.

almost completely the reorganization of the Catholic monasteries conducted in Lombardy in 1769. What is more, simultaneously with the reorganization of the monasteries of the metropolis of Karlovci, the Habsburg authorities were conducting reforms along exactly the same lines in Galicia.[25]

The most surprising aspect of the reforms of the Orthodox monasteries is that Joseph paid no attention to them at all. At the beginning of his reign he did ensure that the new monastic regulations, which the Orthodox bishops had started compiling towards the end of Maria Theresa's reign, were finished and published and introduced into the monasteries.[26] After that, the only sign that Vienna had not completely lost interest in them is the reminder sent to the metropolitan that his report on the financial situation in the monasteries for 1785 was due.[27]

Education

For the newly envisaged parish-based church, the proper education of both priests and laity was of crucial importance. This applied to the Orthodox population of the metropolis as well. At the very beginning of the reform process it was proposed that priests be given a higher level of education. The state was not, however, prepared to finance seminaries for the Orthodox clergy, and it was left to the bishops to find means to open a seminary in each eparchy.[28] As the request was made at the very moment when the bishops' revenues were being reduced and were coming under closer scrutiny of the state, the bishops were extremely reluctant to commit themselves.[29] Maria Theresa realised in the end that it was impossible for every eparchy to support a seminary, and in 1775-76 it was decided that one central seminary for the whole metropolis should be

---

[25] Beales, *Prosperity and Plunder*, 190-91.

[26] Dimitrije Ruvarac, "Pravila za kaludjere mitropolita Vićentija Jovanovića Vidaka od 1777. i 1780.," *Srpski Sion* 17 (1907): 402-07.

[27] A short survey of several monasteries of the archeparchy from the end of the 1780s shows a fairly similar picture to the one from the end of the 1770s. Dimitrije Ruvarac, "Stanje pravoslavnih manastira 1787-1791," *Arhiv* 1 (1911): 90-107.

[28] The plan to open the seminaries was included in the *Regulament*, though finances were not mentioned at all. §§ 33, 34 and 36, *Regulament* (Vienna, 1770).

[29] The bishops simply claimed that they did not have enough resources to sponsor students or open schools. MPA, Collection 'A'; Over the next couple of years the Illyrische Hofdeputation continued asking for seminaries, but without any effect. MPA, Collection 'A,' 45/1770; 34/1771, February 1771; 222/1772, March 1772; 304/1772, September 1772; 341/1772, November 1772.

opened in Temeswar (Temesvár/Timişoara).[30] The bishop of Temeswar even prepared a plan for the new building, the ground floor of which was to be let out to local merchants, so that the school could collect the rent.[31] The plan was never adopted and put into action, presumably again because of financial problems.[32] After these unsuccessful attempts, Maria Theresa abandoned the idea of opening an Orthodox seminary.

It looked as if Joseph II's accession would have an impact on this issue. As he worked to open a series of seminaries for the future Catholic clergy, Joseph turned his attention to the Orthodox seminaries as well. He planned to open one central seminary in Temeswar. The state proposed to pay for the construction of a brand new school building. The proposal went far enough for an architect to be engaged and the plans for the future building to be drawn up.[33] At the same time, the local bishop and the metropolitan were also deeply engaged in negotiations with Vienna about the curriculum for the school.[34] However, after a few years it became obvious that there would not be enough money to build a whole new school. Therefore, the Orthodox were offered a building of the recently abolished Franciscan monastery in Temeswar. Even this plan was in the end abandoned, again probably because of the lack of money.[35] The first Orthodox seminary in the Habsburg lands was opened only four years after Joseph's death, but as a private school financed by the metropolitan.[36]

The state proved much more successful in introducing general elementary education reform among the Orthodox. This was, in fact, possibly the only sphere of the reforms where something close to full uniformity was achieved between what was being introduced in society at large and among the Orthodox. Orthodox schools also lagged slightly behind in the general educational reform process.[37] The first director of the

---

[30] 29 March 1774, MPA, Collection 'A,' 34/1774; Dimitrije Ruvarac, "Rad sinodski 1774 i 1775 godine," *Srpski Sion* 13 (1903): 677-78.

[31] MPA, Collection 'A,' 185/1774.

[32] Dimitrije Ruvarac, "Rad arhijerejskog Sinoda 1776," *Srpski Sion* 14 (1904): 300.

[33] MPA, Collection 'A,' 150, 160 and 170/1785; 314/1786.

[34] MPA, Collection 'A,' 432, 567 and 570/1786.

[35] MPA, Collection 'A,' 318/1788.

[36] For Metropolitan Stratimirović's seminary, see Djoko Slijepčević, *Stevan Stratimirović, mitropolit Karlovački, kao poglavar crkve, prosvetni i nacionalno-politički radnik* (Belgrade: V. N. Rajković i komp., 1936), ch. 5; Nikola Gavrilović, *Karlovačka bogoslovija* (Belgrade: Srpska pravoslavna bogoslovija Svetog Arsenija, 1984).

[37] For a discussion of the general school reforms see Helmut Engelbrecht, *Geschichte des österreichischen Bildungswesens*, vol. 3 (Vienna: Österreichischer Bundesverlag, 1984), and James van H. Melton, *Absolutism and the Eighteenth-Century Origins of Compulsory Schooling in Prussia and Austria* (Cambridge: Cambridge University Press, 1988).

Orthodox schools, Teodor Janković-Mirijevski, was appointed a year before the full reforms of the schools in the Hereditary Lands started in 1774.[38] Within the next two years both new teachers' manuals and all the necessary new textbooks were translated and published in Slavonic.[39] The official document (*Školski ustav*), which regulated the organization of the Orthodox schools, was issued at the end of 1776.[40]

The organization of the schools copied what had already been prescribed in the *Allgemeine Schulordnung* in terms of teacher training, compulsory attendance, methods of teaching, schoolbooks, financing of the school buildings and teachers' salaries. The document made significant special provisions for the Orthodox. Thus, teaching was carried out in the vernacular (either Slavonic/Serbian or Romanian) while only Orthodox schoolmasters were to be employed to teach Orthodox children (Catholics could be employed only if no suitable Orthodox person could be found). These teachers were to be trained in a special *Normal Schule* (teacher training college) for the Orthodox, which was opened in Temeswar in 1777.[41] Teaching at this college, as well as the supervision of the Orthodox schools, was to be done by special Orthodox school directors. Children were required to attend a Catholic school only if there was no Orthodox one in the village. The Orthodox were even allowed to have their own catechism, rather than the translation of Johann Ignaz von Felbiger's prescribed book.[42] When the schools in Hungary were

---

[38] MPA, Collection 'A,' 390/1773.

[39] Three key works dealing with the elementary education reform in the metropolis of Karlovci are Strahinja Kostić, "Kulturorientierung und Volksschule der Serben in der Donaumonarchie zur Zeit Maria Theresias," in *Österreich im Europa der Aufklärung*, ed. Richard G. Plaschka and Grete Klingenstein (Vienna: Verlag der Österreichischen Akademie der Wissenschaften, 1985), 845-65; Philip J. Adler, "Habsburg School Reform among the Orthodox Minorities, 1770-1780," *Slavic Review* 33 (1974): 23-45; Dimitrije Kirilović, *Srpske osnovne škole u Vojvodini u 18. veku* (Sremski Karlovci: Srpska manastirska štamparija, 1929).

[40] *Školski ustav*, in German and Slavonic, was published as the appendix in Kirilović, *Srpske osnovne škole u Vojvodini*. To begin with, new regulations applied only to the Banat, but similar provisions were later introduced in Hungary. See n. 43.

[41] MPA, Collection 'A,' 231/1777.

[42] The catechism was written by the Serbian historian and theologian Jovan Rajić at the synod's request and published under the synod's name in 1776. The publication of the book did not proceed without problems of its own. For the problems with the first edition of Rajić's *Catechism*, see Dimitrije Ruvarac, *Arhimandrit Jovan Rajić, 1726-1801* (Sremski Karlovci: Srpska manastirska štamparija, 1901) and idem, "Arhimandrita Jovana Rajića Istorija katihizma," *Arhiv* 2 (1912): 225-310; also Marija Petrović, "Josephinist Reforms and the Serbian Church Hierarchy in the Habsburg Lands" (DPhil. thesis, Oxford University, 2009), 170-78.

reorganised a year later, similar provision for linguistic and religious freedom was made for the Orthodox.[43]

Overall, the schools proved fairly successful among the Orthodox. In 1780-81 Mirijevski reported that in the district of Grosswardein (Nagyvárad/Oradea) almost half of the male school children attended school regularly, while another third came occasionally (the number of girls attending was approximately half that of the boys).[44] Joseph's accession did not significantly change things for the Orthodox. Even the proclamation of Toleration brought few innovations. Mirijevski went as the representative of the Orthodox schools to a meeting in Vienna in 1782, where the benefits of toleration for the Lutheran, Calvinist, and Orthodox schools were discussed. In a slightly smug report he sent to the metropolitan in Karlovci, he claimed that while toleration would have a significant impact on the Lutheran and Calvinist schools, it would not change much for the Orthodox in the metropolis.[45] One aspect of the school reform, which left the Orthodox dissatisfied, was that the special provisions for Orthodox schools did not extend to the Military Frontier where, because of the importance of German, all children had to attend German-speaking schools. Nor did the proclamation of religious toleration change this.[46]

Two things that happened during the 1780s did, however, have a negative effect on the Orthodox schools. One was the departure of the most energetic and competent school director, Teodor Janković, for Russia, where Catherine the Great had invited him to supervise the reorganization of schools. Another was the war with Turkey, which disrupted normal life in southern Hungary and thus further reduced the already declining school attendance.

Religious Customs and Popular Worship

Various aspects of everyday life and popular religious customs were very much a target of the Josephinist reforms. Here I will concentrate on

---

[43] When in 1778 the Banat was incorporated into Hungary, the *Ratio Educationis* was applied to Serbian schools there as well, although the religious and linguistic freedoms given to Orthodox schools in the *Školski ustav* were kept. Kostić, "Kulturorientierung und Volksschule der Serben," 860.

[44] Adler, "Habsburg School Reform," 44.

[45] MPA, Collection 'A,' 66/1782.

[46] The increased stress Joseph's administration placed on uniformity actually reduced even further the number of church-run Orthodox schools in the Frontier. MPA, Collection 'A,' 196 and 270/1783, 642/1784.

two issues which the authorities considered important enough to be included in the regulations: the number of feast days, and practices regarding burials.

The reduction of the number of feast days began again by establishing the actual state of things, the number of feast days observed. This list, compiled in 1769, showed that the Orthodox at that point had about 130 non-working feast days excluding Sundays.[47] This was extreme not only by today's standards, but even if compared with the number of feast days observed in the Catholic church at that time.[48] The first reduction was therefore agreed upon in 1770 and took the number of non-working feast days down to about eighty. However, once the number of Catholic feast days was further reduced in 1771, even this number seemed excessive. Therefore several years later another reduction was introduced, which brought the number of feast days down to slightly more than forty.[49] The third reduction, introduced by Joseph II, finally reduced the number of non-working feast days to about thirty-five.[50]

The reform of the calendar did not only have a restrictive impact. It allowed for certain exceptions, which meant that on the local level the changes were felt less acutely.[51] Also, as the main aim of the calendar reform was to increase productivity, it forbade the Orthodox to work only on four major Catholic feasts (Christmas, Corpus Christi, Easter, and Pentecost - two of which were Sundays anyway). On the other Catholic

---

[47] Work was not allowed on 120 fixed feast days, on four Saturdays, and on a series of moveable feasts of the Easter cycle. The list completed by the synod in 1769 has been lost, but the numbers can be reconstructed from the list of feasts on which work was allowed after 1770 and from the calendar indicating the remaining non-working feast days. Appendix D, *Regulament*, 1770; *Mesjacoslov vostočnago pravoslavnago ispovjedanija* (Vienna, 1771); Ruvarac gave a slightly smaller number of non-working feast days in Dimitrije Ruvarac, *Kako je postao današnji broj zapovednih parznika kod Srbalja* (Belgrade: J. J. Medecijan i Kimpanović, 1888).

[48] Hersche's conservative estimate is that about fifty feast days were observed in towns and about eighty or ninety in villages. The Catholics of the Habsburg lands also went through two reforms of the calendar in this period, first in 1753-54 and then in October 1771. Peter Hersche, "Wieder 'Müßigang' und 'Ausschweifung,'" *Innsbrucker Historische Studien* 12/13 (1990): 99-106.

[49] The list of non working feast days was published in Appendix E, *Regulament*, 1777.

[50] MPA, Collection 'A,' 486/1786, Appendix A.

[51] Every family, village, town, and region was allowed to continue celebrating its own patron saint (though not to choose a new one) even if his/her feast was not a non-working feast day any more. §71, *Regulament*, 1770; §72, *Regulament*, 1777; §74, "Declaratorium."

feast days they only had to refrain from noisy and outdoor work from eight till eleven in the morning.[52]

Much more "picturesque" were the attempts to regulate the burial customs of the Orthodox. As early as the 1750s, the state started to introduce rules for burials as a sanitary measure to protect the health of the population. Cemeteries were moved from churchyards to the outskirts of towns and villages, while burials within churches were banned altogether. A strict time frame was also imposed, which was meant to ensure that the person was really dead before the body was buried, but that the corpse was not left above ground too long.[53]

Orthodox burial customs made the introduction of new rules both more and less pressing. On the one hand, among the Orthodox there was almost no practice of burying people in churches with the exception of church hierarchs and a few very notable people.[54] On the other hand, the religious customs accompanying burial did give cause for concern. Customarily the body was kept and carried in an open coffin to the church, where a memorial service was celebrated. During the service there was a point when it was the custom for the family to come and kiss the body of the deceased.[55] By the 1770s, observance of this custom had become exaggerated; the local authorities reported that not only family, but relatives, friends, and people simply present at the funeral all came forward to give the last kiss. Moreover, on the way from the home of the deceased to the church the procession stopped in the streets and squares, and people approached to kiss the body.[56]

The first attempts to introduce new burial regulations among the Orthodox only came rather late, in 1770, and were enforced only half-

---

[52] §71, *Regulament*, 1770; §72, *Regulament*, 1777; §74, "Declaratorium." This was also confirmed in the new calendar issued during Joseph II's reign. MPA, Collection 'A,' 486/1786, Appendix A.

[53] This was a compromise between two major fears of that era: that one would be buried alive and that corpses polluted the air, thus endangering the health of those in the vicinity (bad air was considered harmful to people's health). John McManners, *Death and the Enlightenment: Changing Attitudes to Death among Christians and Unbelievers in Eighteenth-Century France* (Oxford: Oxford University Press, 1981), esp. chs. 9 and 10; Erna Lesky, "Österreichisches Gesundheitswesen im Zeitalter des aufgeklärten Absolutismus," *Archiv für Österreichische Geschichte,*122 (1959): 1-228, esp. 175-94.

[54] Miroslav Timotijević, *Manastir Krušedol*, 2 vols. (Belgrade: Draganić, 2009), 2:121-58.

[55] The burial customs of the Orthodox are described with a fair amount of detail in Johann von Csaplovics, *Slavonien und zum Theil Croatien*, 2 vols. (Pest: Hartleben's Verlag, 1819), 1:181-84.

[56] MPA, Collection 'A,' 384/1770 and 88/1771.

heartedly.[57] Over the following six years there were numerous attempts by various administrative bodies not only to impose the new time framework for burials, but also to move cemeteries out of churchyards and most importantly to ban open coffins.[58] It was only in 1777 that the authorities tried to enforce them properly. While the time frame for burials, and even the removal of the cemeteries outside built-up areas, were accepted without much protest, the order to have coffins closed was one of the major causes of the riots that erupted in Novi Sad and Vršac in the autumn of 1777.[59] The situation became so tense that Vienna decided to partly withdraw the new regulations, allowing the Orthodox to keep coffins open except when infectious disease was the suspected cause of death.[60]

Joseph II's reign again was a period of calm after the turmoil of the 1770s. Even his 1784 decree introducing reusable coffins never reached the Orthodox, and therefore neither did the protests that the decree caused. Towards the end of his reign, Joseph's administration managed to enforce the removal of cemeteries to the outskirts of towns and villages, and that without any problems or public protests.[61] The question of open coffins was not addressed again, although by the early nineteenth century the practice was slowly dying out.[62]

Role of the Bishops

What was the role, if any, of the Orthodox church hierarchy in this whole reform process? As we have seen, despite some local peculiarities, the reforms of the metropolis of Karlovci were on the whole very much a part of the general reforms introduced by Maria Theresa and Joseph II. The overall agenda was set in Vienna. However, despite this it would not be right to assume that the reforms were completely a one-way process.

Before this major period of reforms, Vienna had already attempted a partial reorganization of the metropolis in the 1750s. These reforms were attempted without consultation with representatives from the Serbian community, and their primary aim was to regulate the position of the metropolis towards two administrative bodies which claimed jurisdiction

---

[57] New rules were included in the *Regulament*, but were not observed. §43, *Regulament*, 1770.

[58] MPA, Collection 'A,' 384/1770; 30 and 88/1771; 533/1773; for another attempt in 1775, see Kostić, *Grof Koler*, 165.

[59] Detailed reports about the Vršac riots are in Hofkammer Archiv, Banater Akten, box 142/1778. Schwicker, *Politische Geschichte*, 277-79.

[60] MPA, Collection 'A,' 663/1778.

[61] MPA, Collection 'A,' 13/1789 (the actual date of the document is 30 September 1788).

[62] Csaplovics, *Slavonien und zum Theil Croatien*, 1:181-82; Schwicker, *Politische Geschichte*, 345.

over it (the Illyrische Hofdeputation and the Hungarian Court Chancellery) and thus to put a halt to constant strife between these two bodies. The proposed reforms, however, only made the dispute worse, and when the Serbian metropolitan also started to complain, the whole project was abandoned.[63] When the next attempt at reform was planned, Vienna decided that any changes were much more likely to be accepted if they were introduced with local support. The church hierarchy was the likeliest candidate to offer such support, so right from the start, although fairly firm about the issues to be raised and the aims to be achieved, Vienna was eager to have the bishops interested and participating in the reform process.

As far as the bishops were concerned, the idea of reforms was not as remote as might be expected. Although there was no intellectual movement in the Serbian Orthodox church to mirror Jansenism, or Reform Catholicism, or even the reform movement in the Russian Orthodox Church, from the mid-eighteenth century there was a certain change in attitude among the Serbian bishops in the Habsburg lands. This was based less on theological and doctrinal considerations, and more on the observation that practical changes were necessary to make the Orthodox Church relevant in its new surroundings, the Habsburg territories. Thus already in the 1730s the first attempts were made to reform the Orthodox monasteries of the metropolis (and enforce stricter discipline), while a survey of the parishes and parish priests of the eparchies of Karlovci and Belgrade was conducted to determine the clergy's level of education and how well they were performing their tasks.[64] Most of these efforts were undone in the 1740s, but was then followed by another period of reforms by the energetic metropolitan Pavle Nenadović (1749-68). He introduced the first permanent schools for clerics, and also worked on regulating life in the monasteries (successfully, but only after he kept some of the most stubborn abbots locked in the cellar of his residence in Karlovci until they consented to the reforms).[65] Although all these reforms were partial and most of them

---

[63] Schwicker, *Politische Geschichte*, 204-16; also Philip J. Adler, "Serbs, Magyars, and Staatsinteresse in Eighteenth Century Austria: A Study in the History of Habsburg Administration," *Austrian History Yearbook* 12 (1976): 116-28.

[64] For a good survey of what was happening during the first couple of decades of the century, see Dimitrije Ruvarac, "Mojsije Petrović, mitropolit beogradski 1713-1730: Prilog istoriji srpske crkve," *Spomenik SKA* 31 (1892): 81-200, and idem, "Mitropolija beogradska oko 1735. godine," *Spomenik SKA* 37 (1905): 101-204.

[65] For metropolitan Nenadović's school policies, see Dimitrije Ruvarac, *Pokrovo-bogorodične škole u Karlovcima 1747-1769* (Sremski Karlovci: Srpska manastirska štamparija, 1926); for

had limited long-term effects, they at least meant that the hierarchy was accustomed to the idea of reform and reorganization in the church.

Counting on the bishops' benevolent attitude, if not full support, Vienna decided right from the start that the new regulations should be passed through the synod before being made public. This gave the bishops a significant role in the procedural side of the process and also an opportunity to influence the actual policies, as the synod could not be made to approve the reforms without having at least some debate on the contents. This obviously led to occasional problems, as there were issues on which Vienna did not really want the bishops' opinion, just their approval. In these situations Vienna had two options: either not to present the issue to the bishops at all and then deal with their protests once the regulation was published, or to give the bishops the opportunity to debate the issue but then to ignore the conclusions of the synod.[66]

This, however, did not mean that the bishops' protests were always futile. The bishops were realistic enough to know that even if they had reservations about Vienna's proposals, they could not gain much by simple stubborn resistance. Thus they were prepared to compromise and yield to the proposals, especially if they thought the issues were regarded as fundamental for the reform process.[67] Vienna, on the other hand, was prepared to listen to objections, provided they were based on rational arguments. An especially striking example of this is the episode with the bishops' revenues. Early in the 1770s, the dues the bishops were allowed to collect were drastically reduced. The bishops of the poorest eparchies (Karlstadt, Buda, and Pakrac) complained that it was impossible to live on their new revenues, and Vienna duly awarded the three bishops state pensions to supplement their incomes.[68] Similarly, at the demand of the

---

his work on reforming the monasteries: Tihomir Ostojić, *Dositej Obradović u Hopovu. Studija iz kulturne i književne istorije* (Novi Sad: Matica srpska, 1910), 27-55.

[66] Most notably, the matter of the metropolitan's right to consider himself a "national" leader not only in spiritual but in secular matters was not brought up for the discussion at any of the synodal meetings in the 1770s, and Vienna even firmly rebuked metropolitans when they tried to raise the issue on other occasions. Ruvarac, "Rad sinodski 1774 i 1775 godine"; idem, "Radnja arhijerejskog Sinoda 1776"; Dimitrije Ruvarac, "Rezolucija carice Marije Terezije mitropolitu Vićentiju Jovanoviću Vidaku, u kojoj se ponavljaju predjašnje rezolucije, da se on ne sme smatrati i držati za glavu narodnu, i o konzistoriji," *Srpski Sion* 16 (1906): 248-50.

[67] Thus the metropolitan dropped his long disputed claim to secular leadership. Similarly, lay participation in the local church institutions (except consistories) was agreed upon, as were the state-imposed rules for the election of abbots. For the summary of the bishops' opinions on these issues, see "Beschwerde des Illyrischen Cleri und Nation."

[68] MPA, Collection 'B,' 33/1772.

bishops the Orthodox were allowed, as has been mentioned above, to use a separate catechism in their schools instead of a translation of Felbiger.[69]

Although on several occasions Vienna tried to avoid problems by simply not raising issues for discussion at the synod, most of the time it accepted that this should be the standard procedure for passing the reforms. Thus the second round of the abolition of Orthodox monasteries was abandoned because of the bishops' complaints that it was planned without the synod's consent.[70] Sekereš's *Monastic Rules* were also withdrawn because, among other things, they were published in the synod's name but without its approval.[71] Although there was less contact, Joseph II continued the same policy of active cooperation with the synod.[72]

The bishops were also entrusted with many executive parts of the reform. Thus the population census from the 1770s was conducted entirely by the senior clergy and eparchial officials, and so was the first survey of the monasteries.[73] The state set the rules for reorganization, but it was left to the bishops not only to establish the actual number of priests, but also to name those who would be made supernumerary. Similarly, the bishops were allowed to decide how to reduce the number of feast days; the state only insisted that the number of feast days be reduced.

Bishops probably played the greatest role in organizing the practicalities of the school reform. Although the state was anxious to reduce the influence of the clergy in matters of education, it had to rely on the bishops to suggest competent laymen who could be effective in the reorganization of schools. The first school director for the Banat, Teodor Janković, was not only the metropolitan's candidate for the job, but was actually at the time of his appointment the long-standing secretary of the bishop of Temeswar.[74] The first group of Serbs who were sent to complete a teacher-training course in Vienna were all recommended by the metropolitan. The people who translated the schoolbooks into Serbian were found through the metropolitan, and the secretary of the bishop of Vršac produced the translations into Romanian.[75] Even when in 1775

---

[69] MPA, Collection 'B,' 18/1774.

[70] §§ 47 and 48. "Beschwerde des Illyrischen Cleri und Nation."

[71] Ad §48. "Beschwerde des Illyrischen Cleri und Nation."

[72] In 1781 the eparchy of Buda was preserved at the synod's plea. And five years later, it was the synod, though at the request of Vienna, that further reduced the number of non-working feast days. Schwicker, *Politische Geschichte*, 348-49. MPA, Collection 'A,' 486/1786, Appendix A.

[73] MPA, Collection 'A,' 375/1773. Ruvarac, "Opis fruškogorskih manastira," 97-99.

[74] MPA, Collection 'A,' 238/1772 and 390/1773.

[75] MPA, Collection 'A,' 156 and 197/1777.

Teodor Janković Mirijevski was late with his translations of Felbiger's manuals, Vienna repeatedly wrote to the metropolitan asking him about the delay. At this stage Janković was a state employee, translating books for use in state schools.[76]

As Vienna predicted, the bishops also played an important part in getting the faithful to accept the innovations, though this did not go as smoothly as was expected. In 1777, when the reform process was in full swing, people realized that Vienna was serious about introducing the reforms. When it became clear that this was happening with the support of the church hierarchy people rebelled, although not against Vienna but against the bishops. The protests escalated to violence in only two towns (Novi Sad and Vršac), but there were several cases of localized unrest and many letters of complaint sent to the bishops.[77] There was a serious danger that the bishops' reputation among the people would be damaged. However, Vienna reacted quickly to the metropolitan's pleas, reduced the pace of the reforms, and even withdrew a couple of the most problematic regulations in order to give the bishops a chance to regain their positions. Things soon calmed down and seemingly with no long-term harm to the bishops' authority. From the 1780s the reform process even began to acquire supporters among the developing Serbian professional class.[78] In the long run it would be precisely this growing professional class that would benefit the most from the changes introduced into the metropolis at this period.

***

As we have seen, in terms of their content, the reforms of the metropolis fit well with the total Josephinist reform program. They were planned centrally (though perhaps with a surprising amount of regard for local peculiarities) and executed, to a large extent, with the help of the progressive church hierarchy. What is noteworthy about them is the division of the roles played by Maria Theresa and Joseph II. Maria Theresa did not just initiate the reforms, she implemented a fully developed and

---

[76] MPA, Collection 'A,' 303, 339, 374, and 497/1775; 30/1776.

[77] For two different versions of the Novi Sad and Vršac riots, see HKA, Banater Akten, box 142/1778, and Schwicker, *Politische Geschichte*, 314-20. For other protests and complaints, see *Spomenici iz Budimskog i Peštanskog arhiva*, ed. Gavrilo Vitković, 6 vols. (Belgrade: Državna štamparija, 1873-75), 3:388-91; MPA, Collection 'A,' 11/1777 and 10/1778; MPA, Collection 'B,' 94/1777, 9 and 63/1778.

[78] Petrović, "Josephinist Reforms," 254-58.

complete programme of reforms, which was codified and together with the privileges determined the position of the metropolis. On the other hand, except to finish a couple of initiatives left from his mother's time, Joseph made hardly any attempt to further reform the metropolis.

It is easier to explain the unusually active stance of Maria Theresa regarding the Orthodox than to find a satisfactory explanation for the almost complete lack of activity on Joseph's part. The reasons that kept Maria Theresa from embarking on a full-blown reform of the Catholic church were absent from her dealings with the Orthodox. In the first place the Orthodox were only a tolerated religion, "schismatics" rather than "heretics" like the Protestants, and protected by imperial privileges, but still far removed from "the one true church" and the emotional importance that held for Maria Theresa. The position and authority of the metropolitan of Karlovci could not in any way be compared to that of the pope. The metropolitan was after all the head of just one small religious group, and a Habsburg subject at that. The Orthodox hierarchy also had very limited political influence within the Habsburg lands, as they did not hold seats in any estates. All this meant that Maria Theresa could be as bold as she wished in her reforms, and she certainly showed that she could be a fairly radical and completely systematic reformer when free of the scruples of her faith.

The motives for Joseph's actions, or rather their absence, are less clear. One could perfectly justifiably claim that the small Orthodox metropolis was too poor and unimportant to spark Joseph's interest, except that in Bukovina, another small, poor, and predominantly Orthodox region, his actions were much more in line with his general policies. It is true that the Orthodox population of the metropolis was protected to a certain extent by imperial privileges, but the case of the Transylvanian Saxons shows that these were by no means a certain guarantee against Joseph's innovations. It could also be said that Joseph was wary of introducing reforms which could have provoked protest in the Military Frontier, although the impatience with which he brushed aside Kaunitz's attempt to suspend the reforms in the Austrian Netherlands in order to calm the protests, do raise doubts whether this sort of reasoning seemed appealing or reasonable to Joseph.

There were two factors which did make the position of the Serbs specific enough to perhaps explain the relative indifference on Joseph's part. In the first place, precisely the fact that Maria Theresa did conduct such thorough and complete reforms left the metropolis in a fairly well-ordered state at the time of Joseph's accession. It is possible that he found the measures introduced by his mother sufficient, and saw no need to interfere further. Equally important, perhaps the Serbian presence provided Vienna with a weapon that could be used against the Hungarians. Although there is no direct evidence that Joseph thought along these lines, Leopold II's actions soon after Joseph's death show that Vienna was well aware of the situation and its potential usefulness.

Every one of the reasons mentioned for Joseph's attitude towards the metropolis is possible, and even probable. It is much more likely that it was a combination of these and some other factors that influenced his policies. Although the case of the metropolis of Karlovci is far too small on the general scale of things to significantly alter our picture of Joseph's involvement in the reforms, it adds an interesting characteristic to the reform process, which very much goes against Joseph's treasured principle of uniformity.

Transnational Conversions:
Migrants in America and Greek Catholic Conversion Movements to Eastern Orthodoxy in the Habsburg Empire, 1890-1914
Joel Brady

In March of 1910, Andrii R., a Greek Catholic migrant laborer who had converted to Russian Orthodoxy in St. Louis, Missouri, returned to his native village of Myscowa in Habsburg Galicia, whereupon the regional Greek Catholic deanery council and bishop launched an inquisition. Just what was taking place in America that had led Andrii to convert? What were the ethno-political implications of his shift in religious identification? Would he and others like him upon their return from America spread a Russian and Orthodox orientation among Austro-Hungary's Greek Catholic faithful? The Greek Catholic priest in Missouri, Fr. Dymytrii Khanak, responded to the Galician bishop's transatlantic query, elicited through the American bishop. In his letter to the Galician bishop, Fr. Khanak requested leniency toward Andrii, because the Greek Catholic priest in Myscowa, Fr. Durkot, had been supporting Greek Catholic migrants to America in their "apostasy" to Russian Orthodoxy. From Myscowa, the Russophile Fr. Durkot had been writing to his flock in St. Louis saying that it was "better to go to confession and to the schismatic [Russian Orthodox] church than [the] Ukrainian." Not only this, Fr. Khanak of St. Louis reported incredulously that Fr. Durkot had been corresponding from Myscowa directly with St. Louis's Russian Orthodox priest, even requesting donations for his own Greek Catholic parish in Myscowa. When Andrii had returned from St. Louis to Myscowa as a Russian Orthodox convert, "not only did [Fr. Durkot] not admonish [Andrii], neither did he try to teach about that filth, which he...publicly denounced in church [namely, Russian Orthodoxy]."[1]

Key elements related in this letter - religious and ethnonational conversion, labor migration and remigration, transatlantic

---

[1] Letter from Fr. Dymytrii Khanak to Bishop Konstantyn Chekhovych of Przemyśl, dated 28 March 1910. Archiwum Państwowe w Przemyślu, Akta Archiwum Greckokatolickiego Biskupstwa w Przemyślu, (1551-1946) (hereafter referred to as ABGK), syg. 4929: 13-14.

correspondence, socioeconomic remittances, and attempts by religious actors in America and Eastern Europe to influence religious conditions across the Atlantic Ocean - intersect in intriguing, if bewildering ways. To make sense of this convoluted story, it is necessary to situate it within the analytical framework of transnationalism. Between 1890 and 1914, large-scale Greek Catholic conversion movements to Russian Orthodoxy proliferated on two continents separated by an ocean, in America and the Habsburg empire. These conversion movements - and the counter-movements they prompted - factored prominently in late-nineteenth and early-twentieth century national discourses (Ukrainian, Rusyn, Russian, Hungarian, and Polish, to name but a few). Several historians have remarked (though always briefly) upon American influences affecting the shifting religious identifications in Eastern Europe; however, the existing studies have largely treated conversions in American and Habsburg regions in isolation.[2]

Conversions on both sides of the Atlantic, however, influenced each other in significant ways. Transatlantic return and cyclical migration, as well as sustained correspondence between America and Habsburg lands, led many actors - migrants and nonmigrants alike - to orient their lives toward both regions of migratory origin and destination, as if together they constituted "a single arena of social action" - a phenomenon which

---

[2] These include, on the East European context: Maria Mayer, *The Rusyns of Hungary* (New York: East European Monographs, Distributed by Columbia University Press, 1997); John-Paul Himka, *Religion and Nationality in Western Ukraine: The Greek Catholic Church and the Ruthenian National Movement in Galicia, 1867-1900* (Montreal: McGill-Queen's University Press, 1999), and "The Propagation of Orthodoxy in Galicia on the Eve of World War I," *Ukraina: Kul'turna spadshchyna, natsional'na svidomist', derzhavnist'. Zbirnyk naukovykh prats'* 9 (2001): 480-96; A.V. Wendland, *Die Russophilen in Galizien: Ukrainische Konservative zwischen Österreich und Russland, 1848-1915* (Vienna: Verlag der Österreichischen Akademie der Wissenschaften, 2000), 498-507. Iaroslav Moklak, "Pravoslav"ia v Halychyni—politychni aspekty," *Zustrich* 1, no. 2 (1990): 147-54, and "Rosiis'ke Pravoslav"ia na Lemkivshchyni v 1911 – 1915 rokakh," *Lemkivshchyna* 19, no. 1 (Spring 1998): 3-8; Bogdan Horbal, "Halytskŷ starorusynŷ i rusofili i odnoshŷnia do nykh habsburskoi i tsarskoi monarkhii," *Rusin* 3 (9) (2007): 122-45. On the American context, see: Keith P. Dyrud, *The Quest for the Rusyn Soul: The Politics of Religion and Culture in Eastern Europe and in America, 1890-World War I* (Philadelphia: Balch Institute Press, 1992); Myron B. Kuropas, *The Ukrainian Americans: Roots and Aspirations, 1884-1954* (Toronto: University of Toronto, 1991); Walter Warzeski, "Religion and National Consciousness in the History of the Rusins of Carpatho-Ruthenia and the Byzantine Rite Pittsburgh Exarchate" (PhD diss., University of Pittsburgh, 1964); and Paul Robert Magocsi, *Our People: Carpatho-Rusyns and Their Descendants in North America* (Wauconda, IL: Bolchazy-Carducci Publishers, Inc., 2005).

many contemporary scholars describe as "transnationalism."[3] Not only did religious behaviors and ideas in America develop in conversation with those in Habsburg Galicia and Subcarpathia, conversion and counter-conversion movements in each migratory region mutually constituted each other across the Atlantic. When Greek Catholic individuals and communities adopted - and resisted - Russian Orthodoxy in America and Habsburg lands during this period, they did so transnationally. Without negating or even minimizing intra-regional factors identified by other scholars in the East European conversions, this essay appeals to theoretical frameworks articulated within the academic subdiscipline of transnationalism studies in order to argue that migrants in America contributed more significantly to Russian Orthodox movements and Greek Catholic counter-movements in Habsburg territories than has been previously acknowledged. Ultimately, I contend that late-nineteenth and early-twentieth century migrants to America did not, by their leap "across the pond," exit Habsburg history.

Transnational Consciousness

As John-Paul Himka has related in his *Religion and Nationality in Western Ukraine*, in 1882 Habsburg authorities accused the Russophile Greek Catholic priest Father Ioann Naumovych of high treason based upon his association with a village-scale "back to Orthodoxy" movement in Galicia. The incident served as a flashpoint, after which the Greek Catholic hierarchy and civil authorities more energetically targeted Russophilism and Orthodoxophilism as threats to church and state.[4] While there is no evidence to suggest that transatlantic migration played any role in this early instance of Greek Catholic-to-Orthodox conversion, the Russian Orthodox hierarchy in America some years later portrayed Fr. Naumovych in its publications as a hero of the faith. Fr. Naumovych also factored prominently in the writings of Fr. Alexis Toth, who famously converted from Greek Catholicism to Russian Orthodoxy upon arriving in America from Subcarpathia around 1890, after which he facilitated the conversion of an estimated twenty-five thousand Greek Catholics to Orthodoxy in America over the next twenty years.[5] It is not difficult to ascertain why Fr. Ioann Naumovych, associated with earlier conversions

---

[3] Maxine Margolis, *Little Brazil: An Ethnography of Brazilian Immigrants in New York City* (Princeton: Princeton University Press, 1994), 29.

[4] Himka, *Religion and Nationality in Western Ukraine*, 74-78.

[5] Magocsi, *Our People*, 26.

of Greek Catholics to Orthodoxy in Habsburg realms, would appear in hagiographies produced by Fr. Toth and other Russian Orthodox authors for an American migrant audience comprised of recent or potential converts from Greek Catholicism to Russian Orthodoxy.

Beginning around 1900 and continuing for the next decade and a half, until 1914 - as Greek Catholic-to-Orthodox movements in America continued to gain numbers - new waves of Orthodox movements began to appear in Habsburg realms, in both Galician and Subcarpathian villages. Historians have rightly highlighted the important role of East European and Russian factors in the conversions, such as pre-existing Russophilism, local conflicts with priests (often economic or ethnonational in character), or the influx of Orthodox missionaries from Russia, beginning around 1911. By 1914 these Orthodox movements culminated in two treason trials in Maramorosh Sighet, Subcarpathia and in Lviv, Galicia.[6]

Many migrants from Galicia and Subcarpathia in America - both Greek Catholic and Orthodox - followed with great interest the conversions in East Europe from Greek Catholicism to Orthodoxy after the turn of the century, especially the 1914 trials most famously known today for their association with the accused Hieromonk Aleksei Kabaliuk in Maramorosh Sighet and Fr. Maksym Sandovych in Lviv.[7] Meanwhile, nonmigrants in Habsburg lands by no means remained unaware of the conversions in America, about which Galician publications like *Nyva* and *Tserkovnii Vostok* regularly included news items and editorials, speculating about the movement's source. A 1907 article, for example, arguing against the introduction of the Hungarian language into the Greek Catholic liturgy in Subcarpathian Rus, suggested that the language disparity between clergy and laity in America had led to the Orthodox schismatic movement there, and would do so in Habsburg realms as well.[8] Habsburg migrants in America were also prone to enlist the conversion movements

---

[6] Determining the number of converts is a difficult enterprise, given that some did so only temporarily or never did so formally. Another way in which to quantify the influence of the Orthodox movements is to count villages. As Himka related of the Galician context, "surveying the scene in the spring of 1914 the Austrian authorities estimated that there were about 400 villages in which 5-10 families had converted 'to the so-called Orthodoxy'...Another 200 villages could pass to Orthodoxy if circumstances were right." ("Propagation of Orthodoxy," 492).

[7] Both these men, like Fr. Alexis Toth of America, are today Orthodox saints.

[8] "Madiars'ka mova v Bohosluzheniu u hreko-kat. Madiariv(!)," *Katolićki List* 12, no. 3, quoted in "Madiars'ka mova v tserkovnim bohosluzheniu a rus'ke dukhovenstvo na Uhorschyni," *Katolyts'kyi Vskhid* 4, no. 2 (1907): 228-29.

in their migratory regions of origin for homiletic purposes, particularly Russophile ones.

Transnationalism: New and Old

Migrant concern with developments in regions of migratory origin - what might be called a "transnational consciousness" - has long been familiar to historians of American immigration. It is not surprising, therefore, that Galician and Subcarpathian migrant readers in America were interested in news from their region of origin.[9] Neither should it be particularly unexpected that nonmigrants in Habsburg lands demonstrated interest in the American context to which fellow family members, friends, and parishioners were migrating. However, beginning especially in the 1990s, scholars of American immigration began to explore, as the subject of an academic subdiscipline, the *ongoing* processes connecting regions of migratory origin and destination: something beyond mere consciousness.

A powerful critique of American immigration studies has issued from within the subdiscipline of transnationalism studies. The emerging field has been an interdisciplinary one; though cultural anthropologists were its pioneers, sociologists, political scientists, economists, historians, and very recently religionists have contributed to the literature. Unfortunately, partly due to its promiscuous dissemination among many disciplines, "transnationalism" has suffered from a certain definitional ambiguity. The most influential definition of transnationalism within American immigration studies, however, was set forth by cultural anthropologists Linda Basch, Nina Glick Schiller, and Christina Szanton Blanc. They argued that transnationalism is "the process by which immigrants forge and sustain multi-stranded social relations that link together their societies of origin and settlement. We call these processes transnationalism to emphasize that many immigrants today build social fields that cross geographic, cultural, and political borders. Immigrants who develop and maintain multiple relationships - familial, economic, social, organizational, religious, and political - that span borders we call 'transmigrants.' An essential element of transnationalism is the multiplicity of involvements that transmigrants sustain in both home and

---

[9] *Svit* 18, no. 32 (20 August 1914): 6.

host societies."[10] Broadly speaking, this statement has provided definitional parameters of "transnationalism" for scholars of American immigration; it informs usage of the term in this essay, though the argument of Basch, Glick Schiller, and Szanton Blanc is not without its limitations.

"Transmigrants" are seen as "living across borders." Ties between sending and receiving regions have developed through kin and friend networks, migrant organizations, and political associations, sometimes achieving such strength and density that migratory sending and receiving regions constitute, as Maxine Margolis has claimed, "a single arena of social action." Not only economic remittances, but also "social remittances," flow through transnational conduits.[11] While improving communication and travel technologies provide the means for transnationalism, scholars have identified as *causal* factors in transnationalism: (a) a global system of economic inequity, in which (b) migrants from economically peripheral regions travelled to economically exploitative core regions, where they (c) encountered racialized prejudice and socioeconomic marginalization. In this model, transnationalism provides a creative response to these challenges - an alternative means of attaining capital, social support, and the bases of personal identity.

The insights of transnationalism studies are vital to American immigration studies (and, I will argue, to Habsburg studies), yet the discipline has been limited, with several prominent exceptions, by the assumption that the category of transnationalism is applicable only to recent waves of migration.[12] The catalysts and means for transnationalism existed in earlier eras. Migration during what Ewa Morawska called the "the long turn of the century" (1870-1914) originated from economically

---

[10] Linda Basch, Nina Glick Schiller, and Christina Szanton Blanc, *Nations Unbound: Transnational Projects, Postcolonial Predicaments, and Deterritorialized Nation-States* (Langhorne, PA: Gordon and Breach, 1994), 7.

[11] Peggy Levitt, *The Transnational Villagers* (Berkeley and Los Angeles: University of California Press, 2001), 11.

[12] Specifically, those following the relaxation of American immigration laws in 1965. For examples of works on transnationalism in earlier eras, see Ewa Morawska, "Immigrants, Transnationalism, and Ethnicization: A Comparison of This Great Wave and the Last," in *E Pluribus Unum? Contemporary and Historical Perspectives on Immigrant Political Incorporation*, ed. Gary Gerstle and John Mollenkopf (New York: Russell Sage Foundation, 2001), 175-98; Donna R. Gabaccia, *Italy's Many Diasporas* (Seattle: University of Washington Press, 2000); and Adam McKeown, *Chinese Migrant Networks and Cultural Change: Peru, Chicago, Hawaii, 1900-1936* (Chicago and London: University of Chicago Press, 2001).

peripheral regions in Southern and Eastern Europe to exploitative core regions in North America.[13] At the same time, as critical whiteness studies have demonstrated, racial (not merely ethnic) discrimination in social and economic spheres also existed for turn-of-the-century East European migrants in America. The "Slav invasion" of the American labor market was portrayed by various employers, labor unions, scientists, and politicians as one of marauding "Asiatic" Huns or "European Chinamen," and "only hunkies [worked blast furnace jobs] too damn dirty and too damn hot for a white man."[14] According to David Roediger, "in such positions Slavic workers would be said to be 'working like niggers' and would, like the most exploited Jews, Sicilians, or Louisana creoles elsewhere, face further questioning of their whiteness based on the very fact of their hard and driven labor."[15]

In addition to these factors, both the Hungarian and Russian governments promoted prototypical forms of "deterritorialized citizenship" among migrant Habsburg Eastern Christians abroad.[16] Finally, while the barriers to social integration in America outlined above likely contributed to transnational behaviors for some migrants, to speak of these as primary motivating factors relies upon a hidden assumption, long discredited among scholars of American immigration: that migrants of "the New Immigration" migrated to America intending to stay - that is, they *im*migrated, consciously, from the outset. This was not the case. The vast majority of migrants from Habsburg regions migrated intending to earn money and return to villages of origin where they would buy land and settle; many of them did exactly this. Thus, it is best to characterize the barriers to social integration in America outlined above not as "motivations to return," but rather as "the absence of reasons to stay."

---

[13] Morawska, "Immigrants, Transnationalism, and Ethnicization," 178, 181.

[14] David Brody, *Steelworkers in America: The Non-Union Era* (New York: Harper & Row, 1960), 120, quoted in David Roediger, *Working toward Whiteness: How America's Immigrants Became White: The Strange Journey from Ellis Island to the Suburbs* (New York: Basic Books, 2005), 49, 43-44, 51.

[15] David Roediger, "Whiteness and Ethnicity in the History of 'White Ethnics' in the United States," in *Toward the Abolition of Whiteness*, ed. David Roediger (London: Verso, 1994), 181-98 (191).

[16] Both the Russian and Hungarian governments attempted to promote Russian- or Hungarian-oriented national identification among migrants in America by directly subsidizing migrant churches and presses, manipulating the appointment of religious officials, and disseminating politico-religious propaganda. See Dyrud, *Quest for the Rusyn Soul.*

Transnational Religion

Returning migrants have possessed the capacity to upset the social, including religious, *status quo* in regions of migratory origin. Mark Wyman, for example, has remarked upon clerical apprehensions regarding migrants' sexual immorality, alcoholism, and greed. Some late nineteenth- and early twentieth-century East European remigrants, Wyman demonstrated, "were disputing the clergy's monopoly on the truth" and "demanding the same freedom to profess their religion as in America."[17] A Galician priest expressed comparable fears in the Galician Greek Catholic periodical *Dushpastyr* in 1894, when he complained of the susceptibility of Greek Catholic migrants in America to "indifferentism" - that is, independence from the Greek Catholic church, leading to conversion to Orthodoxy and comparable evils, like Protestantism - and the infectious potential of such a sensibility on Habsburg soil:

> And still for us here in "the old country" such a principle [i.e. "indifferentism"], widespread in America, may be dangerous, because from America many return to their ancestral place, and some of them already leave here, and a second time again go to America. When such Americans, soaked in an indifferent spirit, return, it also begins to spread among our people, to work many afflictions, because our people have some inclination to indifferentism. They don't want to be without faith and without church, but (those called Lemko) easily forsake the Divine Services in church when the priest does not impress that they ought properly to go to church. [18]

Scholars of transnational religion point out that religious resources (priests, money, literature, practices, etc.) have at first flowed from regions of migratory origin to regions of migratory destination. Such was the case for migrants from Habsburg lands to America. However, increasing stability in migrant communities has resulted after a time in a partial reversal in the direction of transnational resources, such that new religious forms (like "indifferentism") have been remitted to sending regions.[19] In fact, several historians of Orthodox conversions in Habsburg realms

---

[17] Mark Wyman, "Churches, Traditions, and the Remigrant," in *Round-Trip to America: The Immigrants Return to Europe, 1880-1930* (Ithaca and London: Cornell University Press, 1993), 169-186 (170-71, 173, 178).

[18] A.T. "Nezhoda mezhy Rusynamy v Amerytsi," *Dushpastyr* 8, no. 7 (1894): 156.

[19] *Religion across Borders: Transnational Immigrant Networks*, ed. Helen Rose Ebaugh and Janet Saltzman Chafetz (Walnut Creek, CA: AltaMira Press, 2002), xii.

beginning around 1900 have acknowledged, though in all cases only briefly, just such a reversal in flow of religious resources. Professor Paul Robert Magocsi has, for instance, remarked upon the role played by the "confluence of American immigrant dollars and Russian 'rolling rubles'...meeting in the valleys of the Carpathians" in promoting conversion movements there.[20] Others have emphasized, again briefly, not only the influx of money, but also anti-Greek Catholic postcards and literature, most famously, Fr. Alexis Toth's pamphlet *Hde iskaty pravdu* (Where to Seek the Truth).[21] It is necessary to attribute an even greater role to American migrants in these conversions than has been previously noted by scholars.[22]

The trials in Galicia and Subcarpathia provided a rallying point - a cause - for the American convert population. Community leaders in America attempted to capitalize upon transnational consciousness of the trials in order to foster ethnoreligious unity. One prominent Orthodox Russophile wrote about *vicha* held in "American Rus'" to publicize the Lviv trial. (In Galicia the word *viche*, plural *vicha*, which originally referred to a popular assembly in ancient Rus', was revived in the late nineteenth century as a designation for public political meetings.) The *vicha* in America

> have continually served in that frame of mind, which appeared with the prosperous conclusion of the so-called Lviv trial. Before we cried with tears, how now do we not rejoice with great joy? As full and sincere as was our sorrow for the martyrs of Subcarpathian Rus': so more widely and higher ought to be our joy - no, I say: victory and triumph! - following [the Galician defendants'] moral national triumph....
>
> It is apparent that it is also necessary that *Russky* people from wherever comprehend one another, unify, be united! It is apparent that we need to teach the systematic conscious work

---

[20] Magocsi, *Our People*, 26-27.

[21] Mayer, *The Rusyns of Hungary*, 124; and Moklak, "Pravoslav"ia v Halychyni," 3.

[22] Since beginning my research on this subject matter, it has come to my attention that Bogdan Horbal issued a similar call: "Mentioning only those...causes, historians often forget to add the personal search of Rusyns themselves, especially those which returned from America" ("Halytskŷ starorusynŷ i rusofili," 133). Paul Best, too, has briefly noted the "very powerful indirect" influence of Russian Orthodoxy via America, in the form of correspondence, money, and publications ("Moscophilism amongst the Lemko Population in the Twentieth Century," paper given at the conference on "Ukrainian Political Thought in the Twentieth Century," Institute of History of the Jagiellonian University, 28-30 May 1990).

of raising the level of the *Russky* people in all relationships. We need schools for our young people....We need political societies for the conducting of internal American politics, in order that here would be acceptable service to our poor, forgotten, least safe *Russky* worker....In eternity, the *Russky* people, in eternity! With unity, with togetherness, with mutual assistance, with brotherly love, with elevation of the *Russky* people to the greater heights of a conscious way of life, culture, and truth. "It is time, time for Holy Rus' to go to ardent battle with our enemies!"[23]

This author, writing in the American publication *Svit* in 1914, enlisted the conversions in Eastern Europe for homiletic purposes - with the subject of that homily comprising educational, political, economic, and cultural reforms of the religio-ethnonational entity, Orthodox "American Rus'" - reforms that would unify the community, together with "Galician Rus'," "Subcarpathian Rus'," (and of course, "Mother Rus'") in one "Holy Rus'."

Evident in the 1914 Lviv trial was the role of economic remittances sent from the American migrant community. Fr. Maksym Sandovych testified that, as a subsidy for his Orthodox missionary efforts, he received from America a daily portion of ten crowns.[24] While awaiting trial in prison, Hieromonk Aleksei Kabaliuk, a central figure in the Maramorosh Sighet trial associated with the Subcarpathian conversions, wrote to the Russian Orthodox Archbishop Platon of America in April of 1914:

> Most humbly I ask Your Eminence...to send me (by telegraph) the needed three hundred (300) dollars in crowns.
>
> I beg you to send me 1430 crowns.
>
> I greet, by the Lord Jesus Christ, the American G.C. [i.e., Orthodox (!)] Holy Church and I ask that you not forget to remember me a sinner in your prayers in the holy Divine Liturgies.
>
> .....
>
> I remain in the service of Christ,
>
> Hieromonk Aleksei Kabaliuk
>
> The money, if you please, send by telegraph to the following address....[25]

---

[23] L. Turkevich, "Veche, kak narodnoe delo," *Svit* 8, no 27 (16 July 1914): 5.

[24] The testimony from the 1914 Lviv trial was originally published in the Polish daily *Słowo Polskie* and subsequently republished between 2004 and 2006 in *Przegląd Prawosławny* 6, no. 228 (2004) -- 7, no. 253 (2006). For the archival sources, see issue 6, no. 228.

[25] *Svit* (8 April 1914).

Kabaliuk solicited both economic and spiritual remittances. Archbishop Platon answered Kabaliuk in the affirmative on both counts, in a letter he had publicized alongside Kabaliuk's in a 1914 issue of *Svit*. By his publication of this correspondence, Archbishop Platon also issued a call for economic support and prayers from his American migrant constituency, thereby promoting transnational consciousness and behaviors.[26] Furthermore, the transnational transaction flowed in two directions, for Archbishop Platon also conveyed how much he had benefited by his awareness of Kabaliuk's suffering and his relationship with such a hero for the faith.[27] These were not the only incidences of economic remissions to aid these missionaries from Russia. *Svit*, for example, organized a collection from the American migrant community for the "sufferers" in the Maramorosh Sighet trial. Thus, it is apparent that both hierarchical and more grassroots sources provided money to Habsburg lands in order to support the Orthodox movements there.

---

[26] If, in fact, Archbishop Platon and others did pray for Kabaliuk in public liturgies, all the more so.

[27] Kabaliuk's biography captures the transnational complexities of these conversion movements. Born a Greek Catholic in Subcarpathia, Kabaliuk visited Orthodox monasteries in Bukovina and then in the Russian Empire in 1905. In 1908 he also visited Jerusalem and a Russian Orthodox monastery on Mount Athos in Greece, where he converted to Orthodoxy in 1909. He then returned to Russia, became a monk, and began theological studies. Under the auspices of the Serbian Orthodox Church, he began in early 1912 conducting missionary work among the Orthodox communities in Subcarpathia, which had begun in conjunction with return migration and correspondence from America. All the while, he retained cross-border contacts with Orthodox officials and Russophiles in the Russian empire, including Count Vladimir Bobrinsky, who was also instrumental in the conversion effort in Galicia. Under threat of arrest from Austro-Hungarian authorities, Kabaliuk left again for Russia, "where the visiting [American] Bishop Platon convinced him to go to the United States to serve in a Rusyn Orthodox parish in Pittsburgh." Thus, even as the role of missionaries from Russia (of which Kabaliuk was representative) increased, the American context remained important, in this case as an outlet for religious freedom for one of the principal figures in the Russian missionary period in Austria-Hungary, 1911-14 (an outlet of which Kabaliuk became aware due to the transnational behaviors of America's Russian Orthodox bishop). Kabaliuk remained in America several months, during which time he continued to encourage and assist Orthodox converts in Subcarpathia through correspondence. He was, of course, also contributing to the migrant convert population in America through his pastoral work there. Kabaliuk returned voluntarily to Subcarpathia to stand trial, after which he wrote the letter published in *Svit*. See: "Alexei Kabaliuk," in Paul Robert Magocsi and Ivan Pop, *Encyclopedia of Rusyn History and Culture* (Toronto: University of Toronto Press, 2002).

Habsburg Greek Catholics Fight Back Transnationally

Peggy Levitt and others have argued that some nonmigrants in regions of migratory origin can become "transnationalized" by their implication in migration processes. Correspondence with, visits from, and interest in news of migrants abroad functioned to incorporate nonmigrant Eastern Christians in Habsburg realms into transnational phenomena. Given the consciousness which Greek Catholics in Habsburg realms possessed of conversions in America and their tendency to spread back across the Atlantic Ocean, it is to be expected that the Habsburg Greek Catholic hierarchy would attempt to intervene in some fashion. As early as 1907, Konstantyn Chekhovych, bishop of Przemyśl, frequently expressed, in his correspondence with American Greek Catholic Bishop Soter Ortynsky, keen interest in the reports which Bishop Ortynsky delivered to him regarding the "Russophile schismatic" movement among migrants in America.[28] As early as 1908, a priest in St. Clair, Pennsylvania sent Bishop Chekhovych in Galicia a report on just who exactly had converted to Orthodoxy in that neighborhood. And beginning in 1909, Bishop Chekhovych became particularly concerned with the subject, inquiring in a pastoral letter to all his priests whether or not among their parishioners there could be found returned migrants spreading Orthodoxy and disseminating American brochures or schismatic newspapers. Between 1910 and as late as 1914, he regularly received dozens and dozens of often extremely detailed reports from parishes reporting who remained "in emigration," who had returned, who had converted to Orthodoxy, and who was promoting Orthodoxy in their villages of origin. Even for parishes reporting no Orthodox movements, this episcopal request served to transnationalize those responding by prompting formal, thorough recordkeeping of migration.

There may be some reason to doubt the accuracy of the reports claiming "no schism" among returned migrants. In 1909, the American Bishop Ortynsky ordered that all migrants returning from America carry with them records of Greek Catholic church membership, marriage, and baptisms, because:

> ...many Rusyn migrants, who converted in America to schism, returning to their country, go to the Greek Catholic Church and approach the Holy Mystery, as if they had not taken on a new life - and still they write to their schismatic friends, in

---

[28] ABGK, syg. 444. See, for example, ff. 20, 29-39, 44, 48.

order that they not be frightened of anything, because in Galicia no one will ask them to which church in America they belonged. When it occurs to them to go out again to America, they go again to the schismatic church and they further agitate for schism.

He further requested that Bishop Chekhovych in Przemyśl "adjust the prescriptions of church laws regarding those who fall away from the faith, but not least also to cut through the source of such schism in places in Galicia."[29] Bishop Ortynsky thus attempted a transnational intervention in migrant religious affairs, both in regions of migratory origin and destination. Furthermore, his "transnationalization" developed in response to migrant transnational behaviors - return migration and continued migrant correspondence of an undesirable character. While Bishop Ortynsky behaved transnationally in order to curb Orthodox movements in Habsburg realms, this report also testified that migrants who returned to Habsburg realms sought transnationally to promote Orthodoxy in America.

Notwithstanding the perhaps dubious "no Orthodoxy" reports, many Galician parishes responded to Bishop Chekhovych that yes, in fact, migrants had been spreading Orthodoxy, either through return migration or correspondence. In many cases, Greek Catholic priest-informers provided confiscated pro-Orthodox literature and transatlantic correspondence as material evidence.[30] Galician Greek Catholic parish and deanery councils also conducted interviews with returned converted migrants, which included question-and-answer sessions such as the following, excerpted from a 1911 interview with one such migrant:

> Q: Was there in that municipality [Yonkers] a Greek Catholic church and a Greek Catholic priest?
> A: There was a Greek Catholic church and priest.
> Q: Which faith did you retain in America? In accordance with which church did you perform religious practices? Before which priest did you confess and secondly receive the Holy Mystery?
> A: In the Orthodox Church, and I conducted all religious practices before the Orthodox priests.
> Q: Who persuaded you to change from the Greek Catholic faith?...
> A: No one convinced me, and I converted by myself.

---

[29] *Nyva* 6, no. 20 (October 1909): 812-13.
[30] These letters and responses, taken from nearly every parish and answering in both affirmative and negative, are available in ABGK, syg. 4928-32.

....

> Q. Do you know the difference between the holy Catholic
> faith and the schismatic faith, and do you recognize your own
> sin in falling away from union with the holy Catholic church?
> A. I recognize - in my opinion - it is a fact, that "Upon us the
> Unia is imposed." There was no sin.[31]

It was also these fact-finding investigations that brought to light the story with which this essay began: the account of the returned migrant Andrii as reported by a Greek Catholic priest, Fr. Khanak, in America to the Greek Catholic bishop of Przemyśl. The transnational implications of Fr. Khanak's letter - what might be called an exercise in "transnational tattle-taling" - are myriad and point to transnationalism at varying social strata. A Greek Catholic bishop in Habsburg lands requested a report on the American context, in response to which a Greek Catholic migrant priest in America not only provided information, he also attempted to influence East European religious dynamics, by (a) asking for leniency toward a converted returned migrant and (b) reporting upon the subterfuge of the Greek Catholic priest in Myscowa. This subterfuge consisted of transnational correspondence by that Greek Catholic priest in Galicia with converted migrants in America and the Orthodox priest who was ministering to them, while at the same time Fr. Durkot publicly denounced the migrant-led Orthodox movement among his congregation in Habsburg realms. The transnational transaction between Fr. Durkot and the American migrant community was bidirectional: this ostensibly Greek Catholic priest in Galicia provided encouragement to the migrants in America in their conversions to Orthodoxy, while at the same time requesting economic remittances for his Greek Catholic parish in Galicia. Finally, underlying the instance of this report in the first place was the transnational behavior of Andrii, namely, his return migration. This letter therefore attests to transnationalism at the level of the individual migrant, of a community of migrants in America, of a community of nonmigrants in Habsburg realms, of migrant and nonmigrant priests in both regions, and finally, of both East European and American bishops.

Transnational Greek Catholic counter-conversion efforts also took place at other levels besides administrative. The Galician priest Fr. T. Lezhohubsky suggestively entitled his early twentieth-century pro-Greek Catholic book *De znaity pravdu* (Where to Find the Truth) - presumably a

---

[31] ABGK 4931, 538-39.

more desirable alternative to merely "seeking" the same, as Fr. Toth's pro-Orthodox pamphlet coming from America had advised. (*Where to Seek the Truth* and *Where to Find the Truth* thus represent a transnational variation on the centuries old tradition of the Orthodox-Uniate polemic.) *Where to Find the Truth* provided a fictional account in which a Galician villager encounters an invidious Orthodox missionary from Russia, only to be saved by an enterprising Greek Catholic priest who knows well his Unia and its superiority to Orthodoxy. The text was published in Lviv in 1912 and again in 1914 in Philadelphia and became a transnational anti-Orthodox resource. Equipped with *Where to Find the Truth*, migrants could resist Orthodox propaganda in America; furthermore, they would be prepared, upon returning to Habsburg realms, to stave off the real-life counterparts to the book's fictional Orthodox missionary from Russia.

Another fascinating attempt to counter Habsburg Greek Catholic migrants' susceptibility to Orthodoxy in America came from one Fr. Volodymyr Herasymovych in Galicia. In a 1911 article in the Galician periodical *Nyva*, Fr. Herasymovych narrated a story about parishioners of his who migrated to America both for monetary purposes and in order to marry against their parents' wishes. No one in the village heard any news of them, until "after two years appeared in the parish office two 'gentlefolk': he in elegant clothes, a small collar *a la* Roosevelt, a polka dot tie, leather shoes, and she in a fashionable dress." Fr. Herasymovych learned from his returned migrants' conversation, peppered with English phrases, that they had no baptismal record for the child, but that everything would be "*all right*," because in a month's time they would be returning to America anyway.[32] Of these transmigrants, Fr. Herasymovych had this to say:

> What can be the benefit, if those emigrants...wander about, to America and then back to their own village. I have such parishioners, that already three and four times have gone and returned back. The worst happens with the girls and young boys....Usually they write in the beginning that they are very well, either that they have work in a cigarette factory or in a textile factory, but afterward no one writes, until someone from there comes and says, that so and so "Marynka is coming to nothing" or that she "lives out of wedlock with some Jew" and so forth. Such then are the benefits from our

---

[32] "Proiekt tserkovnoi kontroli nad nashoiu emihratsiieiu do Ameryky," *Nyva* 8, no. 22 (1911): 676-88 (666).

emigration...because they go without control, without any
papers....[33]

The meat of Fr. Herasymovych's "Proposal for Church Control over
Our Emigration to America" consisted of a 24-30 page *Viroispovidna
legitymatsiina knyzhochka* (Religious Legitimation Booklet), modeled after
the Habsburg *Militär-Pass* of the time.[34] He suggested that parish priests
send along with their migrants to America this handy booklet, specifying
the city of migratory destination as well the region, county, parish, and
eparchy of origin. The bearer was to be instructed:

> Immediately after your arrival to America you must, with this
> book, announce yourself to that place's Greek Catholic parish
> council, where your acceptance into the parish will be confirmed
> in this book. Only make sure you ask well, whether that church
> to which you approach is chartered to our Bishop Most Reverend
> Soter Ortynsky, who lives in Philadelphia. Because, if not, that is
> a sign that you have been led to a church of another faith, which
> only cloaks itself under the name of Greek-Catholic [i.e., it is
> "Russian Orthodox Greek Catholic" or "Independent Greek
> Catholic"].

The booklet also admonished the prospective migrant not to forget
that "our people in the old country are very poor and need much" and to
make sure to send a percentage of earnings home: first to the church and
then to the migrant's "familial village," or for some charitable cause like
the *Ridna Shkola*. The booklet also wedded retention of Greek Catholic
religious identity to maintenance of Ukrainian national identity. The
migrant was not to forget the native tongue, to remember the poetry of
"our greatest poet, Taras Shevchenko" (a sampling of whose poetry was
reprinted), and to answer, when asked, that one's nationality is "Rusyn-
Ukrainian" and not "Galician" or "Austrian."

Fr. Herasymovych also maintained affiliations with Lviv's Society of
St. Raphael, founded in the early 1900s to conduct pastoral care for Greek
Catholic migrants. The masthead of its official organ, *Emigrant*, read:

> Dear Countrymen! Don't discard your ancestral land
> thoughtlessly and forever! When desire compels you to emigrate,
> then would to God that you not sell your ancestral farmstead, in

---

[33] Ibid., 667.
[34] Ibid., 680-88.

order that you would have something to which to return. Go
more gladly to your earnings, save, don't take to drink; with your
earnings return and with them improve your community. Don't
attend only to profits, but also pay attention to your soul – don't
allow yourself to be carried away into the sea of corruption,
because you will drown unto eternity! Don't forget to seek
counsel in the Society of St. Raphael before going out.

Emigrant also regularly warned migrants of the dangers of the Russian
Orthodox in America. The Society published the booklet *Pamiatka dlia
ruskykh robitnykiv* (Memorial Book for Rusyn Workers) written by
Metropolitan Andrei Sheptytsky, published twice before the outbreak of
war, in which migrants were also warned of the dangers of Orthodoxy in
America. The activities of the Society of St. Raphael served to
transnationalize its members and the readers of its official organ by
orienting not only their consciousness toward migrant communities in
America, but also their behaviors. The society sought also to promote the
transnational ties (social, economic, cultural, religious) which migrants
retained with kin, friend, and religious networks in Habsburg regions of
migratory origin.

Conclusions

This survey of the ways in which transnationalism influenced
Orthodox conversion movements in Habsburg lands following the turn of
the century permits a few initial conclusions. In the first place, the
American migrant context was an extremely important variable in the East
European conversions. While East European factors were significant in
Habsburg Orthodox movements in 1911-14, it is necessary to recall that in
1909, fully two years before the arrival of the first missionary priest from
Russia, the primary concern of the bishop of Przemyśl was with lay
Orthodox missionaries coming from another direction: America. And
even as missionaries from Russia began to arrive, the bishop continued to
collect detailed reports from his parishes devoted exclusively to the
interaction of migration to and from America, on the one hand, and
Orthodox conversions, on the other.

Secondly, my research also calls for an expansion of the temporal and
thematic boundaries currently limiting transnationalism studies. In this
earlier period, transnationalism was a vital reality for many migrants and
nonmigrants alike. Moreover, religion constituted an important
transnational variable. Remaining questions include: How much money

and other resources flowed across the Atlantic to support Orthodox movements in Habsburg realms? Who exactly donated it, where did it go, and what was its specific impact? And relative to other factors, just how much of a role did the American migrant context play in the East European conversions? Answers to these questions will contribute not only to American migrant history, but to Habsburg history as well.

The Art of the Greek Catholic Eparchy of Mukachevo: Sacral Painting of the Eighteenth Century

Bernadett Puskás

1. Introduction

The art of a single eparchy rarely constitutes such an easily identifiable entity that it can be studied on its own.[1] But the art of what was historically the Mukachevo eparchy does invite analysis within its ecclesiastical jurisdictional boundaries. The eparchy had been founded within historical Hungary and later became part of the Habsburg Monarchy. The territory under its jurisdiction expanded over time. In the first centuries of its existence, a large proportion of its faithful were Ruthenians; a smaller proportion were Romanians as well as Slovaks and Hungarians. According to eighteenth-century censuses, the Mukachevo bishopric had jurisdiction in thirteen northeastern counties of Hungary and encompassed about seven hundred parishes.[2] As a result of its unique geographical and ecclesiastical-political location and no less because of the particularity of its history, it has been a meeting place of the Eastern and Western churches and of the culture of several nations. At the same time, however, it has been a kind of solid nugget within the culture of historical Hungary; that is, along with being open to outside influences, it also preserved its distinct identity, faith, and rituals.

A survey of the parallel development of the eparchy's sacral art, of its various genres and functions, makes it possible to give this art its due – an art that is sometimes considered provincial in relation to the official art of the country – and to define its significance in the pan-European context. The synthetic study of the art of this single eparchy, however large in expanse it may have been, allows us to appreciate its connections over considerable distances with the artistic influences of Central Europe and neighboring lands, the activity of Galician artists in the Máramaros region

---

[1] This chapter was translated by John-Paul Himka.

[2] István Bendász and István Koi, *A munkácsi Görögkatolikus Egyházmegye lelkészségeinek 1792. évi katalógusa* (Nyíregyháza: Szent Atanáz Görögkatolikus Főiskola, 1994), 31; *A munkácsi görögkatolikus püspökség lelkészségeinek 1806. évi összeírása*, ed. István Udvari; Vasvári Pál Társaság Füzetei, 3 (Nyíregyháza: Vasvári Pál Társaság, 1990), 6, 17.

and Transylvania, and the role of baroque spirituality and culture in the Carpathian region.

The research currently being conducted is aimed at as full as possible an acquaintance with the set of cultural artifacts that can be found in the possession of parish communities of the historical Mukachevo eparchy or that were acquired by collections in Hungary or elsewhere; the project is also engaged in locating archival sources connected with these artifacts as well as working through the relevant professional literature. The most important collections are in Slovakia and in Ukraine. Among the Hungarian collections, two stand out: the Greek Catholic Church Art Collection in Nyíregyháza and the collection of church paraphernalia and icons of the Museum of Ethnography (Néprajzi Múzeum) in Budapest, most of whose items are currently in need of restoration. A number of icons from the territory of the historical Mukachevo eparchy are preserved in the Ottó Herman Museum in Miskolc and in the Museum of Applied Art and the National Gallery in Budapest. Liturgical books should also be included in the artistic heritage of Mukachevo eparchy; relatively few are manuscripts – most are printed Cyrillic books, primarily from Galician printing presses. These materials can be found in the National Széchényi Library, in the Library of the University of Debrecen, and in the Library of the St. Athanasius Greek Catholic Theological Institute.[3]

Aside from the main archive of Mukachevo eparchy, which since 1947 has been located in the State Archive of Transcarpathia Oblast in Berehovo, additional documentary sources can be researched in the archepiscopal archive in Eger, in the National Archives of Hungary, in the archive of the Order of St. Basil the Great in Máriapócs, in the Hajdúdorog eparchial archive, and in the archive of the Prešov Greek Catholic metropolis. The archives of individual parish communities usually have gaps, especially in documentation from the beginning of the nineteenth century.

The art history of a local metabyzantine church is the history of complicated stylistic changes and, closely connected with them, changes in worldview. The interpretation of the role that works of sacral art were supposed to fulfill, and the changes over time in how they were perceived, were part of a dynamic process that involved the local church directly commissioning work as well as the person charged with producing it, but also the requirements of a given ecclesiastical community as a whole. The

---

[3] Eszter Ojtozi, *A Görögkatolikus Hittudományi Főiskola Könyvtárának szláv és román cirillbetűs könyvei*, Régi Tiszántúli Könyvtárak, 4 (Debrecen: Kossuth Lajos Tudományegyetem Könyvtára, 1985).

question of how an icon was viewed and how that view changed is intimately connected with the set of problems arising from desires to preserve tradition and also to renew, to bring up to date. The art works of this local church – as in the case of the art of other Byzantine churches that came into contact with West European art – raise questions about the development of a style formed between poles of tradition and modernization. These processes and their impact on the icons and their evolution make sense if we think in certain key terms, namely sacrality and art and, in the first place, traditional and modern.

It would seem that it would be proper to approach the borderland between the Eastern and Western church, and the investigation of perceptual changes, by using a conceptual distinction already known from another context, that between the era of the image and the era of art.[4] But if we look more closely at the works under investigation – and this comes out most clearly in the study of visual art – we see that after the era of the icon, which emphasizes that the icon is an image in a theological sense, comes a period that at first glance can be considered transitional, in which the icon, its meaning supplemented by a new dimension, functions also as a work of art. For the modern postbyzantine culture and church of the Carpathian region this was a formative era that held within it the perspective of a renewal from within. However, the potential of this path to modernity could not be realized. The distancing from tradition led not only to an obscuring of the iconic point of view and its almost complete oblivion and loss, but owing to the specific local circumstances it sometimes ultimately resulted in the disappearance of artistry itself.

By European or Central European standards, or even by comparison to the metabyzantine artifacts of the Carpathian region as a whole, in the circumscribed area we are investigating, we find relatively few works of outstanding quality. From the point of view of the civilization of both East and West, this is a borderland territory, where partly because of its geography there were few noteworthy economic and cultural centers. But this cultural sphere, in spite of its peripheral character and provincialism, is nonetheless worthy of the attention of art historians, primarily because of the numerous unique and interesting ways these works of local sacred visual art solved artistic problems. This becomes especially clear when we move beyond the sphere of ethnographic research; this is, among other

---

[4] Hans Belting, *Likeness and Presence: A History of the Image before the Era of Art* (Chicago: University of Chicago Press, 1994).

things, an iconographic terrain where Eastern and Western artistic patterns crossed each other's path and influenced each other.

2. The Problematic of Sacral Painting

Scholars have been most interested in sacral painting. With regard to the Eastern, Byzantine tradition this is completely natural. The role of the icon in Eastern culture is well known: it is an image that has the immanent capacity to make the transcendental sphere present. The first task of research is to explore the materials that have been preserved to our day, to systematize them, and eventually to reconstruct any gaps. After this, it becomes possible to analyze in more detail stylistic connections, characteristic iconographic types, and iconology, i.e., the investigation of changes in iconographic types or in their reception and interpretation under different historical conditions. When relevant documentary sources are extant, it also becomes possible to investigate when buildings were erected and icons painted, who ordered them, and the role of or changes in the meaning of icons and the iconostasis in the everyday liturgical or paraliturgical practice of a particular community.

2.1 Painters' Workshops and Painters in the Eighteenth Century

A survey of the activity of painters' workshops and painters active in this land in the eighteenth century is only one starting point. In researching these issues, one should not forget that the icon at this time was usually not a stand-alone object but part of an iconostasis, a system of images that was already in place, although sometimes changes in its architectonics can be observed.

Several dozen iconostases were erected in Mukachevo eparchy in the course of the eighteenth century. But written documentation on their creation stems mainly from the end of the century. The majority of works are unsigned, and only rarely do we find the year an iconostasis was painted or the name of the person who ordered it in a donor's inscription. The variety in the eparchy's essentially baroque icons testifies to the activity of several workshops and painters. The painters were often from abroad, particularly from Galicia, but especially from the middle of the century local painters also played their part.

There is no reason to believe that the icon at this time had lost its original significance, but it carried out its role as the manifestation of the transcendental in the world with new methods; for instance, it abandoned reverse perspective and made use of landscape scenes, more realistically drawn clothing, and chiaroscuro. The way icons were painted at the turn of the eighteenth century bears the characteristic features of a transition from the stylistic features of the late renaissance to the formal language of the baroque. Metal coverings (*ryzy*) continued to be produced only for those icons in particular veneration, i.e., for miracle-working icons (unknown Viennese master: silver *ryza* for the second Pócs icon of the Mother of God, 1771, Exhibition of the Collection of the Basilian Fathers, Máriapócs). Imitations of the relief of the *ryza* – but carved from the surface of the icon itself and gilded or painted – testify to the intention to be similar to a miracle-working icon (the principal [*namisna*] icon of the Mother of God from the iconostasis in Nyíracsad, 1792).

The majority of iconostases from the second half of the eighteenth century were produced by the folk painters, especially popular since the second half of the seventeenth century, who came from the Rybotycze workshop or were influenced by it. Their iconostases can be found in Ladomirov (1742), Šemetkovce (after 1752), Miroľa (1770), Kalná Roztoka (end of the eighteenth century), and Topoľa (end of the eighteenth century).[5] In the icon-painting center of Rybotycze over the course of the seventeenth and eighteenth centuries, several generations of painters produced icons, and their own extensive activities as well as their stylistic influences on others also reached historical Hungary. Their works have been preserved above all in the northern part of Mukachevo eparchy. Among the very many icons they produced, all of more or less the same quality, are the Last Supper from Kečkovce (second half of the eighteenth century, Museum of Ukrainian-Rusyn Culture, Svidník, Slovakia) and the festal tier of the iconostasis from Vladiča (also in Svidník). There are also icons that have been neither restored nor studied in the collection of the Ethnographic Museum in Budapest.

In this period there already emerges a need for stylistic uniformity of church furnishings, but at first this has no negative implications for the role of icons, which maintain their preeminence vis-à-vis woodcarving and carpentry work. Alongside iconostases, painters of the Rybotycze circle produced other furnishings that required artistic embellishment, such as

---

[5] V.P. Otkovych, *Narodna techiia v ukrains'komu zhyvopysu XVII-XVIII st.* (Kyiv: Naukova dumka, 1990), 62-63. On the basis of archival documents Volodymyr Aleksandrovych warns against ascribing so many painters to the Rybotycze group over the course of two centuries. Volodymyr Aleksandrovych, "Novi dani pro rybotyts'kyi maliars'kyi oseredok druhoi polovyny XVII st.," *Narodna tvorchist' ta etnohrafiia*, no. 1 (1992): 62. Nonetheless, the great number of icons produced in this style requires at present that we consider them as belonging at least in a wider sense to the Rybotycze artistic current.

Illustration 6.1: Flight into Egypt, predella of the iconostasis in Uzhok.

main altars, on which were now placed an altar icon of the Pietà (the Pietà of Niklová, now Mikulášová, end of seventeenth/early eighteenth century, Šariš Museum, Bardejov, Slovakia) or of the Descent from the Cross. They also painted double-sided processional crosses with images of the crucified Christ and of the Theophany (Baktakék) as well as banners (Christ the Teacher from Tročany, Slovakia, 1750, Šariš Museum). Artists who painted in the Rybotycze manner went all the way to Sighetu Marmației looking for work. They influenced a number of local painters of the Maramureş region: Mihai, Zaharia, Filip, Nicolai Cepschin (Nicolae Cepsin), and one of the most famous, the mural and icon painter

Alexandru Ponehalski was the leader of an itinerant workshop, numerous works of whom have been preserved in the Maramureş region and Transylvania from the 1750s-1770s.[6] The painters in the Rybotycze style sometimes enriched traditional themes with additional scenes (icons on the predellas of the iconostasis in Uzhok: the flight into Egypt, the stoning of St. Stephen, St. George on his horse, carrying the cross; second half of the

[6] V.P. Otkovych, "Tvory rybotyts'koi narodnoi shkoly maliarstva na Ukraini, u Slovachchyni ta Rumunii," in *Ukrains'ke mystetstvo u mizhnarodnykh zv"iazkakh. Dozhovtnevyi period,* ed. V.A. Afanas'iev et al. (Kyiv: Naukova dumka, 1983), 90-91. Marius Porumb, *Pictura românească din Transilvania,* vol. 1 (Cluj-Napoca: Dacia, 1981).

eighteenth century). (See Illustration 6.1.) Works produced by the Rybotycze masters and local folk painters remained very popular in spite of the contemporary church hierarchy's official condemnation of primitive images (Bishop Bradach's circular of 26 July 1769).[7]

At that time painters and craftsmen from Sudova Vyshnia also worked in Mukachevo eparchy. Their iconostases are preserved, among other places, in Pylypka, Repynne (repainted), and Pryslip.[8] The iconostasis of the church of St. John the Forerunner in Sukhyi was painted in 1701 by the Sudova-Vyshnia master Stefan.[9] The iconostases are simple four-tier constructions with modest baroque embellishment. A characteristic feature of their icons is that individual figures, such as the apostles in the Deesis tier, completely fill the space allotted to them, tightly enclosed between the carved columns. The altar in Sukhyi, made in 1771, is probably also the work of craftsmen and painters from Sudova Vyshnia; the altar icon of the Protection of the Mother of God has an architectural-style frame with baroque carving.

One can identify two streams in the work of local masters: traditional and Central European. The differences predominantly affect style, but the adaptation to Western style also precipitated changes in the iconography and in the perception of icons.

The itinerant artists who came from the two Galician centers brought with them primarily the iconographic, but to some degree also the stylistic traditions of the second half of the previous century. Local artists followed their traditional approach, and as a result of their activities the local Eastern iconographic tradition was able to continue, preserving traces of the Carpathian region's medieval understanding of icons. This showed above all in the devotion to canonical images, the role of which was sometimes assumed by models found in baroque engravings. Characteristic too were the outlined and flat images and the extraordinary decorativeness in the choice of colors and in the ornamentation, which elevates even naively painted icons to another level.

A representative of this artistic current was the very skilled master who painted the series of principal icons in Runina (Vihorlat Museum in Humenné, Slovakia).[10] His icons in this baroque iconostasis from the first

---

[7] István Udvari, *Ruszinok a XVIII. században. Történelmi és művelődéstörténeti tanulmányok* , Vasvári Pál Társaság füzetei, 9 (Nyíregyháza: Bessenyei György Kiadó, 1992), 190.

[8] P.M. Zholtovs'kyi, *Ukrains'kyi zhyvopys XVII-XVIII st.* (Kyiv: Naukova dumka, 1978), 42-45.

[9] Otkovych, *Narodna techiia*, 86-87.

[10] Bernadett Puskás, *Between East and West: Icons in the Carpathian Region in the 15th-18th Centuries* (Budapest: Magyar Nemzeti Galéria, 1991), catalogue 92-93.

Illustration 6.2: Apostles, including St. Peter, from the iconostasis of Kolodne, József Boksay Transcarpathian Oblast Museum of Art, Uzhhorod.

half of the eighteenth century demonstrate a relatively high level among the works of the folk iconographers. Others of the many, unfortunately mainly unsigned works include the principal icons of the Hodegetria with Child and of Christ the Teacher in Baktakék, the principal icons of St. Nicholas and Christ the High Priest in Gagyvendégi, which were once part of a single iconostasis, and also the altar icon of the Descent from the Cross in Gagyvendégi (second half of the eighteenth century).[11] The original iconostasis was clearly painted by several artists. Of the icons, the one of highest quality is the icon of St. Nicholas, based on an etching.

Fragments remain of another iconostasis based on the same approach, that is, the collaboration of several artists producing works at varying levels, in Boldogkőváralja (second half of the eighteenth century).[12] The prophet tier, composed of two tablets, stands out from this group because of its more demanding formulation.

The tradition-preserving tendency can also be identified in works from the southern part of the eparchy. Among those from Transcarpathia, the fragments of the iconostasis from Kolodne stand out. They are painted in the folk baroque style and at the same time follow the local visual-arts tradition. They are distinguished, however, by their interesting details,

---

[11] Reproduced in Bernadett Puskás, *Ikon és liturgia. A görög katolikus egyház művészeti emlékei, 17–19. század* (Nyíregyháza: Jósa András Múzeum, 1996), 4–32, catalogue 4.
[12] Ibid., catalogue 39-45.

Illustration 6.3: Transfer of the Relics of St. Nicholas to Bari, from the iconostasis of Kolodne.

such as the figure of St. Peter, which – playing on his name – shows him stepping emphatically on a block of stone (József Boksay Transcarpathian Oblast Museum of Art, Uzhhorod). (See Illustration 6.2.) The iconostasis was reworked several times. An inscription on its royal doors says that it was renovated in November 1737 by Iliia, painter from Khust. According to another inscription, the icon on the predella, of the Transfer of the Relics of St. Nicholas to Bari, was painted in 1773. (See Illustration 6.3.) The iconostasis comprised predellas, principal icons, festal icons, a tier of the apostles (painted on two long boards with the Trimorphion in the center), and the prophet tier (painted on four tablets), with an icon of God the Father in the center. The best artistry in the iconostasis was in the tier of apostles, who stand two in every tablet. The painter used cartoons, repeating them several times. Thus the figures of the apostles John and Philip are identical, and sometimes figures differ only by a hand gesture or are the mirror image of another.

In the Máramaros region one also finds a very local tendency, true to traditions, which at the same time reflects specifically Balkan influences (the Mother of God with child, of unknown provenance, in the National Gallery in Budapest, and the icon of Christ the Teacher, also of unknown provenance, in the Museum of Ethnography in Budapest). In Szabolcs county, icons of local masters are also preserved, such as fragments of the iconostasis of the church that was once in Hodász.[13] As the date on the icon of Christ the Teacher shows, the iconostasis was made in 1779, but it also used some icons from the turn or beginning of the eighteenth century.

In addition to the demand for work in the traditional style there was also a market for the work of those local artists whose style was closer to the Central European baroque, and this entailed more distance from the local icon-painting of the Eastern tradition. The scenes on the pedestal of the altar of the church of St. Nicholas in Podobovets are framed in shell-like rocailles, artistically painted, and enriched with landscape elements: the Sacrifice of Abraham, Christ on the Mount of Olives, and the Archangel Raphael with Tobias. We can find out about the artists from the ever more frequent signatures on their works. We know that in Roztoka the icon of the Annunciation was painted by Liavets Kitsan[14] (1709) and the icon of the Mother of God by Roman Tiaskailo, while the royal doors were carved by Ilko Holovchyn.[15] The principal icons in Lukov-Venecia (1736) were painted, according to an inscription on the icon of the Mother of God, by Andrei Gaietsky. In Jedlinka, in the wooden church built in 1763, a rococo iconostasis with a carved tracery framework in the form of seashells with combs was installed at the end of the eighteenth century. Near it are three older principal icons. A donor's inscription in Polish on the icon of Christ the Teacher tells us that Mikolay Gajecki, a painter from Bardejov, painted them in 1744.[16] In Krainykovo (Mihálka), according to the donor's inscription under the principal icon of the Mother of God, the artist Yavorsky from Vylok worked in the village in 1766-69.[17] In 1782

---

[13] Puskás, *Between East and West*, catalogue 148-59. Puskás, *Ikon és liturgia*, catalogue 10-12, 15-20.

[14] In Hungarian transcription Ljavic Kiszan. – Translator.

[15] P.M. Zholtovs'kyi, *Khudozhnie zhyttia na Ukraini v XVI-XVIII st.* (Kyiv: Naukova dumka, 1983), 137. V. Sakhanev, "Novyi karpartorusskii epigraficheskii material," *Naukovyi zbirnyk Tovarystva Prosvita* 9 (1932): 68-100. Mykhailo Syrokhman, *Tserkvy Ukrainy. Zakarpattia* (Lviv: Vydavnytstvo "Ms," 2000), 459.

[16] Zholtovs'kyi, *Khudozhnie zhyttia*, 123. M. Dubai, "Z mystetstva nashykh derev''ianykh tserkov," *Narodnii kalendar* (Bratislava: Slovenské vydatel'stvo politickej literatúry, 1966), 93-97.

[17] Zholtovs'kyi, *Khudozhnie zhyttia*, 176-77.

František Ferdinándi painted an icon for the altar in the church of Buják.[18]
In Príkra Ivan Yuhasevych (1741-1814) painted several icons.[19]

Their work in the Eastern artistic tradition incorporated more and more characteristics of the baroque style, and the odd result was that as a taste for this gradually spread in society, the baroque became an inseparable component of the local iconographic tradition (the Acheiropoietos of Ortuťová, with a crown of thorns, painted as Veronica's veil, first half of the eighteenth century; the Archangel Michael from Nižný Hrabovec, 1780-1800, Šariš Museum, Bardejov). This process took place in parallel with the change in style one finds in other Greek Catholic territories on the other side of the Carpathians. In addition, in more aesthetically conservative Mukachevo eparchy, the better trained Galician artists who came here played at least the same kind of role as mediators in the acquisition of the baroque language of expression as did the authentic baroque artists who also worked here for the local Roman Catholic church.

In the northern part of Mukachevo eparchy, Prešov continued in the eighteenth century to be, as it had been in the previous century, one of the most significant artistic centers in the region, with its own local traditions. But from the perspective of the icon-painting of the eparchy in the second half of the eighteenth century, even such strong local centers did not play a major role in the popularization of the baroque style. For example, the portraitist Jonas Gottlieb Kramer (1716-71) had many commissions in Prešov, including in the realm of sacral art, but as far as we know, he only produced one work for the Greek Catholic church: in 1769 he painted a copy of the miraculous icon of Klokočov.[20]

Painters who worked with a fully baroque plasticity of style could produce iconostases for village churches, such as the unknown artist who worked in Abaújszolnok and painted the icons for the former iconostasis as well as icons for the church's main altar;[21] most of the artists who filled orders for the villages, however, subordinated baroque methods to traditional artistic solutions. (See Illustration 6.4.)

---

[18] Ibid., 172. Dubai, "Z mystetstva," 94.

[19] Dubai, "Z mystetstva," 94.

[20] Klára Garas, Magyarországi festészet a XVIII. században (Budapest: Akadémiai Kiadó, 1955), 143, 225.

[21] Pál Bacsóka and László Puskás, Házad ékessége. Görögkatolikus templomok, ikonok, ikonosztázok Magyarországon (Nyíregyháza: Görögkatolikus Hittudományi Főiskola, 1991), 93–94, illustrations. Puskás, Ikon és liturgia, catalogue 64.

Illustration 6.4: Crucifixion, Abaújszolnok.

The most prominent artistic personalities in Mukachevo eparchy in the second half of the eighteenth century were two artists from Galicia who appeared in Hungary around the same time in mid-century, probably brothers: Tadei and Mykhail Spalinsky. As artists whose work was of the highest quality, they stood out from the semiprofessional and folk artists and received the most important commissions in that period.[22]

Tadei Spalinsky, who was born in Western or Eastern Galicia around 1747, ended up in the monastery on Chernecha Hora near Mukachevo as a monk of the Order of St. Basil the Great in 1767. We do not know whether he received professional training prior to that. Later we find his name mentioned in the minutes of meetings of the Basilian order's chapter: in 1772 he was still referred to as Brother Tadei, but by 1784 he was a hieromonk. The minutes of 1789 mention that he was a painter (*pictor*) of Mukachevo. From the minutes we also glimpse his peripatetic lifestyle. Over the course of forty years he had lived in almost all the northeastern Basilian monasteries of Hungary. In 1807 Tadei Spalinsky was named pastor of the town Mezőzombor in Zemplén county, where he died in 1809.[23]

Some pictures once hanging in the refectory of the Mukachevo monastery were ascribed to Spalinsky: two images of St. John, with the names of the donors – Dömöczki i Csendes, a life-size portrait of the founder of the Mukachevo monastery, the Lithuanian prince Feodor Koriatovych, and also an equestrian portrait of the founder of the monastery's church, Demeter Rácz. Among his early works were images that were once placed on both balustrades of the monastery church in Malyi Bereznyi monastery, a well-known series of portraits of saints, and another series illustrating the eight beatitudes (Boksay Museum, Uzhhorod). The compositions of the latter, allegorical scenes – thematically rare and painted on wooden tablets – are extremely simple. The artist generally painted a figure representing the beatitude on a bare hillock set among clouds. Thus the first picture, which has the inscription

---

[22] Bernadett Puskás [Pushkash], "Braty rodom z Pol'shchi na sluzhbi v mukachivs'koho iepyskopa: Fadei ta Mykhailo Spalins'ki, druha polovyna XVIII stolittia," in *Sztuka cerkiewna w diecezji przemyskiej. Materiały z międzynarodowej konferencji naukowej 25-26 marca 1995 roku*, ed. Jarosław Giemza and Andrzej Stepan (Łańcut: Muzeum Zamek w Łańcucie, Redakcja czasopisma "Peremys'ki Dzwony," Wydawnictwo "STEPAN design," 1999), 163-76.

[23] Károly Lyka, "Adatok művészetünk történetéhez," *Művészet* 8, no. 1 (1909): 58–59; László Éber, *Művészeti lexikon*, vol. 2 (Budapest: Győző Andor, 1935), 459. Garas, *Magyarországi festészet a XVIII. században*, 252.

Illustration 6.5: Mykhail Spalinsky, "Blessed Are the Poor in Spirit," from Malyi Bereznyi monastery, Boksay Museum, Uzhhorod.

"Blessed are the poor in spirit: for theirs is the kingdom of heaven," shows a young man with his hands folded in prayer; an angel gives him monastic clothing, while beneath him are strewn a crown, a plumed helmet, an overturned cup, and coins rolling out of a purse, symbolizing superfluous earthly goods and ephemeral achievements. (See Illustration 6.5.) The series in its individual scenes urges the choice of a monastic life, different

Illustration 6.6: Mykhail and Tadei Spalinsky,
St. Mark, iconostasis of Máriapócs, Greek
Catholic Church Art Collection in Nyíregyháza.

from life in the world. Details that show that the series was commissioned by the Basilian order – the Eastern monastic garb and the appearance of a fiery column, which was the Basilians' emblem – and the simple and even sometimes naive interpretation of the theme indicate that Spalinsky painted the series in accordance with a program designed in the monastery and so did not make use of known iconographic prototypes. The somewhat crudely painted personages, the sketchy treatment of the drapery, splotches of paint, and the simplified resolutions of chiaroscuro indicate a beginner or an insufficiently trained painter. In the last period of his life Tadei Spalinsky served as the priest in Mezőzombor for two years, and during this time he painted an iconostasis for the parish without charge,[24] which was destroyed in a fire in 1944.

We do not yet have much biographical information about Mykhail Spalinsky. In 1785 the painter signed a document in the Ruthenian language that confirmed that he was undertaking to paint all the icons on the Máriapócs iconostasis for 130 German Gulden and that he has received a down payment of 12 German Gulden. On 10 April 1787 he submitted an invoice for paints he used on the pulpit and also for painting the four

---

[24] Lyka, "Adatok művészetünk történetéhez," 55.

evangelists and St. John the Forerunner.[25] At the end of the nineteenth century, when some of the icons in the Máriapócs iconostasis were being replaced, only some of the older icons had still been preserved, from the apostles' tier: the evangelists Matthew, Mark, and John and the apostle Bartholomew (Greek Catholic Church Art Collection in Nyíregyháza) as well as Christ the High Priest (in a private collection). (See Illustration 6.6.) The exact proportions of the figures of the apostles, their three-dimensionality, the treatment of the faces and hands indicate a well-trained master. We see the figures in a variety of active baroque poses before a landscape with a low horizon. The image of Christ – dressed in the vestments of a high priest and sitting on a high-backed throne against a gold background – in spite of a few flaws in the draftsmanship, is characterized by a wealth of detail, by the representation of spatiality, nuances of light and shadow, and by a translucent, tender manner of painting.

Further research is necessary to determine whether we can identify Mykhail Spalinsky with the carpenter-painter "of Tokaj," referred to in correspondence between Bishop Manuil Olshavsky and Károly Ferenc from 1752 to 1758. They were corresponding about painting the Máriapócs church, its vestry and altars, as well as some painting in the monastery with regard to the former murals of the benefactors who had built the monastery. Bishop Olshavsky mentioned Michael of Tokaj as the person to whom he was entrusting the most important tasks. But we can ascribe with certainty to Mykhail Spalinsky the scene of the Sacrifice of Abraham on the smaller pedestal which was once perhaps the proskomedia table (now it is to the left of the altar with the miraculous icon). Here it is worth mentioning that the construction of the Máriapócs church was carried out according to an Eastern three-apsed plan made in 1730. The transverse apses served as the location for side altars funded by local Roman Catholic gentry, but are so accented as to form cleroses. A cleros (*krylos* in Ukrainian) was a semicircular space for the choir just off the nave. The inclusion of cleroses, probably under the influence of Moldavian monasteries, became characteristic of stone construction in the eparchy from the middle of the century. According to documents in the Eger archive, an architect from Košice named Nikodém Lický (earlier referred to as Nický) designed the church in accordance with a request that it be arranged "ad normam ruthenicam," which we understand to indicate the inclusion of cleroses. The composition of the facade was influenced by the contemporary Roman Catholic architecture of Košice. The iconostasis,

---

[25] Máriapócs, Basilian archive, documents from 1785.

which was finished after 1748, also makes evident the artistic connections of that era. The carving shows parallels with the iconostasis in Blaj, Transylvania. The carver of the iconostasis was the Greek Konstantinos Taliodoros (meaning Carver), which explains why just below the Crucifixion at the top of the iconostasis there are Balkan motifs of serpents.[26]

The name of Mykhail Spalinsky also appears in connection with another, even more reworked iconostasis, the one in Tokaj. In the iconostasis of the Greek Catholic church there, only the icons of the apostles' tier can be considered original, dating from the eighteenth century, as well as certain details in the frames, cornices, and articulating elements of the prophets' tier. The icons are linked to Spalinsky by an inscription on the back side of the apostles' tier: "Anno 1787 pinxit Michael Spalisky Paroche Michael Gregorovics Curatore Ecclesiae Ioanne Zavodkay Tokaine." The icons of the apostles follow a scheme related to that of the apostles of Máriapócs, which was the usual iconographic scheme in that period, the prototypes of which had come from Galician engravings: full-length figures holding their attributes and adopting various poses. The figures are somewhat stouter than those of Máriapócs, but the plasticity of the drapery and the naturalness and ease of the movements can be considered confirmation of Mykhail Spalinsky's authorship.

The Tokaj icon of Christ the High Priest had first been painted on a late baroque tablet in the shape of a lute (the addition to the tablet is readily visible from behind the iconostasis). The identification of three former principal icons was possible because of the characteristic shape of the tablets and on the basis of their measurements. The three are: the Mother of God with child (with an inscription of 1787), Christ the Teacher (both are in the Greek Catholic Church Art Collection in Nyíregyháza), and St. Nicholas (presently on the back tablet of the pulpit in the Greek Catholic church in Tokaj). The icon of Christ the High Priest and the principal icons are even more carefully rendered than the icons of the apostles, especially with regard to details, the embroidery of the episcopal vestments, and the facial features.

---

[26] Eger, Érseki Levéltár, Archivum Vetus, 238. Szilvester János Terdik, "Rácz Demeter, egy XVIII. századi görög katolikus mecénás," *A Nyíregyházi Jósa András Múzeum Évkönyve* 49 (2007): 365.

Illustration 6.7: Mykhail and Tadei Spalinsky, iconostasis in Sátoraljaújhely.

The icon of the Protection of the Mother of God from Hunkovce, Ung county (1781, National Gallery, Budapest) can also be linked to Spalinsky on the basis of its stylistic characteristics and artistic quality. Judging by its size and theme, it could have been the patronal icon of the church in Hunkovce. The iconography is rooted in the middle ages and unites into one two incidents of the Protection. At the head of a group to the right is St. Andrew the Fool for Christ's Sake (ninth century); he points to his vision in the Hagia Sophia cathedral in Constantinople of Mary, who spreads her veil over those present in a gesture of protection, and of the heavenly powers who accompany her. In the center, on the ambo, we see St. Roman the Melodist, who through Mary's agency praises her in wondrous song (sixth century); various important personages stand by and listen to him. One of the interesting features of the icon is that the place of the Byzantine emperor is taken by Maria Theresa and Joseph II, which was the equivalent of a similar iconographic development on the territory of Poland.[27] There is also a portrait of the Mukachevo bishop Andrei Bachynsky, which not only underscores the desire for portraiture in the icon, but makes a point of honoring the primary commissioner of

---

[27] For more detail, see Bernadett Puskás, "Az Istenszülő oltalma-ikonok az Északkelet-Kárpátok vidékén," *Athanasiana* 21 (2005): 57-68.

Illustration 6.8: Mykhail and Tadei Spalinsky, principal icon of the Mother of God, iconostasis in Sátoraljaújhely.

artistic works in the eparchy and suggests the significance of politics. (See the cover illustration.)

The icons on the iconostasis in Sátoraljaújhely are also linked with the Spalinsky brothers. The articulated, corniced structure follows the traditional order. The four-tier construction with its carving can be dated to the second or third quarter of the eighteenth century. The symmetrical

Illustration 6.9: Mykhail and Tadei Spalinsky, St. Bartholomew, iconsostasis in the cathedral church in Uzhhorod.

structure is closed in by the walls; it is painted bluish grey to look like marble. The prophets' tier is composed of circular icons with rocaille frames placed above the topmost cornice. This composition was characteristic of late renaissance iconostases in seventeenth-century Galicia, so for the eighteenth century it is considered conservative. The icons could have been painted not long after the iconostasis was installed. (See Illustration 6.7.) The principal icon of the Mother of God bears the date of its production: 1759 or, more likely, 1769. (See Illustration 6.8.) In 1773, with papal permission, the church of St. Nicholas in Sátoraljaújhely was renamed the church of the Dormition of the Mother of God. This required adjustments to the iconostasis. It was at this time that the patronal icon in the principal tier could have been painted (it was repainted after a fire) and its predella, which depicted the Dormition of the Mother of God with her lying on her deathbed surrounded by the apostles. On the icon of St. Paul in the apostles' tier, a signature was found on his sword. Once erroneously thought to be the Latin letters AR, it is now clear that it was instead the old Cyrillic letter ѳ (*fita*), based on the Greek theta. This was the first letter in the name Tadei (Thaddeus) when written in Church Slavonic, so the letter can be considered the signature of Tadei Spalinsky. The same signature, in the same calligraphy, was also discovered on the blade of the knife held by St. Bartholomew after the icons in two other iconostases had been cleaned: the one in Máriapócs and in the cathedral church in Uzhhorod. (See Illustration 6.9.) The brothers Spalinsky probably – and in the case of Máriapócs, certainly – worked together. Because of their similar artistic perspectives, more research is required to distinguish the stylistic characteristics of the two painters, especially in the case of large iconostases in which the work of additional assistants is evident.[28] The installation of the Uzhhorod iconostasis would have taken place after 1776, when the former Jesuit church was reworked and adapted to the Byzantine rite.[29] Of the dates that appear on the back of the iconostasis, the earliest is 1777, which research suggests could be the year the reconfiguration of the church commenced, and later dates can be understood as subsequent renovations. We also learn that in 1799 Ferenc Teck took part in work on the iconostasis.[30] The traditional, four-tiered iconostasis in rococo style fills the opening of the sanctuary's high triumphal arc. The iconostasis is divided by wide cornices, and the icons of the festal tier are elongated vertically. A significant number of its icons underwent repainting in the nineteenth century, but the manner of painting, so characteristic of the Spalinsky brothers, and the painter's signature letter, which here too, as in Máriapócs, can be found on the apostle Bartholomew's knife blade, indicate with certainty that Tadei Spalinsky also played a major role in painting the Uzhhorod iconostasis.

The icons of the Spalinsky brothers are qualitatively much superior to those of their contemporaries in the eparchy, mainly folk artists. Mykhail Spalinsky's depictions of Bishop Manuil Olshavsky (a full-length portrait made after 1758, a copy painted in 1767 after the bishop died, and also images on the catafalque)[31] and the style of his icons show that he was the senior of the two brothers and a better trained artist. But the plasticity in modelling   characteristic of them both, the richness of the tonality, and the carefully crafted details in the execution of figures, drapery, and landscape backgrounds earned these brothers a reputation as the most distinguished painters of Mukachevo eparchy. The subsequent fate of their workshop is not known, but their influence on certain compositions is attested later even in some of the eparchy's smaller churches.

---

[28] See Bernadett Puskás, "A történelmi munkácsi egyházmegye ikonfestészete a 18. században – Újabb adatok a vezető mesterek tevékenységével kapcsolatban," *Athanasiana* 14 (2002): 153-62.

[29] Maria Theresa donated liturgical paraphernalia made in Vienna to the cathedral church: a dikerion and trikerion and an episcopal epignation made by the monogrammist IL and a cruet and tray made by IWP and Franz Hellmayr.

[30] Syrokhman, *Tserkvy Ukrainy. Zakarpattia*, 18.

[31] Antal Hodinka [A. Romanuv], *Perepyska epyskopa nashoho bl. p. Mykhaila Manuila Olshavs'koho †1767 z tohdashnymy humenamy: Hedeonom z Pazynom i Ioannykiem z Skrypkom* (Zhovkva, 1937), 38.

*Illustration 6.10: Descent of the Holy Spirit with coat of arms
of Austria, iconostasis in Huklyvyi. Descent of the Holy Spirit
with coat of arms of Austria, iconostasis in Huklyvyi.*

Also to be mentioned among the iconostases of the eighteenth century
is the one in Huklyvyi. According to an inscription on it and a reference
in the Huklyvyi chronicle, it was made in 1784 by Frants Peier.[32] The

---

[32] Mykhailo Pryimych, *Pered lytsem tvoim. Zakarpats'kyi ikonostas* (Uzhhorod: Karpaty-
Grazhda, 2007), 131. The likely German spelling is Franz Beier. -- Editors.

Illustration 6.11: Iconostasis in Hajdúdorog.

iconostasis is noteworthy because of some rarely found iconographical details. One of the predellas shows the Baptism of Rus' with the figure of Volodymyr on a throne; there are archangels on the deacon doors, the door on the right depicting the archangel Barachiel, with the white roses that are his attribute. Above the principal icons are coats of arms: of the

Hungarian kingdom with the Austrian double-headed eagle and of Bishop Andrei Bachynsky; the bishop's coat of arms indicates that he was the primary benefactor of the church (the coat of arms of Bishop Manuil Olshavsky was placed on the facade of the church in Máriapócs). (See Illustration 6.10.) An inscription under an image of the crucified Christ, both painted directly on the eastern wall of the Huklyvyi church, informs us that this Crucifixion was a memorial commission to mark the death of the pastor's daughter on 6 June 1784.

At the very end of the century, in 1799, a contract was signed to prepare an iconostasis and altar for the church in Hajdúdorog. Nikola Janković, who undertook this project, was a well-known Serbian carver in Eger; he and his assistants produced several large iconostases in Orthodox churches for Serbs and Greeks in Hungary. But in Hajdúdorog, the contract gave him rather explicit instructions: the structure had to be modelled on the iconostasis in Sremski Karlovci (in Vojvodina), its disposition of images on the iconostasis in Uzhhorod, and its altar on that in the Orthodox church in Eger. (See Illustration 6.11.)

2.2 Tradition and Innovation in Iconography and the Function of Icons

The major moments in the history of the Mukachevo eparchy were not always decisive in the eparchy's artistic life. Although the episcopal center should have been a determining factor in this sphere, it was not until the end of the eighteenth century that it acquired sufficient authority and material resources to prescribe with regard to artistic issues. Every period in the art of Mukachevo eparchy has its own specific set of issues, requiring its own methodological approaches and consideration of insights from style criticism, the history of styles, source criticism, iconography, and intellectual history. One of the most distinctive periods in the history and art of Mukachevo eparchy was the eighteenth century, when, according to censuses, the eparchy had 839 Greek Catholic parishes with over four hundred thousand faithful under its jurisdiction. Problems surrounding the legal status of the Mukachevo bishops had become exacerbated: the king named the Greek Catholic hierarchs as bishops of Mukachevo and the pope named them as apostolic vicars, but the Roman Catholic bishop of Eger considered them only his own vicars of the Greek rite, who could ordain priests and build churches only with his permission.[33] Given these limitations, the bishops of Mukachevo were not

---

[33] Tihamér Aladár Vanyó, *A bécsi pápai követség levéltárának iratai Magyarországról 1611–1786* (Budapest: Akadémiai Kiadó, 1986), 108-12.

able to assume leadership in the sphere of sacral art or to establish artistic models. What was needed was a change in the eparchy's juridical and canonical status.

This finally came about through the intervention of Empress-Queen Maria Theresa. On 19 September 1771 the papal bull *Eximia regalium* regulated the status of Mukachevo eparchy; the bishop would be named by the king, and the eparchy would be part of the metropolis of Esztergom.[34] On 24 February 1773 the queen called a synod in Vienna for Catholic bishops of the Eastern rite, which dealt, among other things, with the publication of liturgical books, the number of church holidays, the fees that could be charged for sacramental services, and pastoral care. With royal acceptance of the synod's decisions, a royal charter of privileges, and material assistance, a new era opened for the Greek Catholics of Hungary – the social status of the clergy was ensured by regulation and the burden of material problems was considerably alleviated.[35]

The influence of enlightened absolutism in church art was first manifest in masonry architecture. In 1779 the Viennese architect Lorenz Lander, at the request of the treasury, prepared a series of designs for Greek Catholic churches, on an elongated plan and minus cleroses. The sketches preserved in the archives of the interiors of the churches show a change in the understanding of sacral space, so that now even the iconostasis was being considered part of the furniture.

2.3 Baroque Religiosity: Images and Practices in the Greek-Catholic Church

In the course of the eighteenth century, following on the change in worldview that had transpired in the previous century, in a process that encompassed the entire Eastern church, unique variants of the baroque emerged, based on local traditions, in both the Greek Catholic and Orthodox churches.[36] At first the baroque affected only the formal side of sacral visual art, and even then only in secondary details such as ornamentation. But later one can notice the new style expanding into the modelling and composition, and still later, from the middle of the century, it became generally accepted in the structure and system of iconostases and throughout the architecture.

---

[34] György Janka, "A munkácsi egyházmegye felállítása," *Szabolcs-Szatmár-Bereg megyei Szemle*, no. 4 (1996): 576-90.

[35] Udvari, *Ruszinok a XVIII. században*, 196-202.

[36] György Janka, "A katolikus barokk szellemiség a magyarországi görög katolikusoknál," *Athanasiana* 1 (1995): 105-13.

Changes in the interior of the church became evident in the eighteenth century. Previous tradition still determined the most accented component, the iconostasis – its system of images and the themes of its icons. Only among the scenes depicted on the predellas do there appear images that follow Roman Catholic models, which had been diffused also by prints of holy pictures; an example is the scene of Christ on the Mount of Olives (Podobovets). In the interior painting of the church, a more receptive space for images influenced by contemporary Roman Catholic iconography were the walls with their murals. The disposition of wall murals had been worked out in the seventeenth century in wooden churches, but only in the eighteenth century did such images appear as the Holy Trinity, in the center of the nave, amid the clouds in heaven, in the company of angels and putti (Serednie Vodiane). In masonry churches the murals on the walls fit into the general tableau of Hungary's monumental art. In Máriapócs the illusionist pseudoarchitecture, modelled on the work of Andrea Pozzo, was painted by the Hungarian artist István Izbeghy Vörös.[37] Baroque features may also be detected in the sacral painting in Hajdúdorog and Uzhhorod; their inspiration came from works seen by the bishops, who were trained by the Jesuits in Trnava. In the second half of the eighteenth century even village churches introduced baroque proskomedia tables, outfitted with an architectural-style frame and an altar icon; there also developed the practice of placing a tabernacle on the main altar. At the end of the eighteenth century and even more so after the turn of the nineteenth century, pulpits and pews came into vogue. Double-sided processional icons, which had taken on a new importance, were placed in richly carved architectural frames (Mother of God with Child/Crucifixion, second half of the eighteenth century, Abaújszolnok).

Visual representations of baroque religiosity and new iconographic motifs in the painting of Mukachevo eparchy appeared in connection with the two perhaps most important trends in that religiosity – the Marian cult and the worship of the Eucharist. In parallel with the flourishing of Marian devotion in the eighteenth century came a more direct reformulation and contamination of the iconography of the Mother of God on the principal icons of iconostases and on the icons of side altars. Although the Mother of God with child, which had ancient origins in the iconographic tradition, was retained, images of the Protection of the Mother of God also gained currency; the eighteenth-century Protection, depicting the Virgin Mary

---

[37] Szilvester Terdik, "A máriapócsi kegytemplom építésére és belső díszítésére vonatkozó, eddig ismeretlen források," *A Nyíregyházi Jósa András Múzeum Évkönyve* 50 (2008): 525-29.

spreading out her cloak, was now modelled on the image of the Mater Misericordiae, which had medieval roots but was decidedly Latin (Ladomirov, icon on the main altar, second half of the eighteenth century). Other popular Marian images showed the Mother of God as royal, wearing a crown (Baktakék, second half of the eighteenth century), Mary being crowned by the Holy Trinity (Lukov, last quarter of the eighteenth century), the Woman Clothed with the Sun. In the eighteenth century one of the most common icon themes on the main altar, which was now outfitted with a baldachin and tabernacle, was the Pietà (Ruská Bystrá, Ladomirov).

The veneration of miraculous icons continued in the eighteenth century as part of the traditional liturgical order in the Mukachevo eparchy. But already in the previous century, in connection with the development of new forms of Marian devotion, pilgrimages in the style of the local Eastern tradition of medieval origin had been giving way to processions and pilgrimages in the style of baroque Catholic practice. Pilgrimages to miraculous icons of the Mother of God, both older and more recent, were major events in the religious life of the eparchy; the clergy and faithful also took part in processions and pilgrimages on the major feasts of the Mother of God. In 1715 the second Pócs miraculous icon, i.e., a copy – probably made in Vienna – of the original miraculous icon taken to Vienna, also shed tears. After this Pócs was rapidly transformed into a center of pilgrimage. The reputation of Pócs throughout the country was reinforced by engraved images of the church and its miraculous icon. The printed liturgical books with engravings and etchings used in the eparchy continued to be purchased primarily from Galician print shops; parishes bought them from itinerant merchants. Similarly, printed images of the Máriapócs miraculous icon continued to be manufactured elsewhere. The first etching to depict the miraculous icon and the church in Máriapócs was made by Franz Feninger (c. 1750). Later, about 1800, a somewhat weaker etching was printed; according to the signature, it came from the workshop of János Fülöp Binder, an artist in Buda. It showed the church from the south, together with the Basilian monastery built near it (finished in 1753). Among the miraculous icons of the Mother of God painted on the territory of historical Hungary in the eighteenth century were two icons from Krychovo, another from Sajópálfala, the previously mentioned copy of the Mother of God of Klokočov, and an icon that was repainted by Tadei Spalinsky in 1769 in Krásny Brod.

Illustration 6.12: Ecce Homo, altar icon in Nyírderzs.

The depiction of the Passion of Christ in the iconography of the Carpathian region reaches back to the Middle Ages. Parallel with traditional depictions, new formulations arose at the end of the seventeenth century and especially in the eighteenth. These were reflections on the Passion and its component elements as well as symbolic representations, such as icons of the suffering Christ and his depiction as the font of the Eucharist. Images of the suffering Christ separate from the Passion cycle were not made for private devotion. In the Carpathian region in the course of the eighteenth century this icon type began to be used on the main altar or on the tabernacle. On the painted tabernacle in Bodružal (1706) we see Christ as the Man of Sorrows, the iconography of which developed in the West in the fifteenth century. The icon shows Christ sitting down for a rest after his crowning with thorns, wearing a loin cloth and a purple cloak, with marks of scourging visible on his body, but not yet the wounds of crucifixion. The altar icon in Nyirderzs (second half of the eighteenth century) shows the suffering Christ as a standing figure from the scene Ecce Homo. (See Illustration 6.12.)

An image for reflecting on Christ's passion that was diffused in the Carpathian region at the end of the seventeenth and in the eighteenth century was the icon of the Unsleeping Eye. Painted on a board or on canvas for private devotion, it showed Christ as a child sleeping on the cross, surrounded by the instruments of the Passion. Paintings of this iconographic type, which was also known in Western baroque art, were inscribed in the Carpathian region with verses, usually concerning the Passion, but sometimes bearing a message of Memento mori ("With patience bear the cross of Jesus; look at this example and be prepared for death"). In Mukachevo eparchy this type of image was mostly painted by folk artists (Jesus Sleeping on the Cross, provenance unknown, c. 1800, privately owned). More popular in Carpathian iconography related to the Passion were symbolic representations of Christ as the source of the Eucharist. The central figure in each of these was the suffering Christ of the Passion that arose under the influence of the iconographic type the King of Glory (of Byzantine origin, c. 1300). In this image, Christ is shown with the wounds from his crucifixion. Another important iconographic element of icons connected with the Eucharist is the traditional symbol of a grapevine, which bends under the weight of the clusters of grapes. The most commonly encountered composition was "Christ the Vinedresser," which shows Christ sitting on a gravestone. From the wound on his side grows a vine, which entwines around the tree of the cross in the background. Christ squeezes wine from the grapes into a chalice held by an angel (Ladomirov, tabernacle, second half of the eighteenth century). Unusually, "Christ the Vinedresser" also appeared in sculpture (Christ Squeezing the Grapes, Budapest, Museum of Ethnography). This composition of Western origin became popular in the Carpathian region in the beginning of the eighteenth century, among other reasons because it appeared in Nykodym Zubrytsky's engravings for liturgical books. A related version was "Christ the Grape Vine," in which Christ presses blood from the wound on his side into a chalice. Also to the series of eucharistic images belongs the icon "Christ in the Chalice."

These symbolic images were primarily used on altars, reflecting the new promotion of eucharistic devotion after the Synod of Zamość (1720). Changes in world view reflective of changing times, a new economic and cultural openness to the West, and the increasing ties with the Western church as a result of the union led to more frequent borrowings in Carpathian art from Roman Catholic models. The adaptation of Western models resulted in a gradual simplification of some parts of the old tradition or even in their disappearance, but at the same time the incorporation of new elements in the Greek Catholic church laid the foundation for new traditions and made it possible to create a new synthesis, the goal of which was the renewal of church life and art. The local environment reinterpreted and reworked the borrowed motifs and themes, adapting them to its own mentality; the borrowings underwent evolution and supplementation until they formed part of a new local tradition (such as the changes noted in the iconography of the Protection). And although the propagation of the Tridentine decrees played a significant role in forming the Greek Catholic art of the Carpathian region, it seems that those Western images sunk roots faster that had some reminiscence in form or content of Byzantine tradition, even if only through familiar liturgical texts.

From the second half of the eighteenth century, images meant to induce meditation, miraculous images, and other sacred images needed for processions and pilgrimages began to absorb the specific functions of icons. Partially in connection with this process, and also because the art became more simplified and devoid of formal elegance, somewhere around the turn of the nineteenth century icons began to be reduced to holy pictures, religiously themed painting, while the iconostasis was beginning to be transformed into a church decoration. An understanding of the liturgical role of the iconostasis was still present, but the theology of the icon incorporated in it had become so unimportant that the ornamentation covering the structure almost became more significant than the icons themselves. The size of the icons shrank; here and there, especially in the costly iconostases in larger cities, the icons were almost lost among the intricate carving. Formal traces of the ancient tradition could only be found in some particularly rooted and fixed images. Even the term "icon" was used less and less; and given the latinizing pictures that appeared in churches, this terminological shift was appropriate.

3. Conclusion and Directions for Further Research

Given the current state of research, it is not possible to flesh out the story in full topographical detail, but it is already possible to attempt to assemble data about the dominant artistic tendencies and linkages and to outline the history of the artistic experience of Mukachevo eparchy. From what has hitherto published we can get a good picture of the art of this church, with its particular status, and this picture is being supplemented continually by many newly published images and data (e.g., the gallery of bishops, funeral images, and printed antimensia).

As the art history of Mukachevo eparchy becomes clearer, however, new questions arise, new thematic approaches, particular problems. The restriction to the boundaries of a single church organization facilitates research into a greater number of questions that had hitherto been peripheral in the literature. These include the role of donors and commissioners, especially of the bishops. The latter increasingly assumed directorship of artistic projects, and as a result there increasingly was a more unified system of demands on artists. By researching on the eparchial level, we can better understand the interesting connections between church politics and artistic phenomena. We can also reach a more profound appreciation of the role of Galician, Viennese, and Hungarian artistic mediators.

Additional Bibliography (2010-17)

Csizmár Sarolta, Puskás Bernadett. Kollár Tibor, Németh Péter, Szatmári István, Szuhóczky Gábor, eds. *Historical Monuments Embraced by the Carpathians and the Tisa*. Nyíregyháza: Szabolcs-Szatmár-Bereg Megyei Önkormányzat, 2010.

Grešlík V. "Z problematiky výskumu ikon na Slovensku." In *Slovenská slavistika včera a dnes*, edited by Peter Žeňuch, 210-12. Bratislava: Slovenský komitét slavistov / Slavistický ústav Jána Stanislava SAV, 2012.

Pryimych Mykhailo. *Ikonostasy Zakarpattia*. Uzhhorod: Karpaty, 2014.

Terdik Szilveszter. " ...*a mostani világnak ízlésse, és a rítusnak módja szerint"*: *Adatok a magyarországi görög katolikusok művészetéhez*, Collectanea Athanasiana 1, 5. Nyíregyháza 2011.

Terdik Szilveszter. *Görögkatolikus püspöki központok Magyarországon a 18. században: művészet és reprezentáció*. Collectanea Athanasiana, 6, Ars Sacra Byzantino-Carpathiensis, 1. Nyíregyháza: Szent Atanáz Görög Katolikus Hittudományi Főiskola, 2014.

Terdik Szilveszter. "Ikonosztázionok a néhai Felső-Magyarországról budapesti múzeumok gyűjteményeiben." *Gömörország az északi magyar peremvidék fóruma* 12, no. 2 (2011): 10-19.

Terdik Szilveszter. "Máramarosi román ikonok egy csoportja a Néprajzi Múzeumban." *Néprajzi értesítő* 98 (2016): 55-65.

Véghseő Tamás, Terdik Szilveszter. "...*You Have Foreseen All of My Paths*...": *Byzantine Rite Catholics in Hungary*. Strasbourg: Éditions Du Signe, 2012.

Publications by the Author

Puskás Bernadett. "Obrazni typy barokovoi relihiinosti v zhyvopysi Mukachivs'koi eparkhii." In *Istoriia relihii v Ukraiini: Naukovyi shchoricnyk 2012 rik*, book 2, edited by O. Kyrychuk, M. Omel'chuk, and I. Orlevych, 445-51. Lviv: Lohos, 2012.

Puskás Bernadett. "Uzhots'ka derev"iana tserkva ta ii ikonostas." In *Istoriia relihii v Ukraiini: Naukovyi shchoricnyk 2015 rik*, edited by O. Kyrychuk, M. Omel'chuk, and I. Orlevych, 305-12. Lviv: Lohos, 2015.

Puskás Bernadett. "Questions Related to the Research of Greek Catholic Art: Debate about the Concept of the Carpathian Region and Its Lessons." In *Symbolae: A görög katolikus örökségkutatás útjai. A Nikolaus Nilles SJ halálának 100. évfordulóján rendezett konferencia tanulmányai*, edited by Véghseő Tamás, 123-40. Collectanea Athanasiana, I, Studia, 3. Nyíregyháza: Szent Atanáz Görög Katolikus Hittudományi Főiskola, 2010.

Puskás Bernadett. "18. századi ikon- és táblafestészet a görög katolikus egyház művészetében Magyarországon." *Barokk. Történelem — Irodalom — Művésze* (2010): 231-46.

Puskás Bernadett. *A Görögkatolikus Egyházművészeti Gyűjtemény anyagai I. Ikonok, festmények*. Nyíregyháza: Görögkatolikus Egyházművészeti Gyűjtemény, 2012.

Puskás Bernadett. "Az ikon a görög katolikusok liturgikus gyakorlatában: a sátoraljaújhelyi ikonosztázion." In (ed.) *Érzékek és vallás*, edited by Barna Gábor, Bodosi-Kocsis Nóra, Gyöngyössy Orsolya, 239-55. Szeged: SZTE Néprajzi és Kulturális Antropológiai Tanszék, 2009.

Puskás Bernadett. "Bacsinszky András püspöki reprezentációjának emlékei". In *Bacsinszky András munkácsi püspök: A Bacsinszky András munkácsi püspök halálának 200. évfordulóján rendezett konferencia tanulmányai. Nyíregyháza, 2009. november 12–14*, edited by Véghseő

Tamás, 173-95. Nyíregyháza: Szent Atanáz Görög Katolikus Hittudományi Főiskola, 2014. Collectanea Athanasiana, I, Studia, 6.

Puskás Bernadett. "Icones de la collection gréco-catholique d'art religieux de Nyíregyháza." *Apulum* 51 (2014): 309-20.

Puskás Bernadett. "Ikonohrafia Khrysta - Velykoho Arhyiereia v rehioni Karpat." In *Ikona – staronovy nástroj evangelizácie: Súbor štúdií*, edited by Šimon Marinčák, 169-79. Košice: Dobrá Kniha, 2012.

Puskás Bernadett. "Kérdések Spalinszky Mihály és Tádé festészetével kapcsolatban." In *Keleti keresztény kultúra határainkon innen és túl: A 2012 november 9-én rendezett jubileumi konferencia tanulmányai*, edited by Bojtos Anita, 120-39. Művelődéstörténeti Műhely, Rendtörténeti konferenciák, 9.192 Budapest: PPKE BTK, 2015.

Puskás Bernadett. "Két kárpátaljai fatemplom és ikonosztázaik." In *Vallásos kultúra és életmód a Kárpát-medencében 10*, edited by Pilipkó Erzsébet and Fogl Krisztián Sándor, 683-707. Veszprém: Laczkó Dezső Múzeum, 2017.

Puskás Bernadett. "Monastyr vasyliian ta Tserkva Sviatoho Arkhanhela Mikhaila v Mariiapovchi i ikh obladnannia XVIII st." In *Rola monasterów w kształtowaniu kultury ukraińskiej w wiekach XI–XX / Rol' monastyriv u formuvanni ukrains'koi kul'tury u XI-XX vikakh*, edited by Agnieszka Gronek and Alicja Nowak, 113-20. Biblioteka Fundacji św. Włodzimierza, 20. Kraków: Wydawnictwo Szwajpolt Fiol, 2014.

Puskás Bernadett. "Pam"iatky mystetstva, pov"iazani z periodom iepyskops'koi khirotonii Andreia Bachyns'koho 1773 r. - v konteksti barokovoi reprezentatsii." In *Gréckokatolícka cirkev na Slovensku vo svetle výročí III*, edited by Jaroslav Coranič, 271-85. Presov: Vydavateľstvo Prešovskej Univerzity, 2013.

Puskás Bernadett. "Zagadnienia sztuki XVIII stulecia mukaczewskiej diecezji greckokatolickiej." In *Wielokulturowość na Sądecczyźnie: Materiały z sympozjum 25-27 listopada 2010 Muzeum Okręgowe w Nowym Sączu*, edited by Barbara Szafran, 73-88. Nowy Sącz: Muzeum Okręgowe w Nowym Sączu, 2010.

Puskás Bernadett. "Znachennia kraievydu v ikonopysi." In *Krajobraz semantyczny wsi i miast*, edited by Józef Marecki and Lucyna Rotter, 225-36. Kraków: Uniwersytet Papieski Jana Pawła II w Krakowie - Wydawnictwo, 2016.

Documentary Collections

Véghseő Tamás, Terdik Szilveszter, and Simon Katalin. *Források a magyarországi görögkatolikus parókiák történetéhez. Az egri egyházmegye területén szolgáló görögkatolikus papok 1741. évi javadalom-összeírása.* Collectanea Athanasiana, II, Textus/Fontes, 5. Nyíregyháza: Szent Atanáz Görögkatolikus Hittudományi Főiskola, 2014.

Véghseő Tamás and Terdik Szilveszter. *Források a magyarországi görögkatolikus parókiák történetéhez. Az 1747. évi javadalom-összeírás.* Collectanea Athanasiana II, Textus/Fontes, 6. Nyíregyháza: Szent Atanáz Görög Katolikus Hittudományi Főiskola, 2015.

Véghseő Tamás, Terdik Szilveszter, Simon Katalin, Majchrics Tiborné, Földvári Katalin, and Lágler Éva. *Források a magyarországi görögkatolikus parókiák történetéhez. Olsavszky Mihály Mánuel munkácsi püspök 1750– 1752. évi egyházlátogatásainak iratai.* Collectanea Athanasiana, II, Textus/Fontes, 7. Nyíregyháza: Szent Atanáz Görög Katolikus Hittudományi Főiskola, 2015.

Véghseő Tamás, Terdik Szilveszter, Majchrics Tiborné, Földvári Katalin, Varga Anett, and Lágler Éva. *Források a magyarországi görögkatolikus parókiák történetéhez. Munkácsi és nagyváradi egyházmegyés parókiák összeírása 1774–1782 között: 1. Szabolcs, Bereg, Szatmár, Ugocsa vármegyék és a hajdúvárosok* Collectanea Athanasiana, II, Textus/Fontes, 8/1. Nyíregyháza: Szent Atanáz Görög Katolikus Hittudományi Főiskola, 2016.

Véghseő Tamás, Terdik Szilveszter, Majchrics Tiborné, Földvári Katalin, and Lágler Éva. *Források a magyarországi görögkatolikus parókiák történetéhez: Munkácsi és nagyváradi egyházmegyés parókiák összeírása 1774–1782 között 2. Szepes, Abaúj, Zemplén és Máramaros vármegyék.* Collectanea Athanasiana, II, Textus/Fontes, 8/2. Nyíregyháza: Szent Atanáz Görög Katolikus Hittudományi Főiskola, 2016.

Véghseő Tamás, Terdik Szilveszter, Majchrics Tiborné, Földvári Katalin, and Varga Anett. *Források a magyarországi görögkatolikus parókiák történetéhez. A munkácsi egyházmegye parókiarendezési iratai 1782–1787. 1. Hajdúvárosok, Szabolcs és Szatmár vármegyék.* Collectanea Athanasiana, II, Textus/Fontes, 9/1. Nyíregyháza: Szent Atanáz Görög Katolikus Hittudományi Főiskola, 2017.

Véghseő Tamás, Terdik Szilveszter, Majchrics Tiborné, Földvári Katalin, Varga Anett, and Lágler Éva. *Források a magyarországi görögkatolikus parókiák történetéhez. A munkácsi egyházmegye parókiarendezési iratai 1782–1787. 2. Abaúj, Torna, Borsod és Gömör vármegyék.* Collectanea Athanasiana, II, Textus/Fontes, 9/2. Nyíregyháza: Szent Atanáz Görög Katolikus Hittudományi Főiskola, 2017.

Véghseő Tamás, Terdik Szilveszter, Majchrics Tiborné, Földvári Katalin, and Csorba Noémi. *Források a magyarországi görögkatolikus parókiák történetéhez. A munkácsi egyházmegye parókiarendezési iratai 1782–1787. 4. Ung vármegye.* Collectanea Athanasiana, II, Textus/Fontes, 9/4. Nyíregyháza: Szent Atanáz Görög Katolikus Hittudományi Főiskola, 2017.

Véghseő Tamás, Terdik Szilveszter, Majchrics Tiborné, Földvári Katalin, Ternovácz Adél, Faragó Dávid, and Bachusz Dóra. *Források a magyarországi görögkatolikus parókiák történetéhez. A munkácsi egyházmegye parókiarendezési iratai 1782–1787. 5. Bereg és Szabolcs vármegye.* Collectanea Athanasiana, II, Textus/Fontes, 9/5. Nyíregyháza: Szent Atanáz Görög Katolikus Hittudományi Főiskola, 2017.

Véghseő Tamás, Terdik Szilveszter, Majchrics Tiborné, Földvári Katalin, Varga Anett, Lágler Éva, Rácz Balázs Viktor, Kis Iván, and Borbás Benjámin, *Források a magyarországi görögkatolikus parókiák történetéhez. A munkácsi egyházmegye parókiarendezési iratai 1782–1787. 6. Zemplén vármegye (első alkötet).* Collectanea Athanasiana, II, Textus/Fontes, 9/6/A. Nyíregyháza: Szent Atanáz Görög Katolikus Hittudományi Főiskola, 2017.

Véghseő Tamás, Terdik Szilveszter, Majchrics Tiborné, Földvári Katalin, Varga Anett, Lágler Éva, Rácz Balázs Viktor, Kis Iván, and Borbás Benjámin, *Források a magyarországi görögkatolikus parókiák történetéhez. A munkácsi egyházmegye parókiarendezési iratai 1782–1787. 6. Zemplén vármegye (második alkötet).* Collectanea Athanasiana, II, Textus/Fontes, 9/6/B. Nyíregyháza: Szent Atanáz Görög Katolikus Hittudományi Főiskola, 2017.

Sacred and Heraldic Images on Ukrainian Banners of the Eighteenth and Nineteenth Centuries

Roksolana Kosiv

Ukrainian lands have belonged to different spheres of influence and have come under various rulers.[1] Ukraine is situated on the border between Eastern Christendom with the Greek (Byzantine) rite and the Roman (Latin) ecclesiastical tradition. As a result, Ukrainian sacral culture and art exhibits diverse tendencies and brings together different traditions and customs. Western influences have always been more palpable in Galicia, Transcarpathia, Volhynia, and Podillia than farther east in Ukraine. As of 1772, part of these Western Ukrainian lands became part of the Habsburg Monarchy. For the Ukrainians of Galicia this can be considered a period of cultural, spiritual, and national awakening. In 1807, after persistent efforts, the metropolis of Halych was renewed – an ecclesiastical institution that had not existed since the time of the Galician-Volhynian principality. The activities of the Greek Catholic church went beyond caring for the spiritual life of the faithful: they also contributed to the educational and cultural development of the Ukrainian population. The political and cultural changes that took place in Galicia during the Austrian period were also reflected in works of art. Styles changed, as did iconography.[2] Heraldic symbols of the Habsburg Monarchy also appeared in various works, especially on a number of banners, which is the subject of this chapter.

From about the fifteenth or sixteenth century, various types of banners existed in Ukrainian lands: military (territorial-administrative), city, guild, church, and funerary banners. Each of these had its specific characteristics, in form and size of the cloth, iconography, and technique of execution;

---

[1] This chapter was translated by John-Paul Himka.

[2] Western influences began to affect Ukrainian sacral art much earlier, at least from the end of the sixteenth century. But a process of "latinization" was accelerated after the Synod of Zamość (1720); this was particularly noticeable in the second half of the eighteenth and in the nineteenth centuries in ritual and church furnishings. It reached such an extent that in the second half of the nineteenth century the Ukrainian intelligentsia sought to return a "national style" to church art. At the same time, in nineteenth-century Galicia many artists came from elsewhere, while some Ukrainian artists received their artistic education in West European schools.

and within each type there were also particular groups of banners with their own individual characteristics. Much depended on where the banner was used and to what institution or person it belonged. Church and funerary banners were little influenced by political and social changes, while military, city, and guild banners reflected these changes more.

Unfortunately, owing to the relatively impermanent material (fabric) from which banners are made as well as to external circumstances (frequent wars, the political situation in Ukrainian lands in the twentieth century), not very many Ukrainian banners have been preserved. All banners were made for processions or in one way or another were used outdoors; this contributed to their rapid deterioration. In fact, a banner on average lasted fifteen to forty years. After that, most of them, especially church banners – as sacral, blessed objects – were burned.[3]

Many more banners have been preserved from the eighteenth and nineteenth centuries than from earlier periods. These include various types, but church banners predominate, particularly from the Lemko region, Galicia, and Transcarpathia. In spite of their different functions, all types of banners from the eighteenth and nineteenth centuries continued the developmental tendencies of earlier ones. We will illustrate this using selected church and guild banners as well as banners of Ukrainian organizations of a military character from the second half of the nineteenth century and beginning of the twentieth.

Church banners were the most conservative in their iconographic themes. Different religious images were affixed to both sides of them. The cloth of a church banner hangs from a horizontal crossbar affixed to the center of the top of a pole. Thus the front side is not covered by the pole, while the reverse is. But all the known banners of the eighteenth and nineteenth centuries have been preserved without their poles, hence it is often impossible to ascertain which side was the front. Some light is thrown on this issue by the inventory descriptions of the property of individual churches. For example, the church of St. Paraskevia in Yasinka Velyka in the Sambir deanery had one large banner with St. Paraskevia on one side and the Mother of God on the other. (It also had three small ones; one depicted St. Michael and St. Barbara and another, St. Nicholas and the Baptism of Christ.)[4] The visitator first named the image of St. Paraskevia, then the

---

[3] The oldest known extant Ukrainian banner dates to the last quarter of the sixteenth century. It came from the church in Stara Sil, Staryi Sambir raion, Lviv oblast (National Museum in Lviv [NML], inventory no. I-1432). There are a few other church banners from Western Ukrainian churches that can be dated to the end of the sixteenth century.

[4] It was not possible to make out what was depicted on the third banner. See "Opys tserkov

Mother of God. One can assume that in this case the image of St. Paraskevia, after whom the church was named, was the front side of the banner.

Visitation documents generally provide minimal characterization of the works of art in churches. The few descriptions of banners that are found in various documents are therefore of particular interest. There is a detailed description of the iconography of a banner, made in 1766, in the church of the Holy Trinity in Limna, Dobromyl deanery. This banner was "newly provided" with an image of the Trinity on one side, and a "well done" image of the Descent of the Holy Spirit on the other. The banner's iconography was thus totally integrated with the patron of the church, the Holy Trinity. The images were placed against a background of "red taffeta with white flowers." The banner had three tassels and a painted pole topped by a cross that was "gilded in silver and gold in marzipan style." In this same church were three old banners "of poor workmanship on canvas."[5] Iconography and the dedication of the church also went hand in hand on a banner described for the Holy Savior Monastery in the Staryi Sambir region. An inventory from 1752 stated that the church had one banner, which depicted the Transfiguration of our Lord against a background of red damask with three silk tassels.[6] The same sort of information about the iconography can also be found in visitation records of the Staryi Sambir and Wysoczany deanery from 1766-93. In the church of St. Demetrius in Yasinka Mala there were three banners. The large banner had St. Demetrius on one side and St. Paraskevia on the other. The two others were "small and frayed."[7] In the church of the archangel Michael in Bystrytsia the "one good large banner" depicted St. Michael and the Holy Trinity. Three little ones depicted the archangel Gabriel and the Baptism of Christ, the Baptism of Christ and St. Nicholas, and the Holy Trinity and the Annunciation.[8] In the church of the archangel Michael in Sozan, there was "one large banner with a depiction of the archangel Michael and the Protection of the Mother of God and two small, frayed banners."[9] In Lviv in the middle of the nineteenth century in the church of

i parokhii dekanatu Starosambirs'koho ta Vysochans'koho 1766-1793 rr.," NML, Viddil rukopysiv ta starodrukiv, Rkl 496, 4.

[5] "Vizytatsiia Dobromyl's'koho dekanatu 1761 r.," NML, Viddil rukopysiv ta starodrukiv, fond Podolyns'koho, vol. 3:2 (98).

[6] T. Hutsalenko, "Dva inventari Sviatospas'koho monastyria," in *Starosambirshchyna III* (Staryi Sambir: Prykarpats'ka asotsiatsiia rozvytku kraiu, 2004), 337.

[7] "Opys tserkov i parokhii dekanatu Starosambirs'koho ta Vysochans'koho 1766-1793 rr.," 5.

[8] Ibid., 14.

[9] Ibid., 45.

St. Nicholas near the castle hill there were banners that "represented St. Nicholas, St. Gregory, Jesus Christ bearing the cross on his shoulders, and the Protection of the Most Holy Mother of God." And in the church of Ss. Peter and Paul, banners portrayed the two apostles as well as St. Thecla (who was converted by St. Paul and was also the first female martyr), Christ in the act of blessing, and the Mother of God. In the church of St. George in Lviv at the same time there were banners depicting not only the Savior and the Protection of the Mother of God, but also Latin-rite images, including Our Lady of Częstochowa.[10] As we see, in all these cases the themes of the major part of the described banners were connected with the church's patronage.

The church visitation records only sketchily describe the condition of the banners, their quantity, and the material of which they were made.[11] In the eighteenth and nineteenth centuries some church banners were bigger than the older banners,[12] as some visitators remarked.[13] In the eighteenth century there were church banners made entirely of canvas, but also banners that had only the central portion (*serednyk*) painted on canvas; there were also embroidered banners and banners on expensive fabric, but many fewer of them.[14] Canvas banners were more frequently

---

[10] T. Bilous, *Opysaniie ikon po tserkvakh russkykh v stolychnom hradi L'vovi* (Lviv, 1858), 35, 46, 55.

[11] For example, we know that the church of St. Theodore in Lviv, which no longer exists, had in 1741 two red banners made of damask with crimson silk tassels. In the brick church of St. Paraskevia in Lviv there were also two red banners of damask. In the church of the Transfiguration in the village of Borynychi in the Zhydachiv region there was a banner painted on red muslin and two canvas ones. "Heneral'na vizytatsiia L'vivs'koi Diietsezii 1740-1743 rr.," NML, Viddil rukopysiv ta starodrukiv, Rkl 17, folios 5, 18, 342.

[12] A banner from the first third of the seventeenth century from the church in Jastrzebik in the Lemko region with a depiction of the Annunciation on one side and the Mother of God Hodegetria on the other measures 76 x 56.5 cm (Muzeum Okręgowe w Nowym Sączu). The banner of Stara Sil from the last quarter of the sixteenth century with a depiction of Christ and St. Nicholas measures 74.8 x 60.4 cm. In both cases, however, the cloth of the banners has not been preserved *in toto*. The size of most banners from the second half of the seventeenth century into the nineteenth century is generally about 120 x 80 cm. The size of large banners can reach 170 x 120 cm. This is roughly the size of a banner of unknown provenance with images of the Mother of God of Mercy on one side and St. Nicholas on the other from the beginning of the eighteenth century (NML I-1236). There are several more large banners like this that date from the nineteenth century.

[13] In the church of Christ's Ascension in Yasnyky, Berezhany deanery, there were "three small, old banners and one big new one." "Vizytatsiia Berezhans'koho dekanatu 1766 r.," Lvivs'ka naukova biblioteka im. V. Stefanyk (LNB), Viddil rukopysiv, Mv-314, op. 1, spr. 336, folio 26.

[14] We are unaware of any Western Ukrainian banners of the eighteenth century that had embroidered images. This technique required a great deal of labor, expense, and practice.

mentioned in the visitation records than banners of other material.[15] In Zhukiv, Berezhany deanery, in the church of St. Nicholas in 1766 there were "three better banners on canvas and two very old ones."[16]

From the visitation records of the eighteenth century we see that the number of banners in a church ranged from one to eight, but usually there were three or four.[17] The records also indicate that there did not have to be an even number of banners in a church and that the banners could be kept against a single wall of the nave. The quantity and placement of the banners in a church depended on the material resources of the parishioners as well as on local tradition. In some inventories banners are not mentioned at all, so we do not know if they were lacking entirely or if the visitator simply did not take note of them.

There is iconographic evidence that banners were used in various processions. They were most often depicted in processions on icons commemorating the translation of saints' relics. Thus, four banners are depicted on an icon from the beginning of the eighteenth century, the translation of the relics of St. Nicholas, in the church in the village of Pryslip in Transcarpathia. Two groups of three banners are painted at the head of the procession on the eighteenth-century icon of the translation of the relics of Ss. Cosmas and Damian from the church of the holy martyrs Cosmas and Damian in the village of Hiiche in the Zhovkva region.[18] The banners are on red and blue fabrics, with decorative streamers (*vyrizy*) and tassels. On this icon one can make out what is depicted on the banners' central portions. In the group on the left, one is painted with the Mother of God and child, the second with a crucifixion and the figures standing around the cross, and the third with St. George the Dragonslayer. On a banner on the right, one can make out the Transfiguration of Our Lord. Two banners are depicted on the image of the translation of the relics of St. Nicholas on a double-sided icon from the village of Sniatynka, Lviv oblast, from the second half of the eighteenth century in the collection of the National Museum in Lviv (NML).[19] All the poles on all the banners are

---

[15] Roksolana Kosiv, *Ukrains'ki khoruhvy* (Kyiv: Oranta, 2009), 99.

[16] "Vizytatsiia Berezhans'koho dekanatu 1758-1766 rr.," LNB, Viddil rukopysiv, f. 3, spr. 314, folio 6.

[17] Kosiv, *Ukrains'ki khoruhvy*, 99-100.

[18] NML, inventory no. I-2520.

[19] NML, inventory no. I-3343.

Illustration 7.1: Church banners in a procession. Detail of the icon "Transfer of the Relics of St. Nicholas." Second half of the eighteenth century. Sniatynka, Lviv oblast. NML.

topped with a cross. Banners of various forms, including church banners, are depicted on an eighteenth-century canvas showing a procession with the wonderworking icon of the Mother of God of Pochaiv monastery. It is worth noting that in all cases where it can be made out, the banners are depicted in men's hands.[20] In the majority of the depictions of banners, the front side of the banner is turned in the direction of the procession's movement, and the reverse is facing the people in the procession. (See Illustration 7.1.)

The iconography of the banners extant from the eighteenth and nineteenth centuries shows variety. As was the case earlier, images of St. Nicholas, St. Michael, and St. George remained popular. The saints retained the traditional iconographic characteristics. The archangel Michael, however, was more frequently than previously shown vanquishing a devil lying at his feet. Noteworthy too is the iconography of St. Nicholas on a banner from the last third of the eighteenth century from Koropets in the Ternopil region. Here a full-length figure of St. Nicholas stands on twelve prostrate figures and holds them down with his bishop's staff. This is a metaphor for overcoming heresies.[21]

The banners of this period also depicted festal scenes. As earlier, the more popular feasts were the Nativity of Christ, the Baptism of Christ, the Annunciation, and the Dormition of the Mother of God. In general, by comparison with the previous period the subjects of the iconography of banners were more diversified. However, as of the mid-eighteenth century there were fewer banners with images of the two St. Paraskevias, the great martyr and the monastic, who had been favorite saints on Western Ukrainian banners of the seventeenth and first third of the eighteenth century. On the other hand, there were frequent depictions of other female saints, such as Ss. Catherine, Barbara, and Helen.

Ukrainian church banners from the end of the seventeenth through the nineteenth century often depict Our Lady of Mercy (Mater Misericordiae).[22] The iconography represents the Mother of God

---

[20] In the icon of the translation of the relics of St. Nicholas from the lowest tier of the church in the village of Sasiv, Lviv region, the two banners are carried by subdeacons following a processional cross.

[21] NML, inventory no. I-3610. In NML there is also an eighteenth-century icon of St. Nicholas from Firleivka that shows the saint standing on top of four figures; this again is a metaphor for the victory over heresies. A similar theme is seen in another icon from this period called "the Mother of God keeping the infidels down with her feet," from a church in Shliakhtova (NML). Such a depiction of St. Nicholas may have been inspired by an engraving for an akathist to St. Nicholas printed in Lviv in 1699; the engraving shows St. Nicholas pushing Arius, who is lying at his feet, with his staff. In general, this iconography has earlier prototypes in the depiction of Roman, and later Byzantine, emperors standing on the prostrate figures of their enemies.

[22] R. Kosiv, "'Shelter of the World, More Spacious than a Cloud': Two Types of Iconography of Virgin Mother of Mercy in Western Ukrainian Icons on Canvas and Church Banners of the 1670–1730s," *Ikon. Journal of iconographic studies* 10 (2017): 387–98.

protecting with her mantle those who come for refuge to her. This theme was inspired on Ukrainian territories by Western models. A specific local icon developed out of it, the Akathist Mother of God – Mother of Mercy. On both icons and banners of the Mother of God of Mercy, various descriptive titles appear: Mother of God of All Who Suffer, the Joy of All Who Mourn, Our Lady of Perpetual Help, and the Protection of the Mother of God. The Mother of God of Mercy is thematically close to the traditional Ukrainian icon of the Protection of the Mother of God, which included St. Roman the Melodist. St. Roman did not appear on pre-nineteenth century banners that we know about, but the variant that included him can be found on various examples from the nineteenth century.

The image of the Mother of God of Mercy is found on five Western Ukrainian church banners. Four of them, of unknown provenance, stem from the end of the seventeenth or beginning of the eighteenth century. The fifth, dated 1712, comes from a church in Drohobych, either the church of St. George or the church of the Exaltation of the Holy Cross. Four of them show the Mother of God covering with her mantle the faithful of various stations, ages, and needs. A variant of this iconography is connected with the akathist and prayer service (*moleben*) to the Mother of God, and this is the variant that achieved the greatest diffusion on Western Ukrainian lands of that period. The iconography of the scene also has parallels on icons of the period. In some cases, it is possible to speak about the authorship of one artist or a group of artists. For example, a banner of unknown provenance in the collection of the Lviv Gallery of Art[23] was executed by the same artist who painted the icon of the Mother of God of Mercy, also of unknown provenance, in the collection of the National Museum in Kraków. Two icons of unknown provenance from the eighteenth century also exhibit a uniform iconography,[24] as do a number of other works.

A somewhat different iconography of the Mother of God of Mercy is on a banner from the end of the seventeenth or beginning of the eighteenth century from the Historical Museum in Sanok.[25] Here representatives of all stations in life stand on both sides of the Mother of God, and in addition there are those who particularly hope for her intercession and aid –

---

[23] On the reverse is the synaxis of the archangel Michael. Inventory no. Zh-4703.

[24] One is in NML, the other in the Historical Museum in Sanok. They are reproduced in V. Svientsits'ka and V. Otkovych, *Ukrains'ke narodne maliarstvo XIII-XX stolit'* (Kyiv: Mystetstvo, 1991), ill. 80; and R. Biskupski, *Ikony w zbiorach polskich* (Warsaw: Wydawnictwa Artystyczne i Filmowe, 1991), ill. 89.

[25] On the reverse is St. Nicholas. Inventory no. MHS/S/2411.

Illustration 7.2: Church banner of the Mother of God Mater Misericordiae. 1712.
From the church of St. George or the church of the Transfiguration in Drohobych.
Author: Ivan Medytsky (?). Canvas, ground, tempera, oil. "Drohobychchyna"
Museum in Drobobych (Lviv oblast).

travelers, sailors, and the poor. Every person standing near the
monumental figure of the crowned Mother of God directs various ribbons
toward her inscribed with words of prayer. The prototype of this

iconography is an icon on canvas from the 1660s-1670s from Stara Sil.[26] In the middle tier of the composition, in the back against a stylized landscape, are depicted travelers and sailors. An iconography very similar to that of the Mother of God of Mercy on this banner can be found on an icon in the parish church in Chornoriky, which – like the banner from the Lviv Gallery of Art and the icon from the National Museum in Kraków – was executed by the same artist from the same sketches.

The banners discussed here have more or less the same variant of the image of the Mother of God, but they treat the lower tier of the composition differently. Thus the Drohobych banner of 1712 shows, instead of the traditional groups of people of various stations and needs, concrete episodes of intercession which are arranged in little groups in two tiers.[27] Among them are rescue from drowning, rescue from assault and robbery, feeding of the hungry, healing of the sick, and protection of travelers – all of which illustrate the words of the akathist. In all the scenes, an angel gives help to those in need. (See Illustration 7.2.) There is a strong iconographic resemblance to a mural from the first third of the eighteenth century on the eastern wall of the narthex, above the entrance to the nave, in the church of St. George, whence the banner itself may have come. The mural is executed more schematically than the banner, on which the details and adornment of the Mother of God's clothing as well as the figures in the scenes are well worked out. In the murals, the scenes are placed in eight squares in a horizontal row in order to fit the size of the wall. (The two scenes on the far left have not been preserved.) A similar layout was used for scenes of the deeds of the archangel Michael in an icon from the 1660s-70s on the principal tier of the iconostasis in the church of the Elevation of the Cross in Drohobych. Comparison with signed works indicates that the author of the Drohobych banner was Ivan Medytsky (the son of Stefan Medytsky).[28]

---

[26] Vira Svientsitska and Vasyl Otkovych suggested that the icon might have been painted by Stefan Medytsky. Svientsits'ka and Otkovych, *Ukrains'ke narodne maliarstvo*, ill. 107.

[27] The banner is preserved in the "Drohobychchyna" museum in Drobhobych, inventory no. 4437/I-110. The reverse depicts the Elevation of the Holy Cross. The depiction of the Elevation on this side of the banner copies the patronal icon of the church of the Elevation in Drohobych. This banner, as well as two other banners dating from around the same time, was found in the belltower of the church of St. George and then given to the museum. It can be assumed that the banners come from that church.

[28] On Ivan Medytsky, see M. Korniecki, "Obrazy i 'ikony' Jana Medyckiego. Przyczynek do dziejów malarstwa na karpatskiej prowincji w początku XVIII wieku," *Biuletyn Historii Sztuki*, no. 2-3 (1993): 249-54.

Illustration 7.3: Church banner of the Mother of God Mater Misericordiae, with a scene of the communion of St. Onuphrius as well as St. John the Baptist. Early eighteenth century. Unknown provenance. Canvas, ground, tempera. Dimensions: 170 x 116.5 cm. NML.

An even more interesting iconography can be found on a banner of unknown provenance in the National Museum in Lviv (NML).[29] Here the

Mother of God is shown covering with her mantle a monastery depicted on the lower tier. On either side of the monastery complex are painted a scene of St. Onuphrius receiving communion and St. John the Baptist. (See Illustration 7.3.) This iconography of the Mother of God of Mercy is unique. The focus of the Mother of God's protection is the monastery with two three-domed, tripartite churches. Although artists of this stylistic school very often painted a monastery or a church of a similar type, here the monastery can be identified as the monastery of St. Onuphrius in Lavriv. The cult of St. Onuphrius was very popular in Przemyśl eparchy because relics of this saint were preserved in the Lavriv monastery, which dates to the era of the medieval Galician principality. Monasteries of St. Onuphrius were also established in Posada Rybotycka and Dobromyl, both also in Przemyśl eparchy. It is not known how exact artists of that time were in representing real architecture, but the connection with Lavriv monastery is clear from the figures of St. Onuphrius and John the Baptist: there once was also a church of St. John the Baptist at the monastery in addition to the church of St. Onuphrius. Unfortunately, it has not been possible to identify from which church the museum acquired the banner. Such information could have enhanced interpretation of the banner's iconography.

The diffusion of various iconographic patterns for the protection of the Mother of God in a rather small circle of painters testifies to the considerable development of this image. This also demonstrates the wide spectrum of creative inspirations that the artists made skilled use of, retaining a national signature in their resolution of the theme. The image of the Mother of God of Mercy is also found on church banners of the nineteenth century. On these, though, can be perceived a more simplified resolution and fewer figures standing near the Mother of God. Also, they lack the traditional connection with the akathist to the Mother of God. A banner from Smerekiv from 1865 stands out because it shows under the Mother of God's protection Ss. Peter and Paul, St. Nicholas, and two other saints.[30] This iconography has analogues in Hutsul icons on glass from the same period, but is nonetheless a deviation from received tradition. A variant of the iconography of the Protection of the Mother of God that was traditional in Ukrainian icon-painting of the sixteenth century can be found in a banner from 183(8?) from Pokuttia,[31] in the center of the lower

---

[29] NML I-1236.

[30] NML I-3095.

[31] NML I-1444.

tier of which is painted St. Roman the Melodist and on either side of him – members of the church brotherhood with candles. The popularity of the theme of the Protection of the Mother of God on banners was not accidental. This image symbolized the intercession and protection of the heavenly church represented by the Mother of God – a theme that was particularly relevant in the context of the difficult social-historical conditions in Ukrainian lands.

Other popular themes in the eighteenth and nineteenth centuries were the images of the Immaculate Conception of the Mother of God and the Coronation of the Mother of God, which entered Ukrainian icon-painting through the influence of West European painting. Their popularity can also be discerned in the literary works of this period. The diffusion of compositions in which particular attention is paid to the glorification of the Mother of God and her virtues, and the emphasis on her role as Queen of Heaven, were manifestations of the Counter-Reformation period. The pictures had parallels in the works of Ukrainian theologians of the seventeenth century such as Ioanikii Galiatovsky, Lazar Baranovych, and Antonii Radyvylovsky, in which considerable attention is devoted to warning against the teachings of "infidel heretics." The main idea of these works is the glorification of the Mother of God and the articulation of her royal status. This is the context for the popularity in the seventeenth through nineteenth centuries of images of the Mother of God and the Child Jesus with crowns and also, at the end of the eighteenth and in the nineteenth century, of the replication of wonderworking crowned icons. In particular, we know about ten church banners from the nineteenth century that bear the image of the Mother of God of Pochaiv, which belongs to the iconographic type of the Mother of God Eleusa. A whole series of banners produced in the nineteenth century by semiprofessional artists depicts the wonderworking Roman or Lydda Mother of God, which was known in various copies and under various local names, such as the Mother of God of Berdychiv, of Letychiv, of Pidkamin, and of Lezhaisk. On Western Ukrainian lands the cult of this image was fostered by the Dominicans.

Let us turn our attention to a rare theme, the Church Militant, which appears on a church banner made in October 1718 for the church of St. George in Drohobych.[32] This is an iconographically complex theme, which is rarely encountered in Ukrainian art; in our opinion, its battle thematics are well suited to the symbolic significance of banners. The iconography

---

[32] "Drohobychchyna" museum in Drohobych, inventory no. 2848 I-14. On the reverse is the Baptism of Christ.

of the Church Militant incorporates the idea of the Most Holy Mother of God, symbolizing here also the Church of Christ as a whole, defending the true church from heretical attacks. It has a clear military program, concentrating on the conflict between the armed forces of heaven and the underworld, the latter army being composed of various heresies.

The depiction on the banner stands out for its complex method of presenting the theme; the banner seems aimed at viewers who have a good grasp of certain theological-philosophical conceptions. The content of the theme is constructed on the basis of a metaphor. The composition can be understood as three-tiered, with the middle tier allotted the most space. This tier shows the full-length figure of the Mother of God with her hands together in a prayerful pose, with a tent in the background. The iconography of the Mother of God exhibits unmistakable features of a Western-style Madonna. Alongside Mary, on the left, stand the Kyivan prince St. Borys and St. Nicholas with an unsheathed sword in his right hand;[33] on the right are an unidentified female martyr also with a raised, unsheathed sword in her right hand and with white flowers in her left hand, as well as the Kyivan prince St. Hlib. The choice of figures accompanying the Mother of God is, of course, also not accidental. The Kyivan princes depicted – St. Borys with a lance and bearing a flag as a symbol of victory as well as a palm branch as a symbol of martyrdom, and St. Hlib with a militantly raised, unsheathed sword – underscore the national allegiance of those who made and commissioned the banner and also declare the correctness of the faith of their fathers. All the accompanying figures, except St. Nicholas, are depicted in crowns and resplendent clothing. The figure of St. Nicholas, who is rarely depicted so militantly in Ukrainian iconography, serves as a clear summons to defend the dogmas of the faith. (See Illustration 7.4.)

In the top tier of the Drohobych banner are two angels in red clothing who hold white signs with quotations from Revelation.[34] Continual parallels with texts from Revelation intensify the symbolic significance of the work and serve as a reminder that those who make sacrifices to idols, i.e., the false prophets, "the synagogue of Satan," will face the Terrible

---

[33] There is no inscription above St. Nicholas, but the depiction of an old man in a hierarch's vestments with a gospel book in his hand corresponds to the iconography of that saint.

[34] On the right: "And after these things I heard a great voice of much people in heaven, saying, Alleluia; Salvation, and glory, and honor, and power, unto the Lord our God" (Rev 19:1). On the left: "For true and righteous are his judgments: for he hath judged the great whore, which did corrupt the earth with her fornication, and hath avenged the blood of his servants at her hand" (Rev 19:2).

Illustration 7.4: Church banner of the Church Militant. 1718. From the church of St.
George (?) in Drohobych. Author: Ivan Medytsky (?). Canvas, ground, tempera, oil.
"Drohobychchyna" Museum in Drobobych (Lviv oblast).

Judgment of Christ. Higher on the icon, a theme from St. John's vision
unfolds. In the clouds is shown the host of heaven riding on white horses
from the left and right corners of the composition. In the middle is a rider

with a crown on his head, dressed in purple and riding a white horse. A sword comes out of his mouth. Detailed inscriptions supplement and explain the painted image. Above the horsemen are ribbons with citations from Revelation.[35] The rider in the middle stands for the apocalyptic appearance of Jesus Christ; a quotation from Revelation explains the image.[36] A militarized image of the apocalyptic Christ in Ukrainian iconography of that time and earlier was rare. An image is known, however, that appeared in both *Tolkovanie na Apoklipsys* (Intepretation of the Apocalypse), published in Kyiv in 1625, and in Lazar Baranovych's *Mech dukhovnyi* (Spiritual Sword) of 1666. The engraving in Baranovych's work shows the apocalyptic hosts in the upper tier, and it is possible that this image became the prototype for the similar image on the 1718 banner.

There must have been serious reasons for the appearance of such a depiction on the banner. Did the painter intend with this theme to frighten off "false prophets," shown in the picture as the founders of various Christian teachings recognized by neither the Orthodox nor Catholic church? Possibly. Let us recall that the overall composition is directed at defending the virtues of the Mother of God as proclaimed at various church councils. In the Reformation era, whose influence extended also to the Western Ukrainian lands in the seventeenth century, Ukrainians were also engaging in polemical disputes. The idea of intercession against heresies is also emphasized by the words inscribed on white ribbons on both sides of the Mother of God. On the left is written: "I will fight against them with the sword of my mouth" (Rev 2:16). Originally these words referred to the ancient sect of the Nicolaitans (Rev 2:14-15), but the author of the banner was using them in reference to heretics contemporary to him. On the right of the Mother of God is the inscription: "[He will] keep thee in all thy ways." On a ribbon above the tent of the Mother of God is this citation: "Though an host should encamp against me, my heart shall not fear; though war should rise against me, in him will I place my hope" (Ps 27:3).

---

[35] "And I saw heaven opened, and behold a white horse; and he that sat upon him was called Faithful and True, and in righteousness he doth judge and make war" (Rev 19:11). An inscription above the group of horsemen on the right continues to quote from Revelation (19:14): "And the armies which were in heaven followed him upon white horses, clothed in fine linen, white and clean."

[36] "His eyes were as a flame of fire, and on his head were many crowns; and he had a name written, that no man knew, but he himself. And he was clothed with a vesture dipped in blood: and his name is called The Word of God....And out of his mouth goeth a sharp sword, that with it he should smite the nations; and he shall rule them with a rod of iron; and he treadeth the winepress of the fierceness and wrath of Almighty God" (Rev 19:12-13, 15).

The heavenly cavalry is supplemented by the scene of a battle of angels with heretics; the angels' leader is the archistratege Michael, who is victorious over the devil. The angels are depicted under the middle tier with the figure of the Mother of God, and Michael is underneath her in an oval; the heretics comprise the lowest register of the whole composition. The heretics are presented on their knees and in the clothing of contemporary Muslims, Jews, and West European gentry. Their faces are vividly portrayed, with exaggerated, ugly features. Among the heretics, as the inscriptions indicate, are Constantine Copronymus (?), Nestorius, a Jew, Apollinaris, Arius, Luther, Calvin, Eutyches, and Decius (?).[37] In as much as the paint has in some places come off, we have listed those names that we were able to make out or almost make out. The Jew and Nestorius, denying the divine nature of Christ, say: "Mary is not the Mother of God." Luther states: "No glory is due to the Mother of God." Calvin: "Mary is the handmaid of the Lord,...not the Lord." Arius and Eutyches: "She is not to be the image of Christ." Others insist that "Mary and Joseph were man and wife; therefore she is not a virgin," that Christ has only a divine nature, that he "did not take the flesh of the Mother of God," and so on. Against the heretics are ranged angels in white clothing with bared swords and shields. On their shields are inscriptions – answers taken from the Old Testament prophets and from the writings of Christian theologians. In the middle of this tier is the prominent image of the battle between the archistratege Michael and the devil, near whose lance are the words: "All who are from Adam have sinned." In answer, these words are inscribed on Michael's shield, in reference to the Mother of God who will conquer the devil: "She herself will bruise your head." Under this scene is depicted the tent of the heretics, as an inscription indicates.

It is important to note that similar texts are found in the writings of Ioanikii Galiatovsky, particularly in his sermon on the tenth Sunday after Pentecost in his collection entitled *Kliuch razumeniia* (The Key of Understanding).[38] It is possible that the painter of the banner consulted Galiatovsky's work. The possibility that the banner replicates a previous work that is no longer extant is not very likely; the entire program of painting in the church of St. George reflects the idea of the Church Militant portrayed on the banner. The artist who made the banner displays a

---

[37] The Roman emperor Decius persecuted Christians. His name is encountered among the heretics in other compositions of the Church Militant, but we cannot be sure that it was actually he that was depicted on the Drohobych banner.

[38] I. Haliatovs'kyi, *Kliuch rozuminnia* (Kyiv: Naukova dumka, 1985), 78-83.

detailed knowledge of the citations and allegories that refer to the Old
Testament prophecies about the Mother of God. Without a doubt, in order
to execute such an extensive and programmatic work, the painter needed
not only artistic talent but also a high level of competence in theological
problems. Of course, an indirect influence on the banner would have been
exercised by educated members of the local brotherhood as well as by the
pastor, Father Stefan Kobryn, who is mentioned in the donor's inscription
placed at the bottom of the banner. In the interior murals and icons of the
Drohobych churches of the Exaltation and of St. George there is no similar
work, but themes concerning the Mother of God are allotted a preeminent
role. An identical composition of the Church Militant is painted on the
outer west gallery on the second story of the church of St. George, near the
entrance to the chapel in the choir loft. The fragment of this mural that has
been preserved shows the same scene as in the upper tier of the banner,
that is, the vision of John the Theologian: the host of heaven on white
horses and Jesus Christ the rider clothed in purple and crowned, with a
double-edged sword proceeding from his mouth. Although some
fragments are damaged, it is possible to recognize a similarity in details:
the movement of the leaders' horses in both groups, the turning of the first
soldier in the group on the right as though he were looking at something,
the almost identical movement of the horse, as well as the clothing and
crown of the apocalyptic Christ. Unfortunately, the lower part of this
mural is not preserved (although certainly it was an abridged version).
This mural could only be seen during services in the upper chapel, which,
of course, took place more rarely and in the presence of a limited group of
people; it could not be seen from below. This may be the reason why this
theme was repeated on the banner. The similarities suggest that both the
mural and the banner were the work of the same artist and executed at
about the same time, i.e., about 1718.

The genesis of the defence of the Mother of God from the onslaught
of the Reformation theologians, as painted on the banner, could not have
occurred earlier than the seventeenth century, when the teachings of
Luther, Calvin, and other Protestants were being propagated in the
Ukrainian lands. It is likely that the theme emerged in the environment of
the Kyiv Caves Monastery at the beginning of the seventeenth century, as
Vira Svientsitska and Vasyl Otkovych have suggested, "in the period of
struggle of the Ukrainian population in connection with the attempt to
implement the [church] union, the invigorated activity of Protestantism,

and the aggressive attacks of the Mohammedans."[39] But the composition which these authors wrote about has a somewhat different iconography. It was about the church itself rather than about the Mother of God as such. This composition also features, aside from the unbelievers already mentioned, a Jesuit and the pope of Rome.[40] The author of the banner did not include them in the list of heretics (although he also did not include Muslims and some others). Perhaps this omission indicates that those who commissioned the mural and banner were Uniates.

The artistic quality of Galician church banners of the nineteenth century, as with most examples of sacral art more generally, was not high. At that time there were two streams in the production of such works. One was the so-called "folk" (*narodna*) stream: the artists employed a flat, decorative treatment of the image and thick local colors. Artists of the artisanal stream made use of academic models and West European iconography.

From the last third of the nineteenth century images of Ss. Cyril and Methodius and Ss. Volodymyr and Olha acquired some popularity on Ukrainian church banners. This was due to the celebration of the nine-hundredth anniversary of the baptism of Ukraine and more generally by the intensification of the national awakening. Images of Ss. Cyril and Methodius are on two church banners: one from 1881 of unknown provenance and the other from 1882 from Pidtemne, Pustomyty raion, Lviv oblast,[41] which were made in the same studio. The images of the Ukrainian princely saints Volodymyr and Olha are on a banner from the late nineteenth century from Khmilno, Radekhiv raion, Lviv oblast and on two banners from 1881 and 1882 of unknown provenance.[42] All these works belong to a single milieu.

***

The themes on guild banners are quite different. Their iconography characterizes the artisan organizations, the guilds, which played an

---

[39] Svientsits'ka and Otkovych, *Ukrains'ke narodne maliarstvo*, ill. 46.

[40] See Kosiv, *Ukrains'ki khoruhvy*, 131 n. 180.

[41] Both are from the "Studion" collection. The 1881 banner is without an inventory number; on the reverse is St. Mary Magdalene. The 1882 banner has an inventory number: St. 1151; on the reverse is Christ Pantocrator.

[42] One is preserved in the collection of Father Zenovii Khorkavy (on the reverse is Christ carrying the cross); the other is in the Museum of the History of Religion in Lviv (on the reverse is St. Paraskevia).

important role in the activities of Ukrainian cities in the eighteenth and
even in the nineteenth century. The banners of Galician guilds often relied
on the artistic traditions of West European banners. This is particularly
evident in the case of the banners of the guilds of Lviv in the second half
of the eighteenth and in the nineteenth century. Some of the guild banners
bear images that are more reflective of local peculiarities. Some of the
banners of that period have the same image on both sides, but others have
different images. The cloth of guild banners could be attached to poles on
one side (as was the case with most military banners), with the other side
hanging down, or it could hang from the top by a cross piece. A particular
feature of guild ensigns was that they depicted the tools of the trade and
sometimes the process of production. Often guild banners were adorned
with images of the saints who were patrons of their trades or guilds.
Because of the small number of Ukrainian guild banners that have
survived to our day, they are considered scarce works.

Artisan guilds were centers with their own regime of work and custom,
where the activities of masters of one or several professions were united. In
addition to mastering the skills of the craft, the artisans had to perform
certain rituals connected with the professional activity of the guild. The
whole brotherhood had the duty to take part in church processions and
festal services. Each guild had its own feast day and took as a patron one of
the saints of the church. Generally, the guild had its own icon or altar in the
church, near which the guild brothers stood during services; sometimes a
guild had its own church banner. These banners and special candles were
also called "the brotherhood."[43] In addition, a guild had its own banner, and
sometimes also a smaller banner with a badge. The guild banner was kept
in the home of the guild president[44] or in the guild chamber (where other
attributes of the guild were kept). The masters of the guild paid a special fee
for the preparation of the banners and guild attributes.[45]

Guild banners were used at various ceremonial events, such as the
election of the guild president. Yukhym Sitsinsky has described the latter
with reference to Dunaivtsi, Ushytsia county (Podillia). Three days before
the election, the officers of the guild removed the banner from the home
of the guild president. After the election, the banner was carried around
the homes of the guild members, and the outgoing president presented

---

[43] Ie. Sitsins'kyi, *Materialy dlia istorii tsekhiv v Podolii* (Kamianets Podilskyi, 1904), 30.

[44] Ibid., 19.

[45] This was the practice of the Kyiv tailors' guild in the second half of the eighteenth century.
A. Vvedens'kyi, "Ekonomichne i politychne stanovyshche Kyieva u XVIII," in *Istoriia
Kyieva* (Kyiv: Vydavnytstvo Akademii nauk Ukrains'koi RSR, 1960), 209-12.

Illustration 7.5: Banner of the tailors' guild, Lviv. 1777. Silk, appliqué, painting. Dimensions: 338 x 200 cm. LIM.

the banner to his successor.[46] The guild banners were also used in funeral processions. At the funerals of famous masters, craftsmen of all the guilds carried their banners before the bier.[47]

Another characteristic feature of the guilds was that they were to serve in defence of the city were the need to arise. Therefore, in the opinion of Yukhym Sitsinsky and Danylo Shcherbakivsky, guild banners originated under the influence of military standards.[48] In the town of Medzhybizh in Podillia, which was on a route taken by Tatars, the weavers' guild was under the obligation "that every master have a musket and ammunition for it, and the guild president should take care that there were all the military appurtenances: a banner and drum."[49] It was in this context, and under the influence of military banners, that some guild signs bore military symbols.

Craftsmen often chose their guild patrons on the basis of associative or symbolic allegories connected with their profession. There are logical

---

[46] Sitsins'kyi, *Materialy dlia istorii tsekhiv v Podolii*, 19.

[47] A. Shafonskii, *Chernigovskogo namestnichestva topograficheskoe opisanie* (Kyiv, 1851), 297.

[48] Sitsins'kyi, *Materialy dlia istorii tsekhiv v Podolii*, 21. D. Shcherbakivs'kyi, *Relikvii staroho kyivs'koho samovriaduvannia* (Kyiv: Vseukrains'ka akademiia nauk, 1925), 35-36.

[49] Sitsins'kyi, *Materialy dlia istorii tsekhiv v Podolii*, 21.

connections in the case of three guild banners from Lviv. Locksmiths on their banner from 1754 depicted the apostle Peter with his keys.[50] Tailors, on a banner from 1777,[51] showed the Transfiguration, since the gospel said that Jesus's clothes became "white as the light" (Mt 17:2). (See Illustration 7.5.) The image on a banner of Lviv carpenters and joiners from 1803[52] shows the Holy Family, and Joseph in particular, who was, of course, a carpenter.

Some of the Western Ukrainian guild banners of the eighteenth and nineteenth centuries are closely modelled on West European banners. An interesting comparison can be made of two banners distant in time and place, namely a banner from the sixteenth or seventeenth century of winemakers from Basel, Switzerland,[53] and a banner from 1837 of coopers from Lviv.[54] Both banners depict St. Urban. Bishop Urban lived in the fourth century in Langres, on the territory of modern-day France. According to legend, he was hiding from persecutors in a vineyard. The vineyard workers rescued him and converted him to Christianity. Later he became the sixth bishop of Langres, and he was canonized after his death. From that time St. Urban was considered the patron saint of vinedressers and winemakers. His cult took hold among the wine producers of Burgundy and surrounding lands. He is portrayed with a bunch of grapes or a branch in his hand, sometimes with a vessel for wine. On the Lviv coopers' banner, St. Urban is shown holding a small basket of grapes and a crozier in his hand; by his feet are painted a barrel of grapes and a compass. Only the basket and compass in this case refer to the profession of the Lviv craftsmen; as far as we know, St. Urban was not generally considered a patron of coopers. On one side of another banner from 1837, that of the weavers of the Galician town of Felshtyn, is depicted the Catholic saint Martin of Tours, who was patron of the weavers of Felshtyn; his cult did not, however, attain popularity in Ukrainian lands.[55]

---

[50] Lviv Historical Museum (LIM), inventory no. Tk. 183.

[51] LIM, inventory no. Tk. 2774.

[52] LIM, inventory no. Tk 3715.

[53] Reproduced in Whitney Smith, *Les drapeaux à travers les âges et dans le monde entier* (Paris: Fayard 1976), 49.

[54] LIM, inventory no. Tk 189.

[55] There was, however, a Roman Catholic church dedicated to St. Martin in Felshtyn (now the village of Skelivka, Drohobych raion, Lviv oblast).

Illustration 7.6: Banner of the junior tailors' and tanners' guild. 1819. Silk, oil. Dimensions: 278 x 220 cm. LIM.

The previously mentioned banner of Lviv tailors from 1777 as well as a weavers' banner of unknown provenance from 1803, preserved in Wawel Castle in Kraków,[56] both show a saint at a tailor's worktable with the inscription "Homobonus." St. Homobonus lived in twelfth-century Cremona. He was a pious merchant who gave over half of his profits to the poor. In the West European tradition he was considered the patron of trade, merchants, and tailors. Guild banners can also depict a work scene. On the 1777 Lviv tailors' banner, St. Homobonus is shown at a worktable with the cloth spread out on it. One side of a banner of Lviv blacksmiths from 1864 shows a smithy, in which a smith is working, against a landscape background.[57]

There is evidence that new guild banners were modelled after their predecessors.[58] There are two banners of the junior guild of Lviv tailors

[56] State Art Collections, Wawel, inventory no. 151.

[57] LIM, inventory no. Tk 187.

[58] Shafonskii, *Chernigovskogo namestnichestva topograficheskoe opisanie*, 480.

and tanners of 1759[59] and 1819[60] that have the same iconography and composition. Both depict the Roman Catholic St. Casimir of Poland praying on his knees before the Mother of God and child.[61] The 1819 banner differs from the older one only by the absence of a crimson-colored strip around the perimeter of the cloth. (See Illustration 7.6.)

Guild banners frequently bore the year of their manufacture, and in the nineteenth century they could also bear the name of the donors as well as of the guild president during whose term the banner was made. Dates are on the Lviv guild banners from the Lviv Historical Museum that have already been mentioned: the banners of the locksmiths of 1754, of the junior guild of tailors and tanners of 1759, of the tailors of 1777, of the carpenters of 1803, and of the junior guild of tailors and tanners of 1819. Aside from the date of manufacture, on the oldest preserved banner of the Lviv locksmiths, from 1754, above the image of the apostle Peter with keys is the inscription in Latin: "Thou art Peter...I will give unto thee [the keys of the kingdom of heaven]" (Mt 16:18-19). The inscription was perhaps not finished, and the last letter (the "o" of dabo) does not fit entirely.[62] There is more text on the banner of the Lviv coopers of 1837. In addition to the names of eleven masters of the guild, there is an inscription in Polish: "During the times of the rule of Emperor Ferdinand I this banner has been made in Lviv for the guild of coopers AD 1837."

Heraldic symbols were widely used on eighteenth-century guild banners. Thus, on the banner of the Lviv tailors' guild of 1777 and on that of the carpenters' guild of 1803 is the coat of arms of Austria – a double-headed black eagle surmounted by a crown and holding a scepter and an orb. The frequent appearance of heraldic images on guild banners is indicated by an instruction issued in 1773 by Piotr Potocki to the cobblers' guild in Dunaivtsi in Podillia: "This guild, whatever the color of its banner, has to use my coat of arms, either painted or cut from cloth, or give expression to the signs of that craft."[63] On the banners of the Lviv junior guild of tailors and tanners of 1759, of tailors of 1777, of carpenters of 1803, and of coopers of 1837 the coat of arms of the city of Lviv is

---

[59] LIM, inventory no. Tk 181.

[60] LIM, inventory no. Tk 191.

[61] Similar iconography can be found in an eighteenth-century mural on the right side nave of the Lviv monastery church of the archangel Michael (formerly the Carmelite church).

[62] The banner has a ribbon with fringes sewn at the edges, which may have been added later when the banner was repaired.

[63] E. Setsinskii, *Trudy podol'skago tserkovnago istoriko-arkheologicheskago obshchestva*, vypusk 2 (Kamianets-Podilskyi, 1911), 48.

included. It is placed beneath the coat of arms of Austria, which in the language of heraldry signified the administrative subordination of Lviv. On two of the banners, that of the junior guild of tailors and tanners of 1777 and the similar one of 1819, the coat of arms shows a lion in a crown standing on all four legs; near him are three hills, with a star over the center hill. On the tailors' banner of 1777 and the coopers' banner of 1837 the lion is placed in the bottom left corner and turned towards the center. He stands on his hind legs, and with his front paws he "holds" the three hills. This particular iconography of the coat of arms of Lviv came into usage at the beginning of the seventeenth century.[64]

It is now possible to summarize the major features of the iconographic and compositional structure of Western Ukrainian guild banners of the eighteenth and nineteenth centuries. Typically they bore the image of the guild's patron or of the Mother of God; less frequently they depicted Christ or a saint or the patronal feast. The depiction of the products of the guild or the tools used was widespread; less frequent were depictions of the process of manufacture. Heraldic symbols were also employed. The compositional variants of the banner were not stable, but were determined by the tradition that had developed in a particular locality. There were guild banners of this period with a complex iconography, with different images on both sides, but there were also simpler ones with a cross and tools of the trade and bearing the same image on both sides.

***

---

[64] This iconography arose as the combination of two earlier coats of arms: a lion rising up in the opening to the entrance of the city (this image was used until 1586) and a lion holding three hills, above which is a star. The latter coat of arms was granted to Lviv by Pope Sixtus V in 1586, when he was visited by the Roman Catholic archbishop of Lviv Jan Dymitr Solikowski. The star above three green hills and two lions were symbols in the personal coat of arms of Pope Sixtus. The symbols were given to Lviv to commemorate its struggle to maintain the Catholic faith. K. Sochaniewicz, *Herb miasta Lwowa* (Lviv, 1933), 28-36, 41; and Iu. Savchuk, "Ukrains'ke mis'ke prapornytstvo v istorychnii perspektyvi (notatky z arkhivnykh ta muzeinykh studii)," in *Spetsial'ni istorychni dystsypliny: pytannia teorii ta metodyky* (Kyiv: Natsional'na akademii nauk Ukrainy, Instytut istorii Ukrainy, 2000), 276.

Illustration 7.7: Banner of the national guard of Yavoriv. 1848. Canvas, appliqué, ribbon with fringes. Dimensions: 105 x 106 cm. NML.

In connection with the revolutions of 1848 that encompassed the Habsburg Monarchy, a Ukrainian national guard was organized under the auspices of the Supreme Ruthenian Council. It existed only in a few cities – Stryi, Zhovkva, Berezhany, Ternopil, and Yavoriv – and then only for a short time. The members of the national guard wore cossack headgear with an insigne of a lion. Their banners were blue, with the image on one side of a golden lion and on the other side the patron saint.[65]

[65] I. Krevets'kyi, "Proby orhanizovania rus'kykh natsional'nykh hvardii u Halychyni 1848-1849," *Zapysky Naukovoho tovarystva imeny Shevchenka* 113, book 1 (1913): 89, 104, 116-114, plates I-II. V. Dzikovs'kyi, "Herb Ukrainy," *Svit*, no. 8 (1917): 133. I. Kryp"iakevych et al., *Istoriia ukrains'koho viis'ka. Vid Kniazhykh chasiv do 20-kh rokiv XX st.*, 4th ed. (Lviv: Svit, 1992), 290.

This was the iconography of the two banners of 1848 reproduced by Ivan Krevetsky, from Berezhany and Yavoriv. The banner of the Yavoriv national guard is preserved in NML.[66] On its dark blue silk is painted in profile a golden lion, turned to the right (or to the left, if we were speaking in heraldic terms) and climbing up a cliff.[67] There is nothing on the other side of the banner. Kyrylo Tryliovsky indicated in his memoirs that this banner was on display at the Ukrainian pavilion in Vienna in 1916.[68] (See Illustration 7.7.) In addition, in 1913 there was some correspondence about a national guard banner between NML and Father Volodymyr Hromnytsky of Ternopil, but the result of the correspondence is unknown, as is the subsequent fate of the banner.[69]

During the mid-nineteenth century political upheaval, the Ukrainian population of Galicia was generally on the side of the Austrian monarchy, while the Poles were generally on the side of the revolutionaries. For his part, Emperor Franz Joseph supported the Ukrainian movement, approving in February 1849 an initiative of the Supreme Ruthenian Council to establish a separate Battalion of Ruthenian Mountain Riflemen. The battalion was set up to guard the Galician-Hungarian border region. Archduchess Sophie of Austria donated a ribbon for the battalion's banner.[70] The banner was inscribed, in German: "Loyalty leads to victory

---

[66] Its size is 105 x 106 cm. The banner has lost two fragments of cloth: in the upper right corner (30 x 33 cm) and on the left side (43.2 x 22 cm). The banner was completely restored in 2007 and displayed in an exhibition of Ukrainian banners held in NML from 13 December 2007 through 30 January 2008.

[67] This heraldic depiction of the lion is known already on a seal from 1316 of the Galician Volhynian principality. Ia. Dashkevych, "Heral'dychne zobrazhennia leva v period Halyts'ko-Volyns'koi derzhavy," Znak, no. 16 (1998): 6-8.

[68] K. Tryl'ovs'kyi, Z moho zhyttia (Kyiv-Edmonton-Toronto: Takson, 1999), 246. In as much as the acquisitions register of NML shows that the banner was given to NML by the Prosvita organization in 1913, the banner was lent to the exhibition already by the museum. Then for a long time the banner was not put on display. In order to preserve it during the Soviet period it was kept in the auxiliary depository of the museum. During the time that the national guard existed in Yavoriv, its banner was kept in the town church. Ivan Krevetsky wrote that it was still there in 1885, but was later given to Prosvita. Krevets'kyi, "Proby orhanizovania rus'kykh natsional'nykh hvardii," 118.

[69] The existence of a letter of 16 April 1913 on this subject from Father Hromnytsky is recorded in NML, Protokol dilovodstva, no. 247. It has not been possible, however, to find the letter itself.

[70] The Supreme Ruthenian Council in Lviv petitioned the emperor for permission to prepare a banner for the battalion. Father Yulian Vyslobotsky in Vienna took up this issue and obtained the agreement of Archduchess Sophie to serve as "mother" of the banner. In early December 1849 the Archduchess gave the ribbon for the battalion's banner to Father Vyslobotsky. The ribbon arrived in Lviv on 10 December, but the battalion had already

Illustration 7.8: Ribbon for the banner of the Battalion of Ruthenian Mountain Riflemen. 1849. Silk, embroidery with metal needles, velvet, ribbon from metal threads, sequins, metal beads, fringes, tassels of metal and silk threads. Dimensions: 137 x 14 cm. NML.

Sophie Archduchess of Austria." The gift was mentioned in the press at the time.[71] The ribbon was embroidered with metal (gold and silver) threads on blue satin. The dominant colors of the ribbon, blue and silver (which in heraldry signifies white), reflect the Bavarian family colors of the donor. At the lower ends of the ribbon are two cartouches: one bears the date 1849, the other – the coat of arms of Archduchess Sophie. The actual banner for which the ribbon was intended was never produced, however, since the battalion was dissolved on 3 January 1850 in Przemyśl, on its way back from Hungary. The Supreme Ruthenian Council decided to keep the ribbon "as a memorial" in the National Home in Lviv.[72] (See Illustration 7.8.) (See Illustration 7.9.) (See Illustration 7.10.)

Revived Ukrainian symbols appeared on the standards of the Western Ukrainian sport and patriotic associations Sokil and Sich, which were

left Lviv, where it underwent training, for Hungary in September. I. Krevets'kyi, "Batalion rus'kykh hirs'kykh stril'tsiv," *Zapysky Naukovoho tovarystva imeny Shevchenka* 107, book 1 (1912): 62-64.

[71] *Zoria Halyts'ka*, no. 1 (1850): 1-2. A panegyric was even composed about the event. Krevets'kyi, "Batalion," 62-63.

[72] In the acquisitions register of NML there is no date for the acquisition of the ribbon. It was first listed on the inventory in 1971. Already in April 1918, however, NML requested that the council of the National Home in Lviv turn over all remaining museum items that had been in the former Museum of the National Home. Knyha dilovodstva NML, 11 August 1914: 28, 30.

Illustration 7.9: Cartouche with date on the ribbon for the Battalion's banner.

founded at the turn of the twentieth century, as well as on the banners of the Ukrainian Sich Riflemen. Not many of the banners of this period have been preserved. This makes the flag from 1911 of the Sokil-Father in Lviv quite valuable; it has been in NML since 1930.[73] The flag has images on both sides, made by appliqué and embroidery. On the front is the coat of arms of Galicia; on the reverse – of the Kyivan land. There are also ribbons for this flag, sent by Ukrainian women from Kyiv, the gymnasium (secondary-school) society in Chernivtsi, and Ukrainians from North America.[74] (See Illustration 7.11.) (See Illustration 7.12.) The flagpole, with a finial in the form of a falcon and name plates of the members, has unfortunately not survived. The gymnastic society Sokil was founded in Lviv on 11 February 1894. The flag held by NML is the first flag of Sokil-

[73] The history of the flag up to the moment of its confiscation by the Polish police during a demonstration at Yaniv cemetery in 1924 is recounted in detail in O. Sova, "Do istorii prapora tovarystva 'Sokil-Bat'ko' u L'vovi," *Znak*, no. 29 (2003): 8-9.

[74] The ribbon from Kyiv was passed on by Lonhyn Tsehelsky. Documents show that there was also a ribbon for the flag from the Zhinocha Hromada (Women's Community) in Lviv (Sova, "Do istorii prapora," 8-9), which is mentioned in the NML acquisitions list. But this ribbon is lost. The two ribbons from North America and a cockade, dated 10 September 1911, arrived only after the flag was consecrated.

*Illustration 7.10: Cartouche with coats of arms on the ribbon for
the Battalion's banner.*

Father in Lviv. The statute of the association specifies that "the flag of the
association is the 'Ruthenian lion,' and the motto is 'let us take courage'
(*bodrim sia*)."[75] Sokil in Lviv formed a special flag commission to prepare
its standard. It was headed by Yaroslav Vintskovsky (pseudonym:
Yaroslav Yaroslavenko) in 1903 and later, in 1908, by M. Kots. Aleksander

---

[75] Sova, "Do istorii prapora."

*Illustration 7.11: Galicia side, banner of the Ukrainian Sokil-Father association
of Lviv. 1911. Silk, embroidery with silk needles, appliqué.
Dimensions 118 x 156.5 cm. NML.*

Czołowski, the director of the Lviv city archive, provided consultation on
the iconography of the heraldic lion and archangel. A meeting of the
officers of Sokil on 11 June 1904 resolved that the flag of the association
had to resemble a hetman's flag and bear the image of the archistratege
Michael. The motto "Struggle, and You Shall Overcome" (*Boritesia,
Poborete!*) was taken from the poetry of Taras Shevchenko. The motto
"Ever Forward!" was taken from the announcement for the First
Crownland Assembly of Sokil in Lviv on 10 September 1911.[76] After long
debates about the iconography it was only in February 1911, at the
initiative of Ivan Bobersky and M. Kots, that Sokil approved the designs
submitted by the painter Oleksander Zinoviev, who at that time was
studying in Paris. The images of the lion and the archangel Michael were
embroidered on silk by the firm Dalger of Lyon. On 30 May 1911 the
association Dostava in Lviv received the flag of Sokil-Father,[77] and on 10

---

[76] I. Bobers'kyi, *Ukrains'ke sokil'stvo (1894-1939)* (Lviv, 1939), 12. Sova, "Do istorii prapora,"
   8-9.
[77] *Visty z Zaporozha*, no. 57 (1911): 1. Sova, "Do istorii prapora," 8-9.

Illustration 7.12: Kyiv land side, banner of Sokil-Father.

September 1911 it was solemnly consecrated. The iconography of the archangel Michael on the flag follows the coat of arms confirmed for the Kyiv palatinate in 1471 – the archangel holds a sword pointed downward.[78] In Ukrainian heraldry the accepted usage is to show the archangel with a raised and unsheathed sword in his right hand. This is how he is depicted on the ribbon for this flag sent by the Ukrainian women from Kyiv in 1911. The tradition of the banners of the national guard and Sich and Sokil societies were followed in the flags of the Ukrainian Sich Riflemen of World War I.

We see, then, that banners form a particular group of artistic works distinctive in purpose and thematics. Banners, with their interesting iconography, have artistic value; the technique of manufacture is complicated, since in most cases banners have images on both sides of the fabric. They are also objects of sociocultural and historical significance. Even though not many have been preserved, we can see that Western Ukrainian banners of the eighteenth and nineteenth centuries reflect their contemporary situation. The church banners have a more traditional, sacral iconography, while guild banners combine religious images, signs

---

[78] V. Rumiantseva, *Emblemy zemel' i gerby gorodov levoberezhnoi Ukrainy perioda feodalizma* (Kyiv: Naukova dumka, 1986), 43-44.

of the profession, and heraldic symbols. As a result of the revolutions of 1848 in the Habsburg Monarchy, banners of the Ukrainian national guards appear, with heraldic designs and images of saints who had a military significance; and we can imagine that this imagery continued traditions that reached back to flags of the medieval, princely era. The iconography of the national guards influenced the themes on the flags of the patriotic sporting associations of the early twentieth century, in which heraldic symbols also predominated. A particularly interesting item, of considerable historical significance, reminding us of Galicia's Habsburg period and its complicated politics, is the ribbon for the flag of the Battalion of Ruthenian Mountain Riflemen donated by Archduchess Sophie of Austria.

Facing East:
References to Eastern Christianity in Lviv's
Representational Public Space ca. 1900
Andriy Zayarnyuk

The presence of the eastern Christian tradition in modern Lviv is usually taken for granted, and for good reason.[1] Some of the city's most ancient churches, including its oldest church, are of the Byzantine rite. Even writers who saw late nineteenth and early twentieth century Lviv (Lwów/Lemberg) as a Polish city acknowledged that the renaissance Orthodox church of the Dormition (the so-called "Wallachian church") constituted one of the city's most beautiful architectural pearls.[2] During Austrian times the significance of Lviv for Christians of the Eastern rite even increased. The city became the see of the Greek Catholic metropolis and the religious capital for the province's Greek Catholics. Greek Catholics, even though a minority, were visible in the city throughout the whole Austrian period. On the other hand, manifestations of Eastern Christian practices were not represented as being of significance to the city's character.

To claim this is not to argue that the Eastern Christian tradition was not on display in the city's public space. Thus, for example, the blessing of the waters during Theophany in nineteenth-century Lviv was a public spectacle watched and enjoyed by city dwellers of all denominations.[3] Nonetheless, there were no visible Eastern Christian elements in the city's representational public space. By representational public space I mean the symbolic part of the city's built environment, open to scrutiny and decoding by both the city's inhabitants and outside observers. Even after the Monarchy, through a series of state-initiated reforms, raised the status of the Greek Catholic church making it comparable to that of its Roman Catholic counterpart, markers pointing specifically to the Eastern

---

[1] I would like to thank Iryna Kotlobulatova for helping to find and sharing images from Ihor Kotlobulatov's collection, which are used in this article.

[2] Karolina Grodziska, ed., *Miasto jak brylant....Księga cytatów o Lwowie* (Kraków: Universitas, 2007), 399-400.

[3] Ostap Sereda, "Masovi urochystosti ta mis'kyi publichnyi prostir," *Istoriia L'vova*, vol. 2, ed. Iaroslav Isaievych, Mykola Lytvyn, Feodosii Steblii (Lviv: Tsentr Ievropy, 2007), 301.

Illustration 8.1: The cityscape of late eighteenth-century Lviv recently annexed by Austria. A print from 1772–1780. Source: "Vue de Lemberg Capitale des Royaumes de Galicie et Lodomerie," the National Digital Library Polona.

Illustration 8.2: The cityscape of mid-nineteenth century Lviv: new public buildings and housing envelop the old baroque town. Aquarelle by T. Czyszkowski, after 1840. Source: "Sands. Lemberg," also known as "View of Lviv from Wronowski's hill," The National Digital Library Polona.

Christian tradition were largely absent from the city's architectural environment.

Visiting Lviv at the end of the eighteenth century, the Austrian emperor stayed at the palace of the Greek Catholic archbishops and metropolitans due to the absence of another adequate residence in the city.[4] But the palace itself was a monument of late baroque architecture, with elements of neoclassicism. The Greek Catholic cathedral located across from the palace was also a rococo structure, richly decorated with sculpture, and only its layout in the form of a modified Greek cross could be read as a reference to the Eastern Christian tradition. Essentially, the city at the end of the eighteenth century appeared as a typical Central European baroque town (see Illustration 8.1). The cityscape of mid-nineteenth century Lviv was still studded with baroque towers,[5] while the new public space that appeared there during the enlightened absolutist and *Vormärz* periods (the wide promenades and green spaces that replaced the old city fortifications, the parks and classicist public buildings) was indifferent to the local historical traditions and ethnic differences to be found among locals. This new architecture reflected the enlightenment ideal of responsible citizenship pursuing universal good in comfortable and healthy environs (see Illustration 8.2).[6]

The restructuring of the state during the constitutional reforms of the 1860s and the introduction of the province's autonomy in their aftermath changed the situation. New venues allowing national appropriation of the city's public space opened up. National monuments were built and patriotic manifestations held.[7] The change was so profound that some Polish writers claimed that the city had completely changed its national physiognomy: "after twenty-five years of self-government Lviv changed unrecognizably from the inside, and from being essentially a German city became completely Polish."[8] This nationalization of the city was accomplished not only through monuments and manifestations but also architecturally, architecture now being seen as both an art and a science capable of shaping a city's total built environment. In Lviv at the end of

---

[4] Stanisław Schnür-Pepłowski, *Obrazy z przeszłóśi Galicyi i Krakowa (1772-1858)*, vol.1 (Lwów: Gubrynowicz i Schmidt, 1896), 152.

[5] Iurii Biriuliov, ed., *Arkhitektura L'vova. Chas i styli XIII-XXI st.* (Lviv: Tsentr Ievropy, 2008), 121.

[6] Markian Prokopovych, *Habsburg Lemberg: Architecture, Public Space, and Politics in the Galician Capital, 1772-1914* (West Lafayette: Purdue University Press, 2009), 21-36.

[7] Daniel Unowsky analyzes the changing spectacle of the province's politics from the middle to the end of the nineteenth century as played out on the streets of the city in connection with royal visits: Daniel L. Unowsky, *The Pomp and Politics of Patriotism: Imperial Celebrations in Habsburg Austria, 1848-1916* (West Lafayette: Purdue University Press, 2005), 33-76. Markian Prokopovych analyzes the earliest Polish national manifestations of the constitutional era that changed the city's topography with the creation of the Union of Lublin Mound: Markian Prokopovych, *Habsburg Lemberg*, 226-41.

[8] *Przewodnik po Lwowie wydany przy wpsółudziale Wydziału gospodarczego V. Zjazdu Lekarzy i Przyrodników polskich* (Lwów: Drukarnia Ludowa, 1888), 52.

*Illustration 8.3: Edgar Kováts. Initial sketch of the Galician pavilion for the 1900
World Exhibition. 1899. Source: Tomasz Szybisty, "Sposób zakopiański i jego
twórca Edgar Kováts (1849–1912)," Rocznik Podhalański 10 (2007), wkładka II.*

the nineteenth century, this new idea about architecture was inseparably
connected with the discussion about, and actual appearance of, national

Illustration 8.4: Kazimierz Mokłowski. Apartment buildings in a hybrid all-Galician style.
Source: <http://uk.wikipedia.org/wiki/%D0%A4%D0%B0%D0%B9%D0%BB:38,
_40_Pekarska_Street,_Lviv.jpg> Author: Aeou.

styles. Polish, Ukrainian, and Jewish secession and modernist movements developed and turned buildings into material identity markers linking the city with the respective nations' imagined past and cultures. To date, references to the Eastern Christian tradition in Lviv's architecture have been discussed only in the context of the Ukrainian national style, and this will be a good place to start this analysis as well.

Beginning with the 1880s, local architects discussed the possibility of creating some distinct local artistic style. Julian Zachariewicz, the patriarch of the Lviv architectural school (he was the first chair of the department of architecture at the local polytechnic) argued in favor of the so-called "Carpathian style" and tried it outside of Lviv. In the 1890s and early 1900s, discussions revolved around the question of what kind of Carpathian style was more appropriate for the city. The Western Galician "Zakopane style," originating from Kraków and based on the folk architecture of Polish mountaineers, appeared and became popular in Lviv. First, it was debatable whether a vernacular style could be applied

Illustration 8.5: Ivan Levynsky and Julian Zachariewicz, the pavilion of the Ukrainian societies at the General Provincial Exhibition of 1894, and the precursor of all other buildings in the Ukrainian style (circled). (The pavilion of Ukrainian religious art was housed in a custom-built wooden Hutsul church.) Source: a photograph from 1894.

in monumental stone architecture, and architect Edgar Kováts, the author of *Sposób Zakopiański* (The Zakopane Mode, 1899), was in favor of combining vernacular motifs with historicist and Art Nouveau elements. He was opposed by the founder of the Zakopane style, Stanisław Witkiewicz.[9] While the majority of Lviv architects sided with Kováts, they also became interested in developing a separate "eastern Galician," or a mixed all-Galician style, based on folk architecture and crafts of mountaineers from both parts of the province. Iurii Biriuliov believes that a particular Eastern Galician style was outlined by Edgar Kováts already in his *Sposób Zakopiański* and can be seen in his works from the 1890s (see Illustration 8.3).[10] The use of the terminology was confusing; there were two Zakopane styles, and the term "Hutsul style" was applied to both an all-Galician "Carpathian" style (see Illustration 8.4) and the so-called "Ukrainian Secession." Eventually, two national styles emerged, both combining *art nouveau* approaches to the building's structure and ornamentation with the adaptation of vernacular motifs. The Polish style used folk architecture and design from the Western Carpathians, while the Ukrainian drew on the traditions of the Eastern Carpathians, Hutsul in particular (see Illustration 8.5).

---

[9] Tomasz Szybisty, "Sposób zakopiański i jego twórca Edgar Kováts (1849–1912)," *Rocznik Podhalański* 10 (2007): 89-94.

[10] Iurii Biriuliov, *Mystetstvo l'vivs'koï setsesii* (Lviv: Tsentr Ievropy, 2005).

Вид Бурси Руского Товариства педаґоґічного у Львові.

Illustration 8.6: "View of the residence of the Ukrainian Pedagogical Society."
Architect: Tadeusz Obmiński (his signature in Ukrainian is on the postcard), 1906.
Source: a postcard from the National Digital Library Polona.

Since the most exciting element of folk architecture in the Carpathians
was the wooden churches, the architects developing local styles tried to
incorporate these churches' shapes, especially their tall steep roofs, into
their building projects. Tadeusz Obmiński, who was very close to
Kazimierz Mokłowski (an important theorist of new national styles) and
in the 1900s did a number of projects in the Ukrainian Secession style,
purposefully studied Hutsul churches and, during a specially organized
trip to the Carpathians, made an album of sketches of these churches.[11]

While both ethnic Poles and ethnic Ukrainians were working in the
Ukrainian Secession style, and the first architectural projects built in Lviv
in vernacular Secession styles defied clear-cut national attribution, on the
eve of World War I the style was explicitly defined as a national one. In
1910 Ivan Levynsky, the Ukrainian owner of the city's largest construction
enterprise, and architect and director of his private architectural firm,
commented: "Builders are members of the nation to which they belong;

---

[11] Biriuliov, *Arkhitektura L'vova*, 397.

Illustration 8.7: "Dniester" insurance company building, 1905. Architects: Ivan Levynsky, Lev Levynsky, Tadeusz Obmiński, Oleksandr Lushpynsky. Source: unidentified photo.

therefore they think, feel and create as a nation....Ruthenians should look for this [national] character of their new buildings only in peasant and church buildings."[12] He was seconded by the well-known ethnographer of the Hutsuls, Volodymyr Shukhevych: "Go to the mountains, where Hutsul churches stand in beauty...raise for us churches in this style, give us projects for the construction of buildings in the national style, then you'll be for us, what Witkiewicz[13] has become for the Polish nation."[14]

---

[12] Iurii Biriuliov, *Mystetstvo l'vivs'koï setsesiï*, 34.

[13] Stanisław Witkiewicz, the founder of the Zakopane style.

[14] Biriuliov, *Arkhitektura L'vova*, 398.

Illustration 8.8: Narodnyi Dim Residence, 1906-1907. Architect: Ivan Levynsky's firm. Source: Unidentified photograph.

Indeed, the shapes of the sharp roofs of the wooden Carpathian churches can be found in well-known works of the Ukrainian Secession – almost all of them done by Tadeusz Obmiński, often in cooperation with Ivan Levynsky and Oleksandr Lopushansky (see Illustrations 8.6, 8.7, 8.8). Tadeusz Obmiński also published an important study of the Ukrainian wooden churches in Galicia, tracing their stylistic features to the peculiarities of the Eastern rite and techniques of building with wood.[15] Projects in the Polish national style (often identified as the Zakopane style) (see Illustration 8.9), and in the hybrid combination of both styles were also built in Lviv in the 1900s (see Illustration 8.10). However, it appears that the Eastern Galician, or Ukrainian style, dominated in the vernacular strand of the Lviv Secession. It seems that references to the region's wooden churches were the defining feature distinguishing the Ukrainian style from the Polish, while the latter in Lviv referred almost exclusively to lay folk architecture. On the other hand, there were more similarities than differences between the two. Both tried to make stonework resemble wooden forms, both used steep tall roofs, for both styles vertical lines and vertical dimensions in general were more important than horizontal

---

[15] Ihor Zhuk, "Tadeusz Obmins'kyi—tvorets' i doslidnyk sakral'noi arkhitektury," *Naukovi zapysky Ukrains'koho katolyts'koho universytetu* 2, no. 1 (2010): 152.

Illustration 8.9: Projected Polish academic home. Drawing by Alfred Zachariewicz and Józef Sosnowski, 1906. Source: "Wikimedia Commons."

orders. Even though the Ukrainian Secession referred to wooden churches, both styles were making use not so much of church or religious but of folk traditions.

As a matter of fact, the Greek Catholic church had problems with this propensity for romanticized folk motifs in the work of Ukrainian architects. In 1902 there was a competition for a Greek Catholic church to be built in the Byzantine style. The reviewer reporting on this competition mentioned that only Yaroslav Rudnytsky's project conformed to the Byzantine character of the church specified by the competition's program; all the rest were national-romantic innovations: "… these are forms of our wooden churches transferred to stone and brick."[16] In all the buildings of the Ukrainian Secession, references to the Byzantine tradition were minimal and could be found only in some elements of decor, metalwork and interior ornaments.

Nonetheless, the Byzantine tradition was also seen as a possible source of inspiration for the new Ukrainian style. Ukrainian activists Vasyl Nahirny, Ilarion Sventsitsky, and Yevhen Bachynsky under the influence

---

[16] Biriuliov, *Arkhitektura L'vova*, 500.

Illustration 8.10: Kazimierz Sołecki's sanatorium. An example of mixed Carpathian style. Architect: Oleksandr Lushpynsky, built in 1906-1908. Source: a postcard from the National Digital Library Polona.

of Mykhailo Boichuk called upon Ukrainian architects to use Byzantine and Romanesque styles for the creation of a Ukrainian one.[17] These references are prominent in the unrealized 1904 project of Obmiński, Levynsky, and Nahirny for a Ukrainian theatre in Lviv. The projected theater displays an eclectic "national" style combining references to the wooden vernacular architecture with Byzantino-Romanesque elements. Its most prominent feature is a highly original dome with a cupola, a clear

---

[17] Ibid., 410.

Illustration 8.11: Invalidenhaus chapel. Source: Postcard (before 1906). Publisher: Jan Bromilski. Source: a postcard from the National Digital Library Polona.

reference to eastern churches in both their vernacular and more "Byzantine" versions.[18]

And yet, modern architecture in the Byzantine tradition in Lviv predates the epoch of national styles. In 1855 the famous Viennese architect Teophil von Hansen drew up a plan for the *Invalidenhaus* in Lviv. This majestic building, which many scholars see as the first original and aesthetically interesting architectural project in nineteenth-century Lviv, was built in the late 1850s and early 1860s in *Rundbogenstil* (round arch style). Hansen also drew up a project for the chapel to stand beside the

---

[18] Oleksandr Noha, *Ivan Levyns'kyi: arkhitektor, pidpryiemets', metsenat* (Lviv: Tsentr Ievropy, 2009), 65-66.

Kościoł Grecki.

Illustration 8.12: The original chapel, used as an Orthodox church, was replaced by St. George's church on present-day Korolenko Street. Source: Tadeusz Mańkowski, Lwów przed laty osiemdziesięciu w współczesnych litografjach Zakładów Pillera (Lwów: Zakłady graficzne Piller-Neumanna, 1928), tablica XXVI.

Invalidenhaus proper and serve the veterans. The chapel was designed in a neo-Byzantine Romantic style. The layout of the building was in the shape

Льво̄въ.   Православная церковь.

Illustration 8.13: St. George's church on Korolenko Street, designed in 1895, built in 1899. Architect: Gustav Sachs. Source: a postcard from Ihor Kotlobulatov's collection.

of a proper Greek cross; windows and portals were Byzantine; and the positioning of the dome at the center was Byzantine as well. Its elongated dome with the lantern on top was highly unusual for mid-nineteenth century Lviv. (see Illustration 8.11). We know that Hansen studied Byzantine architecture during his stay in Greece and was using both

В И Д Ъ

церкви при Народномъ Домѣ въ

Львовѣ

Illustration 8.14: Havryshkevych's original design for the Transfiguration church. Frontal view. Source: Slovo do russkogo naroda po povidu stroeniia obitnoi tserkvi pry Narodnom Domi vo L'vovi (Lviv, 1876).

Byzantine and "eastern," Muslim motifs in his work. Some of the latter can be found in this chapel as well: the towers at the corners of each side

Illustration 8.15: The Transfiguration church's final appearance. Back view, a photograph by Teodozii Bahrynovych, 1910. Source: Ihor Kotlobulatov's collection.

and in front of the facade are minaret-like. It is highly likely that the location of this project – the city of Lviv, capital of the empire's eastern province, where a living Byzantine tradition was present, influenced

Hansen's choice of architectural style. His other projects are quite often context-specific, as is, for example, the Greek Orthodox church in Vienna.

The only other explicitly Byzantine building in Lviv in the 1900s that also did not belong to the local Greek Catholic tradition was the Orthodox church on present-day Korolenko Street. The Lviv Orthodox parish was subordinated to the Bukovinian metropolitan and in the second half of the nineteenth century it used a small two-storey classicist building as its parish church (see Illustration 8.12). Tadeusz Mańkowski was the first to note that this chapel featured no "Eastern" traits: "If not for the small spirelet with the bell, and crosses, its appearance would not betray a building dedicated to a religious cult of the Eastern rite."[19]

However, since by the 1890s that building had become dilapidated and was no longer usable, a competition was announced for a new one. Gustav Sachs, a Viennese architect and chief engineer of the Department of Continental Construction, won the competition in 1895.[20] The Byzantine-Romanesque structure he built in due course had the layout of a Greek cross with five domes, the central one being located above the square nave (see Illustration 8.13). Thus, both neo-Byzantine architectural monuments of Austrian Lviv were not done by local architects nor commissioned by the local church of the Byzantine rite.

When it comes to the local tradition of church architecture, nineteenth-century Lviv had two kinds of churches – ancient stone churches located in the city itself and dating back to medieval and early modern times, and wooden churches located in the suburbs (St. George's cathedral does not fit into this classification, its wooden structures having been rebuilt into a magnificent church in the mid-eighteenth century). In the second half of the nineteenth century the construction project of foremost importance for the city's Greek Catholics was the church of the Transfiguration. The land on which this church was built had been the location of the university, which was housed in the former Trinitarian monastery there. The university building burnt down in 1848 and the land was given to the Ruthenians in the aftermath of the revolution. The so-called "People's House" (*Narodnyi Dim*) was the first building that appeared on this site, and the church of the Transfiguration was to accompany it. This was to be the second Ruthenian church in the city center proper, inside the old city walls.

---

[19] Tadeusz Mańkowski, *Lwów przed laty osiemdziesięciu w współczesnych litografjach Zakładów Pillera* (Lwów: Zakłady graficzne Piller-Neumanna, 1928), 7.

[20] Volodymyr Vuitsyk, *Vybrani pratsi. Do 70-richchia z dnia narodzhennia* (Lviv: Ukrzakhidproektrestavratsiia, 2004), 78.

Illustration 8.16: The ruins of the Trinitarian Monastery, ca.1850. Source: "Ukrainian Wikipedia" <http://uk.wikipedia.org/wiki/%D0%A4%D0%B0%D0%B9%D0%BB: Trinitarian_church,_Lviv_%282%29.jpg>.

The original project for this church dates to 1850. It envisioned three domes on the longitudinal axis, surrounded by the buildings for priests and organizations.[21]   But in 1874 the committee found this project unsatisfactory. New times called for new architectural solutions, and the Ruthenian architect Sylvestr Havyrshkevych drew up a new one. Havryshkevych's project also envisioned three longitudinal domes, but he added two domes on the facade towers as well (see Illustration 8.14). In the process of construction, the three longitudinal domes were replaced with one large dome over the transept. When construction was about to start in 1876, a proclamation was issued to the "Ruthenian Nation" by the board governing the so-called "People's House" (*Narodnyi Dim*). It stated that "the task is to build in Lviv not some crammed Ruthenian church of which we have several here, churches that, as if in mockery, point to the oppression of our church rite; it would befit us to build a magnificent temple of God to the glory of the Almighty, in memory of our revival, in thankful remembrance of our liberation from heavy oppression, from disgraceful and sorrowful slavery, from painful and shameful humiliation."[22]

---

[21] Ibid., 65.

[22] *Slovo do russkogo naroda po povidu stroeniia obitnoi tserkvi pry Narodnom Domi vo L'vovi* (Lviv, 1876), 4.

Illustration 8.17: The Drum of the Transfiguration church with the sculptures of the apostles by Leonard Marconi. A photograph by Dmytro Kadnichansky.

The church that was eventually built had some Byzantine elements, but its main reference was to the Renaissance (see Illustration 8.15). Thus, a model neo-Renaissance church appeared in Lviv, in a way paralleling the old church of the Dormition, which was a Renaissance monument with some Byzantine elements. Beside the Renaissance master code, there was another significant aspect in the church's architecture. It incorporated the ruins of the older Trinitarian church, especially its Baroque façade (see Illustration 8.16, compare with Illustration 8.14) creating an architectural palimpsest. The layout of the new church and of the Trinitarian one was essentially the same; the principal change in the façade was the replacement of the pyramidal roofs and spires of the old towers with neo-Renaissance domes. These domes closely resemble the dome of the *Invalidenhaus* chapel. The Transfiguration church itself became the largest Greek Catholic church in Lviv.

The church of the Transfiguration became a model for the new stone churches that were replacing the old wooden ones throughout the entire province in the 1890s-1900s. Vasyl Nahirny designed a great number of them in the same "neo-Byzantine" style. A characteristic combination of

Illustration 8.18: The Lviv skyline. The Transfiguration church is at the forefront, the bell tower of the Armenian cathedral is to the right of its main dome, and the three green domes of the Assumption church with its Korniakt tower are still further to the right. A photograph by Raskalov. Source: Tim Louzonis, "Guest Post: Lviv, Ukraine: Europe's Hidden Gem," Monday, 29 October 2012 <http://travelshopgirl.blogspot.ca/2012/10/guest-post-lviv-ukraine-europes-hidden.html>.

the cross-shaped layout with a large central dome became the trademark of his style.[23] To decorate the church of the Transfiguration, the board of directors of the Ruthenian People's House hired in 1898, among others, Leonard Marconi, the most famous local sculptor of the time, whose sculptures embellished the city's streets and numerous public buildings. He executed the sculptures of the apostles located along the drum of the main dome. (see Illustration 8.17.) Even though art historians sometimes are puzzled why Marconi and not one of several available Ukrainian sculptors was hired, the answer seems to be simple. The church was supposed to be something more than just a Ruthenian church, it had to be on a par with other imposing buildings in the city. The domes of this church had become an important part of Lviv's cityscape, fitting well with the shapes and elevations of other grand buildings of late nineteenth-century Lviv. (see Illustration 8.18.)

---

[23] Khrystyna Lev, Vasyl' Slobodian, Natalia Filevych, eds., *100 tserkov Nahirnykh. Chastyna persha: Tserkvy Vasylia Nahirnoho* (Lviv, 2013).

Illustration 8.19: The Ascension church in Znesinnia. Built: 1897-1901.
Photograph by Aeou: July 2011.

It is worth comparing this new central church with a similar smaller
venture. In 1897 the project for a new stone church in Znesinnia, a Lviv
suburb, was approved. The church had a modified Byzantine-
Romanesque layout, in the form of a Greek cross with unusually short
shoulders and a central square nave covered with a round dome. Arches
and pendentives holding the transept resembled Byzantine structures, but
the dome itself was hardly Byzantine, and the Romanesque character of
the walls was to resemble Lviv's oldest churches of both rites located in
the suburban belt along the northern foot of the High Castle. (see
Illustration 8.19.) The ancient stone churches themselves were at that time
being "restored" or, to be more precise, rebuilt according to the architects'
ideas about their original appearance. Two of the most celebrated cases of
such imaginative restorations were the church of St. John and the

Illustrations 8.20 and 8.21: St. John's church before and after the "restoration." Sources: Illustration 8.20: Karol Lang, fragment from a photograph from 1861-1863. Iryna Kotlobulatova. L'viv na fotohrafiï-2 (Lviv: Tsentr Ievropy, 2011), 16. Illustration 8: 21: "Ivana Khrestytelia kostel. Muzei davnikh pam"iatok L'vova (bl. 1371, 1887),"
Oko, arkhitekturno-kraieznavchyi sait <http://oko.kiev.ua/m190_k_lviv_ivana_xrestitel ya_kostel_muzey_davnix_pamyatok_lvova.zsp>.

Armenian cathedral. The "restoration" of the Armenian cathedral, which would have changed its appearance completely, was stopped by the intervention of the Imperial Society for the Preservation of Historical Monuments, while the "restoration" of St. John's went through. After the "restoration," a church whose original architecture on these confessional borderlands could have been read as either Western or Byzantine became explicitly Roman Catholic (see Illustrations 8.20 and 8.21).

Something very similar occurred with the ancient churches of the Byzantine rite, all of which underwent "restoration" in the first quarter of the twentieth century. The church that changed its appearance least was St. Paraskevia, restored in 1904 according to plans of Mykola Luzhetsky.[24] The only major change here was the replacement of the tent-like roof of the main tower with a more Eastern onion dome surrounded by four smaller lanterns. (see Illustrations

---

[24] Biriuliov, *Arkhitektura L'vova*, 53-54.

Illustration 8.22 and 8.23: St. Paraskevia church before and after the "restoration."
Sources: Illustration 8.22: A photograph from ca. 1900-1907 from Ihor Kotlobulatov's
collection. Illustration 8.23: "Paraskevy sv. Tserkva (1645)," Oko, arkhitekturno-
kraieznavchyi sait <http://oko.kiev.ua/img/Lvivska/Pustomytivskyy/2005.10.30--
414_~193.jpg>.

8.22 and 8.23.) St. Onuphrius, a church famous because of the old
Orthodox graveyard and monastery located nearby, was originally built
in the sixteenth century and had been incessantly renovated and changed
since then. It also underwent the most radical "reconstruction" in 1902.
Edgar Kováts, the proponent of the "eastern Galician style," who designed
and supervised the reconstruction, decided to make this church resemble
the church of St. Nicholas (as far as we know the oldest Orthodox church
in the city). He added another nave to the church, turning it into a three-
nave church.[25] Finally, in the 1920s, even though it is beyond our
chronological framework, the church of St. Nicholas itself underwent
major reconstruction and acquired its present-day, more Byzantine
appearance (see Illustration 8.24). Because of these "reconstructions,"
church buildings that in the mid-nineteenth century (and, perhaps,
originally as well) looked very much the same, turned into distinct
"Eastern" or "Western" historical monuments.

---

[25] Volodymyr Vuitsyk, *Vybrani pratsi. Do 70-richchia z dnia narodzhennia* (Lviv:
Ukrzakhidproektrestavratsiia, 2004), 57.

Illustration 8.24: St. Nicholas church after reconstruction. Source: cerkiew św. Mikołaja by Adam Lenkiewicz, The National Digital Library Polona. It still maintains its Baroque façade.

Provincial self-government had little influence over what was built in Lviv and how it was built. But the building of the Galician Diet, the province's elected legislature, was the only governmental building with

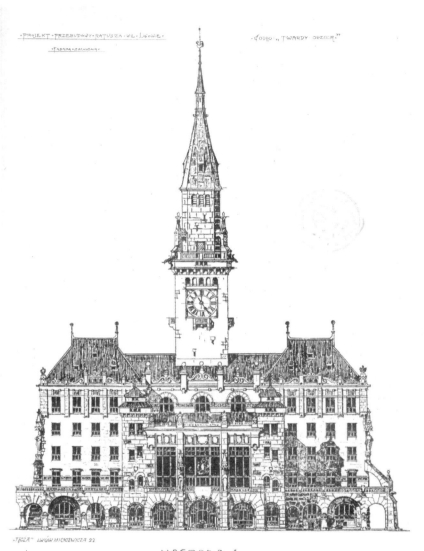

NAGRODA I

PROJEKTOWAŁ ARCHITEKT: ROMAN BANDURSKI z KRAKOWA.

Illustration 8.25: The "Hard Nut" project for the reconstructionmof the Lviv City Hall by Kraków architect Roman Bandurski. Source: Czasopismo techniczne 26 (1908), tablica 2.

an explicit reference to Ruthenian history. That reference belonged to the chisel of a Polish sculptor, Zygmunt Trembecki. On one side of the main staircase of the Galician diet, a neo-Renaissance structure built in the 1870s, statues of Volodymyr the Great and Yaroslav the Wise were erected and paired with Mieszko the Old and Bolesław the Brave on the sides of the main staircase.

The municipal authorities, on the other hand, did try to give Lviv an unmistakably Polish character. The city council and its magistrate had to approve all building projects on the city's territory. The building code itself was neutral when it came to matters of style. Only technical issues connected with public conveniences, public safety, and general city development had to be conformed to. Some general aesthetic considerations were also often raised by the magistrate's representatives during the debates about new building projects, but actual stylistic solutions were left to the architects and the bodies that commissioned the project. The City Council's ideological preferences become obvious from the stance it took on its own home, the city hall (*Rathaus*). After some discussions in the 1890s, a competition for the "reconstruction" of the city hall was announced in 1900. The city council claimed that it planned reconstruction primarily for aesthetic reasons: "The Lviv *Rathaus* resembles a large barracks, and, together with its tower that looks like a square chimney, makes no aesthetic impression."[26] Alfred Zachariewicz's project won first prize. The experts described his design as "made in a Baroque style, most probably for the reason that the architecture of the present-day *Rathaus* cannot be characterized as belonging to any particular style and therefore there is nothing to be preserved in it, while the most beautiful monuments of Lviv are done in the Baroque style."[27] But this project was never carried out, and in 1908 another competition was held. This time a neo-Gothic project entitled "Hard Nut" won the competition, but was in turn also never implemented because of the lack of money. The Gothic style of the project was an explicit reference to the city's Polishness, while its title referred to the city's glorious military history in the Polish-Lithuanian Commonwealth (see Illustration 8.25). The City Council also did not care much about the destruction of old buildings connected with the Eastern rite. The approved 1908 project of developing a new railway crossing through Zhovkivska (now Khmelnytsky Street) to solve traffic problems foresaw the destruction of St. Onuphrius' church, so important to the Ruthenian community of early modern Lviv. It was only because of the intervention of local intellectuals

---

[26] "Rekonstrukcja Lwowskiego ratusza," *Czasopismo techniczne* 8 (1900): 70.
[27] Ibid.

Illustration 8.26: Franciszek Biesiadecki's villa. Architects: Alfred Zachariewicz and Józef Sosnowski. A 2008 photograph by Vodnik. Source: <http://ru.wikipedia.org/wiki/%D0%A4%D0%B0%D0%B9%D0%BB:%D0%92%D0%9F_%D0%94%D0%BE%D0%BC_%D0%BD%D0%B0_%D0%9F%D1%83%D1%88%D0%BA%D0%B8%D0%BD%D0%B0.jpg>.

and art historians, and subsequently the Imperial Central Commission for Research and Maintenance of Architectural Monuments (founded in 1850), that the project was suspended.[28]

The streets of a modern city are not exclusively a public space; rather, they form a space where the private intersects with the public. Private dwellings, even when designed according to the taste of their owners, make public statements with their facades, which form an integral part of the street's architectural spectacle. Around 1900, the Secession movement introduced the idea that architecture should shape the totality of urban space and should be inseparable from the arts and crafts used for the finer

---

[28] The correspondence regarding planned reconstruction. Central State Historical Archive of Ukraine in Lviv (*Tsentral'nyi Derzhavnyi Istorychnyi Arkhiv Ukrainy u L'vovi*, TsDIAL), f. 146, op. 68, spr. 2111, folios 1-38, 119-121, 169.

Illustration 8.27 and 8.28: The Heller Villa, Melnyk Street 7 and a fragment of the exterior ornament from the villa's exterior. Source: unidentified photographs from 2011.

decorations of buildings. This integration of decorative arts into architectural projects, together with the generally accepted eclecticism of historical references, provided plentiful opportunities for architects and real estate owners to play with historical narratives and local traditions.

Around 1900 private housing grew rapidly in volume and became an increasingly important part of the city's representational public space. These private houses built after 1900 also include many references to the Eastern Christian tradition. We can take as an example a villa designed by Jan Sosnowski and Alfred Zachariewicz in 1907. According to art historians, this villa represents "a mixture of Eastern motifs with a Renaissance body, which, in addition, became connected with a number of Byzantine, folk and proto-Secession themes in the details of the interior

Illustration 8.29: The Panchyshyn Villa. Karmeliuk Street 3. Source: a photograph by Aeou, May 2012, Ukrainian Wikipedia, <http://uk.wikipedia.org/wiki/%D0%A4%D 0%B0%D0%B9%D0%BB:3_Karmeliuka_St reet,_Lviv.jpg>.

and exterior..." (see Illustration 8.26).[29] Many villas used some folk motifs, including those from Hutsul sacral art, even if not built in one of the "Carpathian" styles. The Heller villa on Melnyk Street 7 is a good example of such a villa (see Illustrations 8.27 and 8.28). The Panchyshyn villa (Karmeliuk Street 3) is another example of a private dwelling built in the Ukrainian style. The Ukrainian style used here appears as a mixture of folk and Byzantine motifs. The villa was built in 1923, and its Ukrainian style signals a departure from the Ukrainian Secession with its overabundant ornamentation, and the beginnings of Ukrainian Modernism. Characteristically, Byzantine elements are more prominent here than in the buildings of the Ukrainian Secession and appear as better suited to the modernist stage in the development of a local Ukrainian architectural style (see Illustration 8.29). Another example of Byzantine motifs not connected with the Ukrainian style can be seen in the house on Kotliarevsky 17, where they are found largely among the decor and minor architectural solutions for particular parts of the building. The same is true of many public buildings already mentioned. Even buildings of the Ukrainian Secession often show more references to the Eastern Christian tradition in exterior and interior detail than in the building's overall form (see Illustrations 8.30, 8.31, and 8.32).

---

[29] Romana Cielątkowska and Lilia Onyszczenko-Szwec, *Detal architektury mieszkaniowej Lwowa XIX i XX wieku* (Gdańsk: Wydział Architektury Politechniki Gdańskiej, 2006), 100.

Illustration 8.30, 8.31, and 8.32. The Narodnyi Dim Residence. Source: Photographs by the author, 2009.

Some art historians claim that "Lviv Historicism did not create any local peculiar interpretations or distinguishing patterns. It was limited to borrowed *Sigismundian Renaissance* and *Vistula brick Gothic*."[30] This does not seem true; both local and guest architects believed that the city had a unique architectural physiognomy and struggled to give the city a unique modern architectural face, developing idiosyncratic local styles. Julian Zachariewicz (1837-98), probably the most prominent Lviv architect of the historicist period, who designed the building of the Lviv Polytechnic Institute and of the Galician Savings Bank, was also actively searching for a specific Eastern Galician style.[31] Around 1900, the local architect Kazimierz Mokłowski stated that "Secession in Lviv could develop on the basis of magnificent examples of ornamental realism, against the native background of Renaissance or Baroque."[32] It seems that both during the Historicism and early Secession periods, the Renaissance with some Baroque remained the predominant point of reference for local architects. The Galician Diet, the Polytechnic Institute, the Provincial Savings Bank, and

---

[30] Cielątkowska and Onyszczenko-Szwec, 89.

[31] Originally, Julian Zachariewicz was appointed to design the Galician pavilion at the World Exhibition in Paris in 1900. He planned to divide it into Western and Eastern Galician to show the province's two distinct artistic traditions. Tomasz Szybisty, "Sposób zakopiański i jego twórca Edgar Kováts (1849–1912)," 80-81.

[32] Biriuliov, *Arkhitektura L'vova*, 395.

Illustration 8.33 and 8.34. The first (1899) and the second (1900) projects of the new main train terminal. Architect: Władysław Sadłowski. Source: "Nowy dworzec kolei państwowej we Lwowie," Architekt 5, no. 7 (1904): 103-06.

many others were done in that neo-Renaissance style. Moreover, neo-Gothic buildings appear in Lviv relatively late and may be connected with the heightening of national tensions in the 1900s.

In the 1880s, the well-known historian of Galicia, Walerian Kalinka, complained about a "lack of tradition in Lviv in comparison with other Polish cities like Warsaw and Kraków." Discussing impressions from the royal tombs in Kraków Castle, Kalinka noted that "Lviv has no comparable monuments; everything here is if not completely fresh then not too old, and much less connected with the Polish soul."[33] This problematic connection with an exclusively Polish tradition was exacerbated by the local architects' attempt to draw on and create new local traditions. The Eastern Christian tradition was one among these local traditions creatively reinvented in the second half of the nineteenth century. [Another prominent tradition, which contributed a lot to the city's more "Eastern" appearance, was the Jewish one.]

References to the Renaissance in Lviv's architecture included a strong Byzantine connection. One of the earliest neo-Renaissance buildings on the city's central boulevard used Venetian-style motifs and decorations extensively, which themselves can be traced to Byzantium. In the context of Polish history, references to the Renaissance had particular political and

---

[33] Grodziska, *Miasto jak brylant*, 139.

Illustration 8.35: The main train station terminal as completed in 1904.
Source: a postcard from the Digital National Library Polona.

ideological connotations. They referred to the period before the Counter-Reformation, to a Polish-Lithuanian Commonwealth of religious toleration and peaceful ethnic coexistence. Since Lviv was seen as the capital of Polish Rus', the idea of the three tribes of the Polish nation was often invoked here. For example, when in 1891 the centennial anniversary of the 3 May Constitution was celebrated, a triumphal arch was built and decorated with the coats of arms of Poland, Lithuania, and Rus'.[34] Educated observers were able to read these references from the architectural cityscape of the provincial capital. In the 1920s Wacław Zyndram Kościałkowski wrote, "for me, a capital dweller coming from northern 'near-Lithuania,' Lviv had the special charm of a southern city, different from other cities of the Commonwealth, which here displayed its old Jagiellonian face."[35] Practicing different rites of the same religion as well as mutual penetration of the "Western" and "Eastern" cultures were for him the best proof of this.

---

[34] Jurij Biriulow, *Rzeźba lwowska od połowy XVIII wieku do 1939 roku. Od zapowiedzi klasycyzmu do awangardy* (Warszawa: Neriton, 2007), 147.
[35] Grodziska, *Miasto jak brylant*, 199.

Illustration 8.36: The train station vestibule. Source: a photograph from 1925, the National Digital Library Polona.

In the process of construction, even buildings that were designed as explicitly anti-Historicist were adjusted to fit the city's architectural environment. The main train station designed in 1899-1900 and built in 1904, for example, is hailed as the second (after the Mikolasch arcade) Secession building in Lviv. The original (1899) plan by Władysław Sadłowski was full of imperial symbolism. The station's central pavilion had the shape of a Roman triumphal arch, looked universally European, and resembled the Beaux-Arts style of the Second Empire (see Illustration 8.33). For some reason, the design of all the pavilions was significantly modified in Sadłowski's second project (from 1900) (see Illustration 8.34). All the pavilions were now crowned with domes, while the central pavilion also obtained two false flanking towers. In the process of construction, the project was further modified. The polygonal dome became more elongated, and the towers became taller. The combination now alluded to the city's Eastern churches and bell towers (see Illustration 8.35, compare to Illustrations 8.15, 8.23, or the bell tower of the Armenian cathedral from Illustration 8.18). The flanking towers referred to the famous Korniakt tower of the church of the Dormition (compare

Illustration 8.37: Tadeusz Obmiński's design. Waiting hall for third-class passengers. Source: a postcard from the National Digital Library Polona.

Illustration 8.30 and the Korniakt tower from Illustration 8.18). Ludwik (Ludwig) Wierzbicki, the Lviv railway director, who also commissioned the original projects from Władysław Sadłowski, made final modifications and oversaw the actual construction of the station. Ludwik Wierzbicki was not only a high-ranking railway official but also an engineer and architect by training. Moreover, he was the author of the first published catalogue of ornaments used in Ukrainian folk crafts in Galicia.[36] He was also interested in the region's historical architectural monuments, especially in sacral architecture and designed several churches himself.[37] New construction techniques, most notably the use of reinforced concrete, eased the task of alluding to the great Byzantine churches of the past. The

[36] Ludwik Wierzbicki, *Wzory przemysłu domowego*, various subtitles, titles and text in Polish, Ukrainian, French and German, 10 vols. (Lviv, 1880-1889). Oleksandr Barvinsky did the Ukrainian version of the text and praised the work highly: Oleksandr Barvins'kyi, *Spomyny z moho zhyttia*, vol. 2, parts 3 and 4 (New York-Kyiv: Stylos, 2009), 702.

[37] Ludwik Wierzbicki, *Bożnica w miasteczku Jabłonowie nad Prutem* (Krakow: Akademia Umiejętności, 1889); Ludwik Wierzbicki, *Zamek w Olesku* (Lviv: W. A. Szyjkowski, 1892); J. D., "Ludwik Wierzbicki, c. k. Radca Dworu, inżynier, em. Dyrektor kolei państw.," *Czasopismo techniczne* 31 (1913): 25-27.

КОСТЕЛЪ СВ. ЕЛИСАВЕТЫ.   KOŚCIÓŁ ŚW. ELŻBIETY.

Illustration 8.38: St. Elizabeth church. Source: a postcard from the National Digital Library Polona.

square vestibule of the railway station covered with a huge dome was a good example of this (see Illustration 8.36).

Local motifs were present not only in the building's elevation but also in the interior. While waiting halls for first- and second-class passengers were decorated in a manner that would satisfy typical bourgeois taste in any country, the waiting hall for third-class passengers was decorated by Tadeusz Obmiński, who used the local Secession style with its references to folk art and wooden architecture (see Illustration 8.37). Against this background, the construction of the St. Elizabeth church on the traveller's way from the station to the city, with its neo-Gothic architecture, was an unmistakable attempt to counter the too Eastern appearance of the city's vistas and of the main train station itself (see Illustration 8.38). Designed by Teodor Talowski in 1902, and built from 1904 to 1911, the church became the city's tallest building, while its spires dominated the cityscape as it appeared from the vicinity of the train station.

To conclude, symbolic references to the Eastern Christian tradition in the material representational space of early twentieth-century Lviv can be grouped into four main classes: 1) The architecture referring to the province's Ruthenian/Ukrainian tradition, using and reworking vernacular motifs. These works were often a conscious attempt to create a distinct Ukrainian national architecture and to mark nationally the city space. 2) The works referring to the purer Byzantine tradition, done by outsiders, connected with Romanticist orientalism and particular visions of the local Eastern tradition. 3) The modern architecture of the local Greek Catholic church, integrating Byzantine elements, historicist styles, and the city's local architectural tradition. 4) The works of Lviv's Secession and Modernist movements that included historical references to both Romanticised Byzantine and local traditions.

Architectural elements that served as explicit markers of Eastern Christian tradition were the invention of the late nineteenth and early twentieth century and not the development of the local Eastern Christian tradition as it existed in premodern and early nineteenth-century Lviv. The focus on distinct local cultural or ethnic traditions led to the remaking of architectural monuments from previous eras, assigning more "Eastern" features to the buildings connected with the Eastern Christian tradition. This also provoked a reaction in the form of neo-Romanesque and neo-Gothic styles used to emphasize Polishness and Roman Catholicism. Moreover, since the Eastern Christian elements came to be seen as a defining element of the city's unique architectural ensemble, abundant references to Eastern traditions gave a more "Eastern" appearance to Lviv's cityscape.

Those references to the Eastern Christian tradition remained highly heterogeneous. Even though ideological codes were present in the city architecture, they did not exhaust its symbolic readings. The agents behind the shaping of Lviv's cityscape were not the authorities or political movements but intellectuals, institutions, organizations, and wealthier citizens. The role of the intellectuals and professionals was of foremost importance. Fortunately, the choices the intellectuals and professionals made about a building's appearance were determined not so much by their politics or national identity, but by their visions of the city, its history, and its future, as well as the purpose of the buildings they were designing. Manifold and varied historical and cultural references in Lviv's eclectic architecture acknowledged the Eastern Christian tradition's important role in the city without giving it any single interpretation.

The Sacred Art of Modest Sosenko:
Lost and Preserved
Olesya Semchyshyn-Huzner

At the turn of the twentieth century, religious and cultural circles in Lviv developed an interest in adorning Ukrainian churches with high-quality works of sacral art that would adhere to Eastern Christian tradition.[1] They were uncomfortable with the longstanding custom – especially in Eastern Galicia – of using cheap, mass-produced, Western-style religious works in churches. Church walls were being painted with a stylistic orientation on classical European models.[2]

The situation was similar with regard to sacral architecture, which lost its connection to traditional local construction and style. The last years of the nineteenth and especially the first decade of the twentieth centuries saw improvements in the quality of church construction. The designs of leading architects incorporated principles of design from masonry churches of Kyivan Rus' as well as from vernacular wooden architecture.[3]

At the same time, a modern (secessionist) style was developing on the Ukrainian artistic scene that encouraged a creative turn to national traditions. This stylistic phenomenon of the early twentieth century has yet to be precisely defined. However, this style definitely searched for methods of national self-expression and entailed a review of the cultural achievements of past eras and their projection in contemporary art.

Exploring the development of Ukrainian sacral painting in the twentieth century, and especially its origins in the first decades, poses difficulties. One of them is the lamentable state in which extant pictures

---

[1] This chapter was translated by Fr. Michael Kwiatkowski (with some modifications by John-Paul Himka).

[2] K. Ustyianovych, "Deshcho o nashii zhyvopysi tserkovnoi," *Dilo* (1888), no. 7:1, no. 9:1, no. 10:1. K. Chaikovskii, "Arkhytektura i shtuka maliarska a nasha ruska tserkov'," *Dilo* (1893), no. 73.

[3] At the turn of the twentieth century there were several serious professional architects who designed sacral structures in Galicia and to some extent competed with one another with regard to church style: Sylvestr Havryshkevych, Vasyl Nahirny, and Ivan Levynsky and his followers.

Illustration 9.1: Modest Sosenko. Photo from the beginning of the twentieth century, NML photoarchive.

are found today, due to the ravages of the First and Second World Wars as well as the destruction of artifacts and churches in the postwar period. No less harmful is the attitude of today's pastors and parish communities towards church decoration. Researchers now have to spend a long time looking for intact images, working with archival manuscripts and photographic materials, and sorting out attributions. Only through taking such pains can we reconstruct the sacral legacy of individual artists and study their articulation of a national style in sacral art at the beginning of the twentieth century.

Modest Sosenko (1875-1920) is rightly regarded as the pioneer artist-monumentalist whose work laid the foundation for the revival of national traditions in the decoration of churches. (See Illustration 9.1.) He acquired excellent professional training in Europe at the Kraków School of Fine Arts (1896-1900),[4] the Royal Academy of Arts in Munich (1900-1902),[5] and the National School of Fine Arts in Paris at Leon Bonnat's studio (1902-1904).[6] He was not only familiar with contemporary artistic trends, but because of his work in the National Museum in Lviv (NML) he also acquired a detailed knowledge of old Ukrainian art.[7] He wanted to develop his own style of artistic expression as well as a universal system of formative principles. He wanted to find the golden mean between East and West, between the traditional and the professional, in order to create a unified Ukrainian style. This artist-intellectual, as his contemporaries called him, throughout his brief life moved step by step toward that goal. Mykola Holubets wrote:

---

[4] *Materiały do dziejów Akademii sztuk pięknych w Krakowie*, vol. 2 (Wrocław-Warsaw-Kraków: Ossolineum, 1969), 396. See also "Svidotstva pro navchannia u shkoli krasnykh mystetstv u Krakovi," National Museum in Lviv (NML), Rk 3239, 1-6.

[5] According to the correspondence between Sosenko and Andrei Sheptytsky, the artist received a stipend from the metropolitan from the start of the twentieth century until he finished his studies in Paris. See "Lysty M. Sosenka do Andreia Sheptyts'koho (1901-1904 rr.)," Tsentral'nyi derzhavnyi istorychnyi arkhiv Ukrainy u L'vovi (TsDIAL), f. 358, op. 2, spr. 259, 12-46. See also Sosenko's certificates from the academy of arts in Munich, NML, Rk 3242, 1, 3-7.

[6] His certificates from the national art school in Paris are in NML, Rk 3244, 1, 3-4. See also L. Voloshyn, "Modest Sosenko – mytets' ukrains'koho modernu (Roky studii: Krakiv, Miunkhen, Paryzh)," *Zapysky NTSh* (2004), vol. 248:210.

[7] Sosenko was a full-time employee of the museum as of 1907. In particular, he was assigned to expand acquisitions. In addition, he was entrusted with the delicate task of restoration, a field which was still in its infancy. See I. Svientsits'kyi, "XXV. lit diial'nosti Natsional'noho muzeiu," in *Dvaitsiat'piat'-littia Natsional'noho muzeiu u L'vovi*, ed. I. Svientsits'kyi (Lviv: Naukova fundatsiia halyts'koho mytropolyta Andreia Sheptyts'koho, 1930), 10-11. See also Sheptytsky's letter to Sosenko of 3 July 1907, NML, Rk 3249; Ilarion Svientsitsky's letter from Lovran to Sheptytsky, 31 July 1909, TsDIAL, f. 358, op. 2, spr. 250/1, 38; Svientsitsky's letters from Lviv to Sheptytsky, 6 November 1909 and 26 March 1912, ibid., 40-41, 71; Svientsitsky's letter to Sosenko in Italy, 25 April 1914, NML Rk 2938, 20; the fragment of Svientsitsky's letter from Kyiv to Sheptytsky, 27 February 1910, NML archive, folder (*papka*) 257; and note (*zapys*) no. 464 of 18 August 1913 in the museum's diary (*dnevnyk*).

Before a Galician public disoriented by the hitherto dominant kitsch, arose and stood up to his full height a stylist-decorator conscious of his goals and means, who sought sources of inspiration in the tradition of ancient Ukrainian iconography, a tradition that had long been forgotten and was therefore incomprehensible in his day. Because it arose on the boundaries of West and East, it was neither Western nor Byzantine, but a synthesis - into the strict framework of the Byzantine canon it poured the young blood of life and its rhythm.... From this synthesis of ancient Byzantine conventions with the artistic achievements of the nation was born in Sosenko the concept of his icons and iconography that he brought to fruition in a whole series of churches....[8]

For the longest time Ukrainian scholars, with the exception of some of his contemporary art critics, especially Ilarion Svientsitsky and Holubets,[9] did not pay much attention to the artist's sacral art. The reason, of course, was the imposition of Soviet rule beginning in 1939. The first studies appeared only at the beginning of the 1990s.[10] The initial results of field research were not very heartening. From what we know from the archival materials and literature, only two churches painted by Sosenko have been preserved in their entirety.[11] Among those lost were the wooden church of St. Elias in the village of Yablunytsia (Yaremche city council, Ivano-Frankivsk oblast),[12] the wooden church of St. Paraskevia in the village of Puzhnyky (Tlumach raion, Ivano-Frankivsk oblast),[13] the polychrome in the wooden three-tiered church of St. Michael in the town of Pechenizhyn

---

[8] Mykola Holubets', *Nacherk istorii ukrains'koho mystetstva* (New York: Vydavnytstvo Chartoryis'kykh, 1973), 34.

[9] I. Svientsits'kyi, "Pam"iati Modesta Sosenka," *Nova Rada* (1920), no. 31. I. Svientsits'kyi, *Modest Sosenko. Zbirna vystava* (Lviv, 1920). M. Holubets', "Modest Sosenko (1875-1920)," *Hromads'ka dumka* (1920), no. 32. M. Holubets', "Spadshchyna Modesta Sosenka," *Ukrains'ka dumka* (1920), no. 13.

[10] V. Radoms'ka, "Povernennia Modesta Sosenka," *Zerna* (1994), no. 1. V. Radoms'ka, "Povernennia Modesta Sosenka," *Obrazotvorche mystetstvo* (1991), no. 1. NML organized an exhibition of Sosenko's works in the museum's collection in 1995; it was curated by Liubov Voloshyn.

[11] This is the information provided by Radoms'ka, "Povernennia," *Zerna* (1994), no. 1:37-38. But today Radomska's list of Sosenko's works has to be verified and supplemented in light of additional information.

[12] *Shematyzm vseho klyra hreko-katolytskoi Eparkhii Stansylavivskoi na rok Bozhii 1910* (Stanyslaviv: Nakladom Klyra eparkhiial'noho, 1910), 162.

[13] Ibid., 229.

(Kolomyia raion, Ivano-Frankivsk oblast),[14] the wooden church of St. Nicholas in the village of Koniushky near Rohatyn (Ivano-Frankivsk oblast),[15] the murals in the brick church of St. Michael in the village of Bilche Zolote (Borshchiv raion, Ternopil oblast). There is also information that Sosenko painted the church of St. George (St. Josaphat) in the village of Deviatnyky (Zhydachiv raion, Lviv oblast)[16] as well as the church in the village of Kholoieve (now Vuzlove, Radekhiv raion, Lviv oblast). The information about the church in Vuzlove, which was destroyed in the 1960s, is wrong, because the polychromes there were not Sosenko's work but Yurii Mahalevsky's.[17]

Sosenko had his first experience in the field of monumental sacral art immediately after finishing the Kraków School of Fine Arts: in 1900 he helped Yulian Makarevych with the work on the murals and iconostasis of the cathedral church of the Ascension of Our Lord in Stanyslaviv (now Ivano-Frankivsk).[18] His first independent undertaking was the polychromes in the sanctuary of the church of St. Elias in Yablunytsia in 1901.[19] Unfortunately, the church burned down in 1918,[20] and we have no idea how it was painted. In summer 1907, at the request of a relative who had raised him, Fr. Mykolai Soviakovsky, Sosenko painted the church of

---

[14] Ibid., 171.

[15] Ibid., 321.

[16] The polychromes in Deviatnyky were first mentioned in Ostap Shandura, "Za domovynoiu Sosenka," *Vpered* (1920) (NML Rk 3291). Violeta Radomska stated that the church was destroyed in August 1945. See Radoms'ka, "Povernennia," *Zerna* (1994), no. 1:38. The Lviv schematism records a brick parish church of St. George in 1904, of which Fr. Mykolai Smyslovsky was pastor. *Shematyzm vseho klyra hreko-katolytskoi Arkhyieparkhii L'vivskoi na rok Bozhii 1910* (Lviv: Iz typohrafii Stavropyhiiskoho instytuta, 1910), 360-61. But in 1910 Metropolitan Andrei Sheptytsky consecrated the church to St. Josaphat. Vasyl Laba, who wrote the history of Deviatnyky and its parish church, states that Sosenko was supposed to paint the church, but something interfered. The church of St. George, in spite of repeated plundering, has survived to our time, but the contemporary wall painting has nothing in common with Sosenko. Vasyl' Laba, *Istoriia sela Dev"iatnyky* (Lviv, 1996), 17.

[17] According to V. Badiak, "Sakral'ne mystetstvo: storinky dramy," *Kyivs'ka tserkva* (2000), no. 2 (8): 96-100, the church in Vuzlove was destroyed in the 1960s and had been painted by Sosenko. But Fr. Volodymyr Yarema mentions Mahalevsky in connection with the wall painting. V. Iarema, *Dyvnyi svit ikon* (Lviv: Lohos, 1994), 65. Because no scholar studying Sosenko has mentioned Vuzlove, nor do any archival documents, we incline to Fr. Yarema's viewpoint.

[18] Voloshyn, "Modest Sosenko," 198.

[19] One can see how seriously Sosenko took his work in Yablunytsia from his letter to Metropolitan Sheptytsky, 1 November 1901, TsDIAL, f. 358, op. 2, spr. 259, 13.

[20] Information from Vasyl Slobodian, 2009.

St. Paraskevia in Puzhnyky, which has not been preserved.[21] Confirmation of this can be found in the memoirs of Yaroslava Sosenko-Ostruk, which were published in the diaspora.[22] She wrote that her uncle painted the church together with his wife Mykhailyna in the year that they married, that is, 1907.[23] Hence, this work of Sosenko's remains today only as a fact in his artistic biography.

The church of St. Michael in the village of Pidberiztsi (Pustomyty raion, Lviv oblast) belongs to the best-preserved artistic complexes painted by Sosenko. The brick church was built by the architectural firm of Ivan Levynsky at the end of the nineteenth century.[24] The pastor at this time was Yevhen Shukhevych, brother of the well-known ethnographer of the Hutsul region, Volodymyr Shukhevych.[25] The artist worked on the polychrome in 1907-1910. Since there was so much work, Sosenko approached the Society for the Advancement of Ruthenian Art with a request to give him some helpers. His request, however, was refused.[26] There were also problems with the technical realization of his painting designs. Sosenko could not convince the parish community of the necessity of using quality paints and real gold leaf in the polychrome *al fresco* technique. Over time, due to poor ventilation in the church, the paints of inferior quality began to run, and no repairs could fully satisfy the artist.[27]

The good condition of the complex allows for an analysis of the work within the context of the formation of the "Sosenko style." Paintings fully cover the ceiling and walls of the church. Based on the canons of Byzantine iconography and wall painting, Sosenko developed his own system of church painting, supplemented with ornamentation borrowed from

---

[21] Svientsitsky gave 1906 as the year the church in Puzhnyky was painted. See I. Svientsits'kyi, *Modest Sosenko. Kataloh vystavy* (Lviv, 1920).

[22] S. Sosenko-Ostruk, *Modest Sosenko. Spohad* (USA? n.d), NML archive.

[23] In the legal papers regarding their divorce in 1916, the date of their marriage is given as 7 February 1907. It took place in Kraków. NML, Rk 2937, 20. So if Sosenko travelled to Puzhnyky to introduce his wife to his family and at the same time painted the church, this had to be 1907 and not 1906 as Svientstitsky mentioned in the catalog to the posthumous exhibition.

[24] O.P. Noha, *Ukrains'kyi styl' v tserkovnomu mystetstvi Halychyny kintsia XIX – pochatku XX stolit'* (Lviv: Ukrains'ki tekhnolohii, 1999), 82.

[25] *Shematyzm Arkhyieparkhii L'vivskoi 1910*, 116.

[26] The official rejection letter of 16 June 1908 is in NML, Rk 3251, 1.

[27] Svientsits'kyi, "Pam"iati Modesta Sosenka," 3.

Illustration 9.2: Painting in the sanctuary of the church of St. Michael in Pidberiztsi. Author's photo from 2008.

national decorative traditions and reworked according to the requirements of monumental painting. In the church at Pidberiztsi we can see the artist working out his own style. The painting in all the components of the church (the sanctuary, the nave, the entrance) has different artistic features. (See Illustration 9.2.) The most concentrated decoration of the sanctuary is the central apsidal wall, which has a majestic, dynamic depiction of the Holy Trinity surrounded by angelic choirs, all against a golden mosaic background. Both the use of *smalti* and the very rendering of the image are reminiscent of church interiors from the time of Kyivan Rus'. One can see the characteristics of Sosenko's mature style in the way he executes the portrait of God the Father, in the decorative, flat manner of treating the angels' halos and wings, and in the subtle arrangement of the heads of the angels with the ornamentation in an arch above the mosaic. In the cupola before the altar area, four ornamental rays that suggest a cross emanate from a magnificent rosette. In the surfaces between them there are four two-winged angels. Lower, divided by a wide ornamental strip on the surfaces between the windows, are medallions with the heads of other angelic creatures. Across the next, more complexly decorated strip and architectural cornice, on triangular areas of the pendentives are the half-length portraits of evangelists, with their symbols on a pillar below; they are accompanied by trumpeting angels. Extraordinarily intricate and heterogeneous ornaments (plant and geometrical forms, and their combination) cover the interior spaces of the arches and the walls of the main and side altars and central part of the church. They not only fill in the walls, but create surfaces for depictions of the saints: Ss. Anthony and Theodosius of the Caves, the holy martyrs Borys and Glib, Ss. Gregory the Theologian and Josaphat, Ss. Basil the Great and John Chrysostom (all in full stature), and busts of the holy martyrs Catherine and Eudokia, Ss. Demetrius and Joseph, Ss. Cyril and Methodius, Ss. Constantine and Helen. These figures are arranged along the walls of the church as if to lead the faithful to the sanctuary. The ceiling of the central part of the church was arranged in a relatively simpler manner than was characteristic for Sosenko's style. It consisted of a decorative rhythm of halos and wings of the cherubim and seraphim. Using Sosenko's designs, Stanisław Gabryel Żeleński's mosaic workshop in Kraków produced the stained glass windows for the church – of Christ blessing the children and of Christ and Mary.[28]

The process of painting the church interior was followed in the contemporary press, and the completion of the painting was a major event in Lviv's artistic circles.[29] The major Ukrainian daily, *Dilo*, published the following:

> The walls and dome of the brick church are covered with the finest checked ornamentation of the sort one can only see in the oldest Rus' manuscript illuminations and in St. Sophia's in Kyiv. The wall paintings of the blessed saints are executed most exactly in the manner of ancient Rus'-Byzantine models, and the images in the domes and altar section are true works of art, executed after studying the very best images of our rite. Mr. Sosenko deserves great recognition for this, because he dared to go beyond the traditional Western-Latin manner and took as his

[28] L. Voloshyn, "Perlyna tserkovnoho rozpysu," *Obrazotvorche mystetstvo* (2001) , no. 2:55.

[29] As we know from the press, among those who travelled to Pidberiztsi to admire Sosenko's work were Metropolitan Sheptytsky, Svientsitsky, Shukhevych, Levynsky, and the Armenian archbishop of Lviv, Józef Teodorowicz. "Stylevo mal'ovana tserkva," *Ruslan* (1909), no. 137. "Tserkov u Pidberiztsiakh," *Dilo* (1909), no. 142. "Saksons'kyi kniaz' i Eks. Sheptyts'kyi na seli," *Dilo* (1910), no. 22.

model our eastern Rus'-Byzantine painting, which was once so magnificent in our land.[30]

The paintings of the wooden church of St. Michael in Pechenizhyn, consecrated in 1880 and painted in 1907-08,[31] no longer exist.[32] We can learn something about them only from a few lines by an unidentified author:

> The church in Pechenizhyn, one of the largest in our land, with three heavy domes, was built in the style of our ancient churches. In painting it, Sosenko took the structure into account. He knew how to apply ornamentation: he achieved a harmony of coloristic meldings that gave the entire structure lightness. Especially beautiful was the main dome – like a Hutsul Easter egg.[33]

In the following year, 1909, the artist worked on several projects: paintings and the iconostasis of the church of the Dormition of the Mother of God in the village of Slavske (Skole raion, Lviv oblast), and the iconostases of the church of the Holy Trinity in Drohobych and the church of St. Onuphrius in Lviv. The church of the Dormition of the Mother of God in Slavske was constructed in brick in 1901, as recorded on the entrance to the church and in the schematism of the Lviv archeparchy.[34] The oldest church in the village dated to the seventeenth century and stood on Holytsia hill. Later, at the beginning of the eighteenth century, the villagers built a wooden church a bit lower on the hill.[35] In 1900, the parishioners took the church apart, and in the following year, thanks to the efforts of the pastor at that time, Fr. Yevstakhii Kachmarsky, they built a new one of brick, "the best church in the High Uplands (*Verkhovyna*)."[36] The church in Slavske was erected according to the plans of Vasyl

---

[30] "Novynky," *Dilo* (1908), no. 281:3.

[31] We are following the dating in Svientsits'kyi, *Modest Sosenko. Kataloh vystavy.*

[32] The church was destroyed by fire in 1944. Information from Vasyl Havryshchuk, *Pechenizhyn. Pam"iat' mynulykh stolit'* (Kolomyia: IuKS, 2011), 67.

[33] "Khystyianstvo, a postup," *Ruslan* (1911), no. 236 (NML Rk 3286, 1).

[34] "Tserkva Uspeniia P.D.M., mur. 1901, kan. viz. 1874....Parokh: Ievstakhii Kachmars'kyi...." *Shematyzm Arkhyieparkhii L'vivskoi 1910*, 385.

[35] "The oldest church, over three hundred years old, stood on a hill called 'Holytsia,' where the cemetery still is. Once a violent storm ripped the cross from the church and carried it to where the church now stands. The parishioners believe that this place was chosen by God for the church." "O. Iosyf Lemishchuk, parokh Slavs'ko. Opys parokhii Slavs'ko. 15.IX.1935 r.," TsDIAL, f. 408, op. 1, spr. 73 (1935-1937), 30-31.

[36] Ibid.

Nahirny, one of the most popular architects of the end of the nineteenth and beginning of the twentieth centuries. The church is of a type widely used by the architect: cross-shaped, with one dome placed upon a light-colored cylinder over the center of the cross. Nahirny had presented his plan for the church in Slavske at an exhibition of the Society for the Advancement of Ruthenian Art already in 1900.[37] Sosenko commenced working on the decoration of the church in Slavske, as already mentioned, in 1909. It is likely that among his assistants was Yuliian Butsmaniuk, then a student at the Kraków Academy of Fine Arts.[38] Pastor Kachmarsky wrote in 1909:

> Now M. Sosenko is finishing painting the church in Slavske. And really, whoever genuinely cares about art should spare no effort to come look at this work of a Ruthenian artist who understood its essence and who sees what is beautiful in the people and tries to convey it in painting.[39]

The first director of the National Museum in Lviv, Svientsitsky, mentioned the work of the artist in Slavske:

> He [Sosenko] worked most easily on the iconostases of the Basilian church [in Lviv] and in Slavske. In both cases he displayed such tender artistic tact in the inevitable – and in our conditions vital – compromises of the artist with everyday life and such great talent that it is not possible not to say a few words about them....
>
> Slavske, one of the most beautiful settlements of the Boiko Carpathians, the cradle of the creativity and work of the Ustyianovychi – father and son – had become even richer after Sosenko. He put into this church all the wealth of his creative spirit, all his ability as a draftsman-ornamentalist, decorator, and colorist. Before undertaking this artistic project he was already entirely prepared, because to his previous artistic training, experience, and knowledge, he added his profound feeling for the old ornament of the manuscripts and books of the

---

[37] *Kataloh vystavy Tovarystva dlia rozvoiu russkoi shtuky v L'vov r. 1900* (Lviv, 1900); see point 136.

[38] In a letter to Metropolitan Sheptytsky, Butsmaniuk wrote that he met Sosenko about 1908. Sosenko lent him money, which he was to pay back by helping paint the church in Slavske. The letter also mentions Fr. Kachmarsky, pastor at that time. TsDIAL, f. 358, op. 2, spr. 111, 115.

[39] Ievstakhii Kachmars'kyi, "V spravi tserkovnoho maliarstva," *Dilo* (1909), no. 235 (NML Rk 3285, 1).

fifteenth and sixteenth centuries of the Lviv museums – the Stavropegial and National museums – and also for the Byzantine-old Rus' ornament of Kyiv and ancient folk art. We must add to this his enthusiasm for our landscape, brightened by the clear, warm sun – and then Sosenko will stand before us, the singer of beauty in lines and the transition of colors of the rainbow. More than that, Sosenko wanted to find the connection between pictures and ritual, which in the distant past was so characteristic of our churches. To this end he made a fundamental study of the archeology of our ecclesiastical painting and ritual. And so he was able to give us not the commonplace drawings of the late baroque or contemporary realism, which look for some particular effects achieved by the great monumentalists of the past, but instead he creates works that stand out because of the noble simplicity of the draftsmanship of the ornaments and because of the variety of color. The wall painting of the church in Slavske is a very fine expression of the ability of the artist to express an immortal creative sprit with the aid of a small number of material means.[40]

Happily, the church survived the turbulent times of the First World War.[41] The renowned Polish ethnographer, Mieczysław Orlowicz, describing his journey through the Skole region, wrote his impressions of the church:

> The principal feature of the village of Slavske is its brick church.... It is one of only a few brick churches in the county, obviously in the Byzantine style with a dome - however, its significance lies not in its rather banal architecture, but in the frescos that cover the dome and the interior walls. The Ukrainian artist Sosenko painted them a few years previously.... Certainly no other village church can compare itself to the church in Slavske with regard to frescos. Its pictures could be an adornment of more than one Eastern or Western church in any large city. Also rather beautiful is the newly carved iconostasis which came from the workshop of Sovinsky in Drohobych. The icons of this iconostasis are also by the hand of Sosenko....[42]

---

[40] Svientsits'kyi, "Pam"iati Modesta Sosenka," 2-3.

[41] Several churches were lost in the Skole region in the first years of the war: in Zhupany, Koziova, and Klymets; the church in Ternavka was damaged by bullets. See the periodical *Svit* for 1917.

[42] "Zapysky," *Svit* (1917), no. 5:87-88, based on M. Orłowicz, "Wrażenia ze Skolskiego," *Kurjer Lwowski* (1917), no. 150:3-4.

Unfortunately, in 1944, as a result of the Soviet bombardment of Slavske, the interior decoration suffered a great deal;[43] in particular, the dome of the church was seriously damaged. For long after the war, the church remained in its damaged condition. Rain, snow, and wind negatively affected the frescos and the iconostasis. Only after the restoration of the dome and the repair of the roof did the urgent restoration of the paintings become possible. As a result of the delay, the original paintings and icons of the iconostasis were covered by an amateur attempt at restoration and were partially (in the dome) probably lost forever.[44] However, on the positive side, photographs were preserved that allow scholars to recreate the original appearance of the interior of the building and analyze it in the context of the stylistic experiments in monumental and easel-painting sacral art of the start of the twentieth century. Pictures in the photo archive of the National Museum in Lviv capture the stage when the interior decoration work was underway in the church, and other photos, made after the completion of the paintings, show how they used to look. The photographic evidence allows us to confirm that the contemporary version (amateur restorative works were undertaken from around the 1960s to the 1980s) retains in the main the author's compositional system of the imagery. Only the dome part of the church was completely repainted. As far as the icons of the iconostasis are concerned, it is evident that for some of them an attempt was made to restore the artist's original version. The carved decoration of the iconostasis lost its original appearance because it was covered with oil paint that seeped deep into the oak wood.

When analyzing the archival material and the contemporary repainting, we can detect a certain commonality between Sosenko's compositional methods and the painting of old-Rus' churches of the eleventh and twelfth centuries, which, incidentally, fit well with the

---

[43] Information from Fr. Andrew, pastor of Slavske, June 2007.

[44] The parishioners repaired the church themselves, since the Soviet authorities were not interested in funding the repair of a religious structure. Archival documentation confirms that Slavske was badly damaged during the war and that much in the city needed to be rebuilt. But among the reconstruction projects approved in 1948 the church was not even mentioned. "Protokoly zasidan' vykonavchoho komitetu Drohobyts'koi Oblasnoi Rady deputativ trudiashchykh ta zatverdzhennia rishen'. Rishennia no. 282 pro vidbudovu raitsentriv Strilky ta Slavs'ko," Derzahvnyi arkhiv L'vivs'koi oblasti, r-2022, op. 1, spr. 1959, 64-65.

Illustration 9.3: Painting in the dome of the church of the Dormition of the Mother of God in Slavske. Photo from the beginning of the twentieth century, NML photoarchive.

artistic and structural ideas of Nahirny's church. (See Illustration 9.3.) First of all, this pertains to the hierarchy of the images: at the highest point of the church - in the cupola - is depicted the Pantocrator accompanied by four angelic creatures; below are angels; on the pendentives are the evangelists. We also can discern similarities in the active use of ornamentation - both separating the individual registers and strengthening the symbolics of the figurative images with signs. The surfaces of both the arches and the walls of the church are filled with plaited ornamentation that suggest the miniatures of old manuscripts and incunabula. Especially valuable, and preserved in the photographs, is the artwork in the cupola area of the church where the center, in terms of both content and composition, is the half-length depiction of the Pantocrator in Glory. The face of Christ is distinct and professionally modelled; his right hand forms a gesture of blessing, his left holds a closed gospel book. The entire image is composed in a circular shape filled with spiral ornamentation that creates the illusion of depth. Emanating from the circle are four rays with plaited ornamentation that simultaneously are perceived to be the bars of a cross. They support the central part of the image in the cupola and unite it with the lower strip of art of the church – with the windows and the spaces between them. In a somewhat lighter manner, but no less precisely, the artist completed the expanse of the cupola between the rays and in the interstices between the windows, where he placed images of the cherubim. In the cylinder, side by side and all turned to the left, are full figures of angels. Under them is an ornamental band made up of circles joined together in a meander fashion within which are cross designs. The old photographs show that the paintings of the evangelists upon triangular vaultings with the two trumpeting angels were expressive and well thought through. A notable feature of Sosenko's work is the combination of fully modelled realistic faces with a flat, decorative treatment of the angels' clothing, halos, and wings. Orłowicz recalled that "in the pendentives are the heads of the four evangelists full of power and expression, among which the head of St. John is excellent."[45]

As a modernist artist, Sosenko was well versed in ornamental motifs. He arranged larger and even very small spaces successfully, with delicate taste and feeling, while respecting the programmatic, symbolic significance of the figurative paintings. Unfortunately, we are unable to analyze the color scheme, since, of course, it differed from the present polychrome. Even the fragments of the artist's work that we see in the faded black and white photographs make a strong impression.

---

[45] "Zapysky," 3-4.

Illustration 9.4: The iconostasis of the church of the Holy Trinity in Drohobych. Author's photo from 2009.

Returning to our only visual source, the archival photographs, we can assume that Sosenko painted the icons for the altar screen in Slavske over several years, probably beginning in his own studio in Lviv prior to 1909. One can gather from the photos that while he was working on the polychrome, some of the iconostasis was already partially filled with icons, notably the festal tier, the apostles' tier (with the exception of the central icon), and the prophets' tier. The work was fully completed considerably later, around 1911, as attested by the invoice for preliminary materials for the icons submitted to Sosenko by the woodcarver Dmytro Stashchyshyn.[46] It difficult to analyze the icons more concretely, because the images in the old photographs are not very clear. However, it may be confirmed that during the repainting of the artists' original composition, the festal icons were not preserved. Tragically, in May 2019, Sosenko's polychromes in Slavske were completely destroyed, the iconostasis dismantled, and only some of the icons were transferred for restoration.

There are reasons to doubt that Svientsitsky and Holubets listed all of Sosenko's works.[47] Sosenko is first mentioned as the author of the

---

[46] "Rakhunok dlia Vysokopovazhnoho Pana Modesta Sosenka u L'vovi," NML Rk 3252, 1-2.

[47] Svientsits'kyi, "Pam"iati Modesta Sosenka," 2-3. Svientsits'kyi, *Kataloh vystavy*. Holubets', "Modest Sosenko." M. Holubets', "Spadshchyna Modesta Sosenka," *Ukrains'ka dumka*

iconostasis of the church of the Holy Trinity in Drohobych in the Catholic newspaper *Nova Zoria* in 1939.[48] (See Illustration 9.4.) Later, in 1994, archpriest Volodymyr Yarema pointed to the work as an example of the innovative Ukrainian sacral art of the beginning of the twentieth century.[49] And in 1996 Larysa Hurevych studied the iconostasis and brought it to the attention of scholars, although the main theme of her study was the decorative carving of the altar screen.[50] The information about the church contained in Vasyl Slobodian's 1998 reference work on the churches of Przemyśl eparchy mentions Sosenko's painting of the iconostasis.[51] In 2003 the researcher Volodymyr Pohranychny attempted a detailed analysis of the iconographic program of Sosenko's altar screen.[52] However, none of these authors examined the church in the context of Sosenko's sacral creativity at the beginning of the twentieth century.

The present church of the Holy Trinity is a three-nave basilica with two low towers on the facade. It was once a Carmelite, Roman Catholic church that was given to the Basilian Fathers in 1790 and reconsecrated as a Greek Catholic church in 1808. The original church had one nave, but when it was adapted for the Greek rite the side naves were built on. Changes were also made to the interior, as a result of which, at the beginning of the twentieth century, the church walls were painted and a new altar screen erected; the latter has been preserved without change to this day.[53] The paintings were begun in 1909; all four icons of the principal (*namisnyi*) row bear that date as well as the artist's signature. The work

---

(1920), no. 13.

[48] O. Nazaruk, "Po nashykh monastyriakh u Drohobychi," *Nova Zoria* (9 April 1939), 9-11.

[49] Iarema, *Dyvnyi svit ikon*, 60.

[50] L. Hurevych, "Motyvy narodnoi derev"ianoi riz'by v ikonostasi tserkvy sv. Triitsi mista Drohobycha," in *Ukrains'ka narodna tvorchist' u poniattiakh mizhnarodnoi terminolohii: prymityv, fol'klor, amatorstvo, naiv, kich....Kolektyvne doslidzhennia za materialamy Druhykh Honchars'kykh chytan'*, ed. M. Selivachov (Kyiv: Muzei Ivana Honchara; Rodovid, 1996), 110-14.

[51] Vasyl' Slobodian, *Tserkvy Ukrainy. Peremys'ka ieparkhiia* (Lviv: Instytut ukrainoznavstva, 1998), 150-52.

[52] We do not share Pohranychny's views on the iconographic and theological interpretation of either individual icons or their integration into the whole of the iconostasis. What is valuable in his work is the detailed description of the iconostasis and careful measurements. V. Pohranychnyi, "Ikonostas tserkvy Sviatoi Triitsi u Drohobychi – vyznachna pam"iatka halyts'koho sakral'noho mystetstva," in *Sakral'ne mystetstvo Boikivshchyny. Zbirnyk statei prysviachenyi kafedral'nomu khramu Presviatoi Triitsi u m. Drohobych* (Drohobych, 2003), 151-90.

[53] The iconostasis was carved by Andrii Sarabai and a certain Gołębiowski. See V. Slobodian, "Novi znakhidky i doslidzennia pro Tserkvu Sviatoi Triitsi u Drohobychi," in *Sakral'ne mystetstvo Boikivshchyny. Zbirnyk statei* (Drohobych: Kolo, 2003), 302.

was probably completed in 1910 according to the dating on the central painting of Christ the High Priest.[54] The church is in good condition, and the images have completely preserved their original character.

The iconostasis of Holy Trinity church has a clearly expressed folk coloration, which is legible in the rhythm of simple decorative motifs of the carving. Open-work decor is present only on the royal doors and on the endings of individual components and of the altar screen as a whole. The carving around the icons of the iconostasis is associatively reminiscent of Hutsul carving or metal work (*mosiazhni vyroby*), but the traditional motif of vines and grape clusters is maintained for the royal doors. This bold resolution of the decor in relief works well with the iconography, which is no less bold, where the portraitist character of the realistically painted faces of the saints in the principal tier are combined with a flat treatment of their dress and attributes on a richly ornamented background that emulates the engraving of Ukrainian icons from the end of the sixteenth to the beginning of the eighteenth centuries. The two-tiered iconostasis is composed of the principal tier (from left to right: St. Nicholas, a deacon's door with a half-length painting of Archdeacon Lawrence, the royal doors with the Archangel Gabriel and the Mother of God, another deacon's door with Archdeacon Stephen, and the icon of the church - the Theophany, in which the Holy Trinity was manifested) and the festal tier, composed in a two-levelled scheme. On the upper level are the Nativity of the Mother of God, the Nativity of Christ, the Transfiguration, and the Descent of the Holy Spirit, while on the lower level are the Encounter, the Annunciation, the Flight into Egypt, the Resurrection of Lazarus, the Mourning, the Entry into Jerusalem, the Crucifixion, the Ascension, the Resurrection, and the Meeting of Christ with Mary Magdalene. Somewhat higher on the axis of symmetry is the central icon of Christ the High Priest accompanied by two angels, and above him the icon "not painted by human hands" (*acheiropoietos*), and at the top the Crucifixion. The principal painting of the Mother of God with child is, in our view, the artist's reworking of an icon from the collection of the Ivano-Frankivsk Regional Museum.[55] There is no mistaking that these are portraits from life. The model for the Mother of God was, naturally, Sosenko's wife Mykhailyna (*née* Leiter).

---

[54] Since I have not been able to examine the icons of the upper tiers myself, for the dating I have relied on Pohranychnyi, "Ikonostas tserkvy Sviatoi Triitsi u Drohobychi," 171.

[55] Ivano-Franivs'kyi kraieznavchyi muzei, inventory no. KM-104535/-62.

At the beginning of the twentieth century (1902), the church and monastery of St. Onuphrius in Lviv underwent changes in architecture and decoration. The church was rebuilt by Levynsky's construction firm in accordance with a design prepared by Edvard Kovach. It now became a three-nave triapsidal church with two symmetrically constructed sacristies adjoined to the central faceted apse. After the completion of the polychrome, work began on a new iconostasis. The carving was done in spring 1908 and for a four-year period beginning in 1907 Sosenko worked on the icons for the altar screen. In 1908 he completed the icons of the upper tiers, that is, of the prophets and the apostles.[56] The St. Onuphrius monastery functioned as a religious site until 1946 and was only returned to the Basilians in 1989. Since that time, the monastery complex has been under the attentive scrutiny of scholars.

The construction of the new iconostasis generally followed the instructions of Sosenko's clients to base it on a lost masterpiece of the baroque period (end of the seventeenth century), the iconostasis of the monastery of St. John the Forerunner in Krasnopushcha (destroyed by fire in 1899) and adapted to the measurements of the St. Onuphrius church.[57] Magnificent, voluminous carving plays a dominant role in the iconostasis. The paintings are seen as an interpolation in the general multitiered composition consisting of the lowest tiers (*predely*) and of the principal and festal icons as well as those of the apostles and prophets. In working out such a complex assignment, Sosenko remained faithful to his creative interpretations, which were oriented toward the iconography of bygone epochs and reconceived from the point of view of contemporary artistic tendencies. Even on the technical-technological level, the painter had recourse to his knowledge of old Ukrainian iconography. The iconostasis was executed on properly prepared linden boards; the painting was in tempera; and the gilding used genuine gold leaf.[58] The icons of the principal, apostles', and prophets' tiers were united by a golden ornamented background, while the upper sections of icons in the lowest and festal tiers were also gilded in the baroque manner. Sosenko also held to the traditional manner of presenting saints' garb, though there are also

---

[56] V. Vuitsyk, "Monastyr Sviatoho Onufriia u L'vovi," *Visnyk instytutu "Ukrzakhidproektrestavratsiia,"* no. 14 (2004): 57-58. Vuitsyk relied on archival materials concerning Basilian monasteries held by the manuscript division of the V. Stefanyk Lviv Scientific Library.

[57] The similarity to the iconostasis of Krasnopushcha has been noted by all previous scholars who have studied the St. Onuphrius iconostasis. These include Svientsits'kyi, "Pam''iati Modesta Sosenka," 3; and Vuitsyk, "Monastyr Sviatoho Onufriia," 57-58.

[58] Svientsits'kyi, "Pam''iati Modesta Sosenka," 3.

some departures from the usual iconography.[59] But in this complex, Sosenko's innovativeness came through as well: in the portraitist, realistic rendering of the apostles, the prophets, and the Mother of God; in his characteristic miniature landscapes in the backgrounds of the events taking place in the festal icons; and also in the saturated, complex ornamental insets based on folk art (especially in the halos). In the lowest tier we see: St. Nicholas, the Meeting of Christ and Mary Magdalene, the Apostle Peter before the Savior, and the Archangel Michael with a flaming sword. In the principal tier, we see: St. Josaphat, the Mother of God with child, Christ with an open gospel book, and then the patronal icon of St. Basil the Great. The festal tier is not complete. It has only six icons, placed according to their sequence in Holy Scripture: the Nativity of Christ, the Theophany, the Transfiguration, the Last Supper, the Resurrection, the Ascension, and the Descent of the Holy Spirit. Above the icon of the Last Supper is the "icon not painted by human hands." The apostles' tier is constructed as a pyramidal composition with a monumental icon of Christ the High Priest in the center. The busts of eight prophets are placed in six cartouches corresponding in size and form to the festal icons. As is traditional, the four evangelists and the Annunciation are painted on small ovals on the royal doors, while on the deacon's doors there is a certain dissonance between the painting and the carvings, where under the cartouches appear the symbols of the evangelists (it is presumed that these could have been prepared for the royal doors, but instead were affixed to the deacon's doors). Sosenko deals with the problem creatively - in the upper cartouches he paints archdeacons and in the lower, angels. His highly cultivated sense of color and his feel for style allow Sosenko to unite into a single whole the greatest achievements of the past in woodcarving with the modernist quests of the beginning of the twentieth century in sacral art. He did not take the simpler path of copying: he solved problems creatively.

During 1911-1913, Sosenko worked on decorating the wooden church of the Holy Resurrection in the village of Rykiv[60] (now Poliany, Zolochiv

---

[59] See R. Vasylyk, "Ikonostas tserkvy sv. Onufriia oo. Vasyliian u L'vovi," in *Ukrains'ka hreko-katolyts'ka tserkva i relihiine mystetstvo. Naukovyi zbirnyk materialiv IV Mizhnarodnoi naukovoi konferentsii* (Lviv: L'vivs'ka dukhovna semynariia sv. Dukha, 2006), 109-14.

[60] *Shematyzm Arkhyieparkhii L'vivskoi 1910*, 310-11. The church was long inactive, and now it is a parish of the Orthodox Church of Ukraine. The preparatory work on the iconostasis began at the end of 1909, and work carried on, as the dates on the icons indicate, until 1913. See "Rakhunok dlia Vysokopovazhnoho Pana Modesta Sosenka u L'vovi," NML, Rk 3252, 1-2.

Illustration 9.5: Painting in the dome of the church of the Holy Resurrection in Poliany (formerly Rykiv). Author's photo from 2009.

raion, Lviv oblast), built in 1903, and on painting the wooden church of St. Nicholas in the village of Koniushky (Rohatyn raion, Ivano-Frankivsk oblast), built in 1902 from Nahirny's design; the latter church burned down in 1944. Sosenko worked on these projects for several years. At present at least, we have no information about the church in Koniushky, not even about its general appearance, let alone about the paintings inside it.[61] But the church of the Holy Resurrection in Rykiv (Poliany) has been preserved to our day, as has Sosenko's work. In the NML photoarchive and manuscript division, one can consult the materials of Mykhailo Drahan, which include photos of the church at the beginning of the twentieth century and detailed notes regarding Sosenko's work on the interior. Also in the NML are the lawyer Volodymyr Starosolsky's materials of the court case between the artist and the parish community of the village of Rykiv regarding the decoration project. In the files are also older detailed photographs of the iconostasis and the paintings. Such abundant information from various sources makes it possible to explain certain moments in the decoration of the church. (See Illustration 9.5.)

---

[61] Slobodian, *Khramy Rohatynshchyny*, 86-87.

The church in Rykiv is trisectional with a developed transept, and was completed with three cupolas. The entrance to the church is from the south side. Researchers unfamiliar with Drahan's handwritten notes write that the only polychromic works of the artist that have survived to our day are in the cupola of the central dome.[62] According to archival materials, however, Sosenko did paint other parts of the church. In the church of the Resurrection the iconostasis and the icons of the side altars are also his.[63] Sosenko's work in Rykiv caused him considerable trouble, since the parish committee, unable to pay him, accused him of not adhering to the agreement. The conflict required judicial intervention.[64] Sosenko even mentioned the village's debt in his will.[65]

When formulating the composition of his paintings, Sosenko used the particularities of the architecture as his starting point. Plaited ornaments fill out figurative images. In the dome there is a rosette from which emanate ornamental strips that give order to the convex surface and create a place to be filled with figurative images, of four angels in motion. In the spaces between the windows, which are as if swaddled in ornaments, are the half-length depictions of the evangelists, with their symbols below them, in the lower part of the polychrome. In the small triangular fields resulting from the transition of a tetragon to an octagon there is a rich ornamental motif. Under the symbols of the evangelists on medallions, in the company of two trumpeting angels, are: over the altar – Christ; to the left - the Mother of God; to the right - John the Forerunner; and across - the Archangel Gabriel. The ornamental finishing in the lower part has not survived. Blue, green, and yellow shades harmoniously mingle and pass into each other and as a whole appear cordial and solemn. As with the painting in the church in Slavske, Sosenko was assisted in his work by Butsmaniuk.[66]

The iconostasis, of simple construction, consists of the principal and prophets' tier. The space in the church did not allow the erection of a high sanctuary partition with more tiers. On the principal tier on either side of the Mother of God and Christ are St. Nicholas and St. Basil the Great. The deacon doors are solid, with full-length depictions of the archdeacons.

---

[62] V. Radoms'ka, "Povernennia Modesta Sosenka," *Zerna* (1994), no. 1:38.

[63] "Materialy Drahana do Sosenka," NML, Rk 2935, 7-10.

[64] Letter of Mykhailo Martyniuk do V. Starosolsky, 24 January 1914, NML, Rk 2935, 5-6.

[65] NML, Rk 3277, 3-4.

[66] Mykhailo Khom"iak, ed., *Iuliian Butsmaniuk. Monohrafichna studiia* (Edmonton: Kanads'ke naukove tovarystvo im. Shevchenka, Oseredok na Zakhidniu Kanadu, 1982), 14.

Illustration 9.6: The Heart of Jesus. Photo from the beginning of the twentieth century, NML photoarchive.

Bust images of the prophets are included in little niches at the edge of the iconostasis and in circular cartouches over the deacon doors, level with the principal icons. The royal doors also retain paintings from the brush of Sosenko - the Annunciation and the evangelists. On the left side altar is a painting of the Protection of the Mother of God. The event takes place symbolically over the background of Rykiv, in which, just off to the right, is also an image of the village church. On the right side-altar is the icon of the feast to which the church is dedicated - the Resurrection.

The varying level of execution of the icons is striking; obviously, the artist's illness had an impact on how he finished individual works. The painting of the icons of St. Nicholas and St. Basil (1912, 1913) are quite detailed, as are the prophets. With regard to the Mother of God with child (1911), however, it is noticeable that the artist spent most of his time on the faces, but the halos appear to be unfinished, even though Sosenko was known for his special approach to their ornamentation. It is somewhat strange that the icons of the deacons appear to be almost as if they were not meant for this iconostasis. Their form seems to suggest that there was carving planned for the deacon's doors. It can be assumed that the limited financial means of the community also influenced the not wholly integrated appearance of the iconostasis. The polychromes of the beginning of the twentieth century make a strong aesthetic impression, but they clash with the contemporary amateur painting of other components of the interior. Even Sosenko's elegant icons become lost in the splendid iconostasis.

In 1912 the artist resided in Bilche Zolote where, according to his contemporaries, he worked on painting the church.[67] In the NML photo archive, a picture of the Heart of Jesus is also preserved that has the notation on the reverse "Bilche Zolote."[68] (See Illustration 9.6.) According to the schematism of 1910, there was a Prosvita reading club in the town headed by Fr. Sofron Levytsky, the pastor of the brick parish church of St. Michael. Also, two Christian organizations were active - the Brotherhood of the Sacred Heart of Jesus Christ and the Charitable Society of St. John the Merciful.[69] Thus it is quite possible that Sosenko executed the painting for the local brotherhood.

The last work of the artist in the field of sacral monumental art was the painting of the church of St. Nicholas in Zolochiv in 1913, including a series of icons for its iconostasis. The latter are now in the collection of the National Museum of Lviv and the Lviv Museum of the History of Religion

---

[67] Letter of Oleksa Novakivsky from Kraków to Metropolitan Sheptytsky, 4 September 1912, TsDIAL, f. 358, op. 2, spr. 67, 68. Svientsitsky note 434 (21 October 1912) and 470 (4 November 1912) in the NML diary; O. Shandura, "Za domovynoiu Sosenka," *Vpered* (1920) (NML, Rk 3291); Svientsits'kyi, "Pam"iati Modesta Sosenka"; Svientsits'kyi, *Modest Sosenko. Zbirna vystava*. The brick church of St. Michael survives, but we do not have sufficient information about changes to the interior. I suspect that Sosenko's painting has been lost.

[68] NML 10466.

[69] *Shematyzm Eparkhii Stanyslavivskoi 1910*, 178-79.

Illustration 9.7: Detail of the painting in the sanctuary of the church of St. Nicholas in Zolochiv. Author's photo from 2008.

(LMHR). The present church has survived to our day with many reconstructions, the last of which dates to the beginning of the twentieth century. A modest-sized brick church with thick walls and narrow windows, it consists of a rectangular narthex, nave, and a semicircular apse. Also added on to the building were a porch and a sacristy. The structure is covered by a gable roof with a false cupola over the central area. The exact date of the building of the church is not known, but the architectural form bears witness to an archaic origin with various interventions over time. Within the interior, ribbed vaults have been preserved in the nave and the apse. With the appointment as pastor of Fr. Stepan Yuryk at the beginning of the twentieth century, the church again underwent reconstruction. Mainly the interior was altered, and by 1913 the church acquired a distinctively national character.[70] Fr. Yuryk was in close contact with the head of the Greek Catholic church – Metropolitan Andrei Sheptytsky – and the National Museum, so it is likely that the

---

[70] N. Hupalo, *Tserkva Sviatoho Mykolaia: Istorychnyi aspekt (Tserkva Sviatoho Mykolaia u Zolochevi* (Lviv: Misioner, 2007), 7-17.

metropolitan was the one who recommended Sosenko to paint the church and renovate the iconostasis.

Polychromes cover the walls and vaults of the church. The Gothic ribbed vaulting forced Sosenko into an absolutely different approach to the composition of his designs than in most of his earlier works. The artist accented ornamentation in his polychromes. On the pilasters of the central space, on the right and on the left, he painted luxurious stylized plant compositions in an intricate palette from cool to warm; they are reminiscent of a distinctive vase or of the Tree of Life, which is frequently encountered in folk art, but here filled with religious content, containing such elements as the cross, heart, and candelabra. In between the ribs of the ceiling is a different plant ornamentation in which one can also discern the influence of folk art, especially that of central Ukraine. It masterfully instantiates the theme of Christ's love through interweaved images and the repetition of the motif of a heart with a cross in it. In the polychromes of Zolochiv we notice, aside from various interesting plant ornaments, other ornamentation that is familiar from earlier works of the artist: plaited and geometric compositions that he used for the lower registers and for the transitions among architectural elements. (See Illustration 9.7.) The composition in the sanctuary was somewhat more easily resolved; here, besides more restrained ornamental insertions, were added angels in motion. In the frescos in the choir loft is an unexpected composition of the Mother of God Oranta in a flaming circle. We are unable to fully appreciate Sosenko's color achievements in the church of St. Nicholas because a considerable part of the painting was already lost when restoration began (1999). The painting on the vaulted ceiling and the walls was damaged by moisture and mold. In the altar area, the figures of angels were destroyed. The coat of paint was falling away, as was the very plaster with the polychrome. Today the presentable interior of the church is the result of restorative toning and reconstruction.[71]

During the pastorship of Fr. Yuryk it became necessary to renovate the baroque iconostasis. This entailed changing the festal tier (perhaps)[72] and to some extent the principal icon tier. Sosenko restored the paintings

---

[71] Taras Otkovych, "Restavratsiia nastiinykh rozpysiv Modesta Sosenka v tserkvi sv. Mykolaia v Zolochevi," *Biuleten'. Informatsiinyi vypusk* (Natsional'nyi naukovo-doslidnyi restavratsiinyi tsentr Ukrainy, L'vivs'kyi filial), no. 1 (10) (2008): 133-34.

[72] It cannot be established whether the iconostasis had a festal tier or not. See V. Zhyshkovych, "Ikonostas tserkvy Sviatoho Mykolaia u Zolochevi: Istorychnyi aspekt," in *Tserkva Sviatoho Mykolaia u Zolochevi*, ed. R. Hrymaliuk et al. (Lviv: Misioner, 2007), 29.

Illustration 9.8: Detail of St. Andrew the First-Called. NML collection.

on the royal doors,[73] replacing the old, destroyed images with new ones that he painted himself. The icons of the tier of festal icons were completely changed. Now in their stead were paired icons of saints, including some Ukrainian saints – Ss. Anthony and Theodosius of the Caves, Ss. Constantine and Helen,[74] Ss. Cyril and Methodius,[75] Ss. Volodymyr and Olha. The outer icons of the principal tier accented the importance of the Ukrainian Greek Catholic church in Galician society and culture. A painting of St. Andrew the First-Called[76] bears some resemblance to Metropolitan Sheptytsky, and there is also a painting of the priest-martyr Josaphat Kuntsevych. (See Illustration 9.8.) The cartouches over the deacon's doors and over the outer icons[77] are filled with refined, stylized national motifs. A certain compensation for the absence of the festal icons in the renewed iconostasis is seen in the two oval icons of the Annunciation[78] and the Veneration of the Angels,[79] which were obviously hung in the place of the outer icons of the principal tier. In 1913 Sosenko also produced two icons, of the Mother of God with Child and St. Josaphat, for the church of the Ascension of Our Lord in the village of Pobochi (Zolochiv raion, Lviv oblast). However, only the icon of the Mother of God is accessible for viewing; the icon of St. Josaphat has been covered by an icon of St. Nicholas for over sixty years, and we only know about it from an archival photograph.

In Soviet times, this church, as most other houses of worship, was not used for its intended purpose. A museum of atheism was established here instead. The iconostasis was dismantled, smashed, and tossed into the waste bin, whence museum workers from Lviv and conscientious parishioners at their own risk saved individual components and preserved them to our day.

Recently another church with monumental painting possibly from Sosenko's brush was photodocumented. In the village of Polove (Radekhiv raion, Lviv oblast), a wooden church of the Descent of the Holy Spirit has been preserved. It contains paintings in the presbytery that were completed around 1912. Although no documentary confirmation has been found to date, the style of the polychrome in certain places suggests Sosenko's authorship. The ornamental strip from the tier of meanders, in which crosses are painted, is also seen in his churches in Slavske and Zolochiv. The decorative frieze with the secession-style protracted profiles

---

[73] NML D-1135.
[74] LHMR Zh-397.
[75] LHMR Zh-371.
[76] NML Zh-2099.
[77] NML D-1136/1, D-1137/1.
[78] NML Zh-1807.
[79] NML, Zh-1806.

Illustration 9.9: Detail of the painting in the sanctuary of the church of the Descent of the Holy Spirit in Polove. Author's photo from 2009.

of the heads of angels with wings are also associated with his monumentalist artistic discoveries (an analogy can be traced in the plans for a polychrome in the "Wallachian," i.e., Dormition church in Lviv). (See Illustration 9.9.) It is, of course, also possible that the artwork may have been done by another artist who was very familiar with Sosenko's style. However, it was not Butsmaniuk, who had often been Sosenko's assistant in monumental works. The question remains open for now. Furthermore, some pictures in the archive of the NML still demand scrupulous research.[80] Some photos still need to be identified with a certain church, which is time-consuming, since churches have been destroyed. It is possible that these are pictures of paintings in the churches of Bilche Zolote, Koniushky, or Pechenizhyn, about which we do not at present have enough information.

Some unrealized proposals of Sosenko's are preserved that were prepared in an open tender for the renovation of the interior of the Dormition church around 1910-1912.[81] Although they were rejected by the commission of the Stauropegial Institute, they still constitute an interesting episode in Sosenko's creative evolution. The designs are

[80] Ft 10454-55, Ft 10457, Ft 10468, Ft 10471, Ft 10474-75, Ft 10478.
[81] NML Hn 1880, Hn 1885-86, Hn 1888-90.

Illustration 9.10: Detail of the design for painting the church of the Dormition in Lviv.

executed for the most part in pastels or gouache with droplets of bronze paint that upon completion were to be replaced by gilding. The refined color composition – with blue predominating, but in conjunction with gold – is most characteristic of this particular artist. It is a testimony to Sosenko's gifts as a colorist that he could operate with the whole spectrum of colors yet not ruin, but rather enhance, the architectonics of the building. The accentuated linear effect and decorativeness, the exquisite symbolic ornament together with the creative placement of figures that are reminiscent of old Ukrainian iconographic models, the bold composition of characteristics of Eastern and Western iconography – these are testament to Sosenko's status as a representative and original interpreter of modern art. Sosenko's work in stained-glass windows, especially as manifest in the church in Pidberiztsi, is also significant. The designs for the Dormition church proposed stained-glass windows of the Nativity of Christ, the Mother of God, and an Archangel. (See Illustration 9.10.)

One of the designs for an iconostasis[82] allows us to see how well Sosenko knew the examples of old Ukrainian art in the NML's collection and how he creatively reworked them and included them in a new artistic interpretation of the iconostasis composition. The works taken into consideration were the Crucifixion from Sniatyn,[83] as well as figures standing by the crucifix, the Mother of God[84] and St. John the Divine,[85] dating from the sixteenth century from the Kolomyia region and Dolyna (Ivano-Frankivsk oblast). This constitutes a renewal of the national sacral patrimony, which became one of the fundamental sources of Sosenko's inspiration.

Some of Sosenko's religious paintings are no longer extant. Icons perished with the destruction of churches. Some works that had been preserved in the NML were assigned to "special deposit" (*spetsfond*) in the 1950s and were burned:[86] the Nativity of Christ, oil on canvas, 50 x 46 cm; the Mother of God, tempera on board, 11 x 10.5 cm; the Savior, tempera on board, 11 x 10.5 cm; the Savior Acheiropoietos from 1910, oil on board.

Sosenko also took orders for individual icons, as we know from his correspondence and Svientsitsky's notes. Fr. Ioan Aleksandrovych, the pastor of Khmeleva (Zalishchyky raion, Ternopil oblast), and Fr. Ksenofont Sosenko, a relative and pastor of Koniukhy (Koziv raion, Ternopil oblast), requested an icon of St. Nicholas in the style of Eastern iconography.[87] Sosenko's innovative approach to icon painting and his

---

[82] NML Hn 1887.

[83] NML I 146.

[84] NML I 1718, I 1450.

[85] NML I 1719, I 1449.

[86] V. Arofikin and D. Posats'ka, *Kataloh vtrachenykh eksponativ Natsional'noho muzeiu u L'vovi* (Kyiv and Lviv: RVA "Triumf," 1996), 35.

[87] Letter of Ioan Aleksandrovych from Khmeleva to Modest Sosenko, 12 June 1904, NML, Rk 2938, 4; letter of Ksenofont Sosenko from Koniukhy to Modest Sosenko, undated, NML,

attempt at combining Eastern and Western iconography in the image of St. Barbara, which the artist painted at the request of nuns from the village of Ozeriany near Chortkiv, failed to please and was returned to him.[88] Around 1912 he painted an icon of the Protection of the Mother of God, which was commissioned by Bishop Nykyta Budka and taken to Canada in that year.[89] A compositional replica with some changes in the landscape and people kneeling in veneration is found at the side altar of the church in Rykiv. Svientsitsky noted that in the left corner of this work Sosenko painted himself on his knees in a prayerful pose with his hands covering his face.[90] A private collection holds a large icon of the Dormition of the Mother of God from 1912 that earlier was known only from an archival photo; we can detect a compositional similarity with designs for painting the Dormition church in Lviv. The picture of the Sacred Heart of Jesus, about which Svientsitsky wrote[91] and which was painted for the church in Zhovtantsi (Kamianka Buzka raion, Lviv oblast), has a long history. It was painted to replace the seventeenth-century icon of the Dormition of the Mother of God, after which the church was named, because the old icon, as an object of considerable value, was to be transferred to the museum.[92] But since the exchange did not actually take place, Svientsitsky requested that Sosenko's icon be returned to the museum. Sosenko also collaborated with the organization Dostava, and it is known that he completed a picture for them of St. Josaphat, which Svientsitsky borrowed for a posthumous exhibition of the artist in 1920.[93]

Thus we see that only a small portion of Sosenko's monumental works in sacral culture has survived to our day and that other works remain to be located. Still, there are things we can say about his art. First, we are able to identify with some precision the sources he drew on in the ornamentation of churches. One is the ornamentation of the old manuscripts in the Stauropegial Museum in Lviv and in the collection of manuscripts from Galician Ukraine from the sixteenth and seventeenth

Rk 2938, 11-12.

[88] Letter from the pastor of Ozeriany, 25 June 1903, NML Rk 2938, 1-2; letter of Sosenko from Paris to the pastor, 30 June 1903, NML Rk 2938, 3-4. See also Voloshyn, "Modest Sosenko," 207-09.

[89] At present the icon is preserved in the church of the Protection of the Mother of God in Winnipeg, where it was donated as the patronal icon by Nykyta Budka. Information from Fr. Michael Kwiatkowski, 2009.

[90] Svientsits'kyi, Modest Sosenko. Zbirna vystava.

[91] Svientsits'kyi, Modest Sosenko. Zbirna vystava.

[92] NML diary, notes 408 (14 July 1913), 470 (22 August 1913), and 501 (17 September 1913).

[93] Svientsits'kyi, Modest Sosenko. Zbirna vystava. NML diary, note 357 (13 October 1920).

centuries at the NML, which Sosenko processed and painted while he was on staff at the NML in 1909 (although this work was only published in 1923, after his death).[94] The characteristic decorative motifs from these manuscripts lay at the basis of his plaited ornamentation and free plant compositions. However, in Sosenko's work we do not encounter any directly borrowed motif - only the artist's own versions. Typically, Sosenko would insert into his plant ornamentation the symbolism of the Sacred Heart – the veneration of which was spreading in the Ukrainian Greek Catholic church at the beginning of the twentieth century especially through the efforts of the Basilian order.[95]

There can be no doubt that Sosenko was also familiar with old Ukrainian monumental art. When he visited Kyiv he probably viewed the interiors of the great churches of St. Sophia, the Golden-domed St. Michael Monastery, and St. Cyril. Also, it was Sosenko who discovered sixteenth-century frescos in the monastery of St. Onuphrius in Lavriv (Staryi Sambir raion, Lviv oblast).[96] What he saw could not have left him indifferent and not have influenced his own practice as a monumentalist.

Sosenko's recourse to ornamental traditions of the past is not accidental, given the important role of ornament in the art of the modern. It was actively adapted to various types of art, where it served not merely as decoration, but bore a profound aesthetic and sensual charge. The functional and symbolic aesthetic significance of ornament in Sosenko's sacral legacy connects him closely to the approach to ornament found in the art of Byzantium, Kyivan Rus', and sixteenth- and seventeenth-century Ukraine. Sosenko understood this well as he maintained hierarchy in the churches not only with figurative images, but with ornaments as well.

A distinctive characteristic of sacral art is the stability of its iconography, as demanded by tradition. Sosenko, while continually searching, also tried as much as possible to retain the features of the traditional iconography of any given picture or subject. Without breaching the logic or symbolism of an image, he would come up with successful compositional, pictorial, and ornamental inventions that he could apply repeatedly in various works. Examples of this are his icons of the Nativity

---

[94] Modest Sosenko, *Prykrasy halyts'kykh rukopysiv XVI i XVII vv. Stavropyhiis'koho muzeia zrysovani Modestom Sosenkom (†1920)* (Lviv, 1923), with 18 plates.

[95] See O. Semchyshyn-Huzner, "Obraz 'Sertse Khrystove' v ukrains'komu zhyvopysi pochatku XX stolittia," in *Ukrains'ka hreko-katolyts'ka tserkva i relihiine mystetstvo*, 103-09.

[96] Mykhailo Vavryk, *Po vasyliians'kykh manastyriakh* (Toronto: Vydavnytstvo i drukarnia oo. Vasyliian, 1958), 82.

of Christ (on iconostases in Drohobych and Zolochiv), of the Theophany (on iconostases in Drohobych and Lviv), and of the Mother of God (the icon from the Ivano-Frankivsk Regional Museum and in the principal row of the iconostasis in Drohobych). Further, there are ways he solved the decoration of domes (polychromes in Pidberiztsi, Slavske, Rykiv, and an unidentified church in an old photo), the evangelists on the pendentives (Pidberiztsi, Slavske), the Mother of God Oranta (polychrome in Zolochiv, design of an iconostasis in the NML graphics collection, an ex libris), Christ the High Priest (iconostasis in Lviv, iconostasis design in the NML graphics collection), the ornamental background behind Christ and the Mother of God (dome in Slavske, polychrome in Zolochiv, designs for the dome of the Dormition church), and the angels surrounding God the Father or Christ (painting of the sanctuary conch in Pidberiztsi, the design for painting the Dormition church).

In sum, from the polychromes, the designed and completed iconostases, as well as the icons which have been preserved or photographed, it is clear that Sosenko possessed an impressive command of both Western and Eastern iconography. He learned Western iconography in Kraków, Munich, and Paris, where he became familiar with rich collections of European art and copied works of Renaissance masters for Metropolitan Sheptytsky. After his return from studies abroad, Sosenko stayed in close contact with the directorship of the National Museum and its founder, the metropolitan. Later he became involved with the restoration of sacred art at the museum. He added to its collection of icons, bringing items from locations where he was working on churches. Immersed in ancient Ukrainian sacral art, Sosenko also drew on the traditions of Byzantine-Rus' art. Reaching back to the cultural achievements of the past was typical of the turn of the twentieth century, but Sosenko's knowledge of the old traditions surpassed that of other Ukrainian artists of his time, based as it was on the study of icons, manuscripts, incunabula, textiles, and folk art (embroidery, carving).

Professional training in European academies and his innate gifts, together with experience gained in Galicia, formed Sosenko as an original and unique artist who breathed new life into Ukrainian sacral art of the twentieth century. His brilliant talent as a monumentalist and his exquisite taste inspired prominent contemporaries like Yulian Butsmaniuk and Mykhailo Boichuk, as well as the next generation of Ukrainian monumentalist artists like Demian Horniatkevych, Yurii Mahalevsky, and Mykhailo Osinchuk. His creative directions have thus not lost their relevance for today.

Sacral Needlework in Eastern Galicia:
Social and Cultural Aspects (Late Nineteenth and Early Twentieth Centuries)
Natalia Dmytryshyn

Sacral needlework,[1] often called "needle painting,"[2] is an expression of Christian worship; along with icon-painting, frescoes, or wood carvings, it is considered an artistic reading of Holy Scripture, with a complex symbolism and a profound content. One of the elements of this content is that over the centuries sacral needlework has been the sphere of Christian women, a fact that has found reflection in apocryphal literature,[3] folklore, and the iconographic tradition.[4] In the early church, when the access of women to the public cult was fundamentally restricted, sacral needlework served as a vehicle allowing women access to church service and to the personal and positive expression of their religious aspirations.[5] The study of this stratum of Christian culture makes it possible to see the female trace, underestimated and marginalized for long centuries by the patriarchal social canon.[6]

The range of items that required sacral needlework was not fixed; over the centuries it expanded and underwent modification as services and the textiles required for them grew more complex. The practical application and symbolism of the needlework was determined by the Eastern Christian (Byzantine) canons as well as by popular notions about the

---

[1] This chapter has been translated by John-Paul Himka.

[2] Ernst Diez, "Moldavian Portrait Textiles," *The Art Bulletin* 10, no. 4 (1928): 378.

[3] The most widespread apocryphal motif is the participation of women in the creation of images not made by human hands (*acheiropoietoi*) on textiles. The legend of St. Veronica became deeply rooted in Ukrainian piety. See Ivan Franko, *Apokryfy i liegendy z ukrains'kykh rukopysiv*, vol. 2 (Lviv: Nakladom Naukovoho Tovarystva im. Shevchenka, 1899), 237-39.

[4] The depiction of the Mother of God with a spindle and yarn became incorporated into the Eastern Christian, including Ukrainian, iconography of the Annunciation; it symbolized the ideal of the unity of handiwork and motherhood.

[5] Tat'iana Bernshtam, "Shit'e i devy-vyshival'shchitsy v tserkovnom i narodnom simvolizme," *Zhenshchina i veshchestvennyi mir kul'tury u narodov Rossii i Evropy. Sbornik Muzeia antropologii i etnografii*, vol. 62, ed. T.A. Bernshtam (St. Petersburg: Nauka, 1999), 226.

[6] Anne-Marie Pelletier, *Khrystyianstvo ta zhinky. Dvadtsiat' stolit' istorii* (Kyiv: Dukh i Litera, 2016), 11-14. This is a translation of *Le christianisme et les femmes*.

aesthetics and beauty appropriate to God's temple. The early baroque era essentially defined the set of sacral needlework items. The Russian anthropologist Tatiana Bernshtam has classifed them into three categories.[7]

To the first category belong items connected with the liturgy: shrouds, chalice covers, *diskos* covers, and *aers* (cloths to cover the Holy Mysteries). To the second category belong textiles for adornment of sacred space: altar cloths, banners, towels, *podeas* (*pidvisni peleny*; decorative cloths to adorn icons, often with embroidery that thematically matched the icons they adorned), *katapetasmas* (curtains behind the royal doors), altar cloths (*endytes*). To the third category belong clerical vestments: *sticharia, epitrachelia*, cinctures, *epimanikia, epigonatia*, sakkoses, *omophoria, phelonia*, dalmatics, and *oraria*.

Sacral needlework is also classified by what is depicted: figurative/iconographic or ornamental representation.[8] In liturgical items figurative needlework dominated, while ornamental needlework dominated in the decoration of the church.

This study strives to analyze the sacral needlework of Eastern Galicia in the context of the deeper strata of Christian culture as well as of the particularities of the space and time under investigation. The chronological focus will be the late nineteenth and early twentieth centuries.

The Institutionalization of Sacral Needlework

Scholars of modern nationalism have long noted the relevance and productivity of the approach that analyzes the new national canon through the prism of its construction by the intellectual elite of that era.[9] The appeal to the ethnographic cultural substratum was an all-European phenomenon that underwent various stages and processes: an interest in antiquities and collecting was transformed into a completely modern understanding of their role for contemporary culture. Discussions about

---

[7] Tat'iana Bernshtam, "Shit'e i devy-vyshival'shchitsy," 227.

[8] Pauline Johnstone, *The Byzantine Tradition in Church Embroidery* (Chicago: Argonaut, Inc., Publishers, 1967), 27–48.

[9] See John-Paul Himka, "The Construction of Nationality in Galician Rus': Icarian Flights in Almost All Directions," in *Intellectuals and the Articulation of the Nation*, ed. Ronald Grigor Suny and Michael D. Kennedy (Ann Arbor: The University of Michigan Press, 1999), 109-64; Jaroslav Hrytsak, "History of Names: A Case of Constructing National Historical Memory in Galicia, 1830 – 1930s," *Jahrbücher für Geschichte Osteuropas* 49, no. 2 (2001): 163-77.

the search for "our own style" in art migrated from all-Galician exhibitions of folk culture to the columns of newspapers and specialized periodicals, and ultimately resulted in processes of institutionalization.

In Eastern Galicia, the Eastern Christian tradition was inherited primarily by the Greek Catholic church. Its synods regulated the development of sacral art, including liturgical needlework, in light of canonical principles and in accordance with a larger vision. The Lviv provincial synod of 1891 instructed the faithful as follows: "Our churches, as the dwelling places of the living God and the havens of angels, should be built and decorated in such a way as is appropriate for such a Guest, i.e., they should be built with all splendor possible, decorated inside and out, equipped with all holy vessels and implements, and furnished with sufficient income for maintenance."[10] The synod mandated uniformity in the colors of sacerdotal vestments. White and all colors close to it, such as gold, silver, and shades of white, were to be worn on Sundays and all the great feasts. Red vestments were for the feast days of holy martyrs. Violet-colored vestments were for Christmas eve and Theophany eve as well as for Great Lent and Passion week. Black vestments were to be used in services and liturgies for the departed. For everyday usage, mixed colors were to be used.

Complementing the activities of the church itself, at the turn of the twentieth century a plethora of various organizations emerged – cultural societies as well as workshops and cooperatives, both secular and religious, both purely artistic and industrial, constructed along old caste or new gender lines – which promoted in various ways the production, distribution, and popularization of sacral products for ritual usage.

The metropolitan of the Greek Catholic church at that time, Andrei Sheptytsky (1865-1944), established the conceptual directives for the development of Eastern Christian sacral art in Galicia. He called upon his countrymen to view artistic artifacts "not as archeological monuments, but as the foundation of national culture for future centuries."[11] His personal enthusiasm for works of art (which he probably received from his mother, Zofia Fredro Szeptycka, herself a talented painter) first evolved into systematic collecting, and then, in 1905, he founded the

---

[10] See *Chynnosti i rishenia ruskoho provyntsial'noho sobora v Halychyni otbuvshoho sia vo L'vovi v rotsi 1891* (Lviv: Iz typohrafii Stavropyhiiskoho Instytuta, 1896), 183, 187-89.

[11] Andrei Sheptyts'kyi, "Z istorii i probliem nashoi shtuky. Vyklad vyholoshenyi na s'viati otvorennia 'Natsional'noho Muzeia' dnia 13 hrudnia 1913 r.," in *Sakral'ne mystetstvo z kolektsii "Studion". Kataloh tvoriv XVI-XX st.* (Lviv: Monastyr Studiis'koho Ustavu Arkhystratyha Mykhaila, 1991), 17.

Church Museum, which in 1913 acquired the status of a National Museum. Professional art historians as well as enthusiasts of the national revival worked under its sponsorship. The collection of sacral textiles of the National Museum was formed as a result of numerous expeditions, which found items that were no longer usable in the vestries of Galician towns and villages;[12] the collection was also enhanced by items purchased at craft exhibitions, donated by collectors, or otherwise obtained.

An interesting case is that of Vadym Shcherbakivsky (1876-1957). It provides insight into the connections between the Dnieper-Ukrainian and Galician artistic intelligentsia and at the same time into the similarity of the challenges of, and solutions for, studying and preserving the cultural heritage. Shcherbakivsky began his career as a scholar with the City Museum of Antiquities and Arts in Kyiv, in whose establishment in 1899 he played an active role. Oksana Franko, who researched his biography, noted: "It was Vadym Shcherbakivsky himself who came up with the idea to supplement the ethnographic collections of the museum with unique items of ancient church embroidery."[13] In 1907 Shcherbakivsky happened to be in Lviv, where he met with Metropolitan Sheptytsky. The metropolitan proposed that he work for the Church Museum. "He spent a rather long time asking me about my work and intentions and then offered me work in his museum.... This determined that I stay on longer in Lviv."[14] Travelling through Galicia and Bukovina, the young scholar photographed and sketched churches and iconostases. He enriched the collection of the National Museum with valuable items of sacral needlework from the environs of Lviv itself.[15] Indeed, church textiles

---

[12] Mariia Helytovych, "Davnia dekoratyvna tkanyna," in *Natsional'nyi muzei u L'vovi: 100 rokiv. Al'bom*, ed. Mariia Helytovych et al. (Kyiv: Rodovid, 2005), 91.

[13] Oksana Franko, "Arkhiv Vadyma Shcherbakivs'koho u Prazi," in *100 rokiv kolektsii Derzhavnoho muzeiu ukrains'koho narodnoho dekoratyvnoho mystetstva. Zbirnyk naukovykh prats'*, ed. M. Selivachov et al. (Kyiv: ArtEk, 2002), 44.

[14] Vadym Shcherbakivs'kyi, "Moie perebuvannia ta pratsia v muzeiu o. mytropolyta A. Sheptyts'koho u L'vovi," in *Dvaitsiat'piat'-littia Natsional'noho Muzeiu u L'vovi*, ed. I. Svientsitskii (Lviv: Dilo, 1930), 22.

[15] "At the beginning of 1909 I was in Zhyravka near Lviv. From there I brought, aside from photographs of the church and belltower, also some church antiquities. In that same period I brought from the village of Vovkiv quite a few very old manuscripts and vestments, in recompense for which the director [of the Church Museum] gave the church new items. The most important acquisition for the museum was a fairly small, wonderful old embroidered shroud, for which the management of the museum gladly exchanged a showy new one.... From here I returned on foot to Lviv. When I brought all my acquisitions to the museum, the director was astonished that I had found so much here, right next to Lviv." Ibid., 23.

constituted the largest group of items he acquired for the museum.[16] Later Vadym Shcherbakivsky worked up the material from his expeditions for publication, and one of the chapters was devoted to church vestments.[17]

The search for a "Ruthenian style"[18] in ecclesiastical and secular art was taken up by the Association for the Development of Ruthenian Art, founded in 1898 in Lviv. The association's initiators were Mykhailo Hrushevsky, Ivan Trush, Vasyl Nahirny, and Yuliian Pankevych. The association's advertising poster proclaimed: "The goal of the association is to elevate our art and create a Ruthenian school of fine arts....The association executes all manner of work from the sphere of artistic painting after compositions of its members, namely religious pictures for iconostases, altars, banners, and tetrapods as well as shrouds and other things."[19] Also in this period the Ruthenian Craft Workshop (*Rus'ka rukodil'nia*) of Volodymyr Ustiensky sold "church paraphernalia," including *phelonia*, banners, shrouds, and flags.[20] In Zolochiv in the interwar period there was the cooperative Selection of Church Embroidered Items (*Vybir tserkovnykh vyshyvanykh richyi*) of Mykola Alyskevych, which specialized in embroidery exclusively.[21]

The companies Ryznytsia ("Vestry") and Dostava specialized in providing practically everything that was necessary for worship services. "The goal was as follows: to furnish churches solid wares at appropriate prices, to elevate native industry and art, and to use the net profit to help poor churches or the families of priests."[22] Ryznytsia (also called the

---

[16] Iaroslava Pavlychko, "Ekspedytsiini zdobutky l'vivs'koho periodu Vadyma Shcherbakivs'koho v diliantsi sakral'noho mystetstva," *Istoriia relihii v Ukraini. Tezy povidomlen' V mizhnarodnoho kruhloho stolu*, part 3, ed. V. Haiuk et al. (Lviv-Kyiv: Lohos, 1995), 314.

[17] Vadym Shcherbakivs'kyi, "Tserkovna odezha," in *Ukrains'ke mystetstvo: Vybrani neopublikovani pratsi*, ed. V. Ul'ianovs'kyi (Kyiv: Lybid', 1995), 117-18.

[18] Oles' Noha, *Ukrains'kyi styl' v tserkovnovu mystetstvi Halychyny kintsia XIX-pochatku XX stolit'* (Lviv: Ukrains'ki tekhnolohii, 1999), 49.

[19] The poster is reproduced in ibid., 73. Another advertisement of the Association can be found at http://uk.wikipedia.org/wiki/Товариство_для_розвою_руської_штуки (accessed 29 June 2018).

[20] The advertising poster of the Ruthenian Craft Workshop of Volodymyr Ustiensky is reproduced in Noha, *Ukrains'kyi styl' v tserkovnovu mystetstvi*, 132.

[21] Tsentral'nyi derzhavnyi istorychnyi arkhiv Ukrainy u L'vovi (TsDIAL), f. 301, op. 1, spr. 19, folios 19, 26, 150.

[22] This quotation, which was published in the newspaper *Nyva* in 1909, is cited from Oles' Noha and Roman Iatsiv, *Mystets'ki tovarystva, ob"iednannia, uhrupuvannia, spilky L'vova 1860-1998* (Lviv: Ukrains'ki tekhnolohii, 1998), 43.

„Ризница" въ Самборѣ.

Illustration 10.1: Postcard showing the Ryznytsia building in Sambir (beginning of the twentieth century). Source: TsDIAL, f. 428, op. 1, spr. 57, 19.

Association for the Manufacture and Sale of Church Vestments,[23] and after 1915 Ukrainian Ryznytsia)[24] was founded in Sambir in 1893. Its first director was the Greek Catholic priest Fr. Teodor Ripetsky. The social composition of the company's members consisted of priests, women from priestly families, and secular intelligentsia. From Ryznytsia's statute we learn that it had two main directions in its activity: it produced and sold vestments and church paraphernalia, and also maintained a savings and credit association.[25] The company bought a building in Sambir which housed a workshop, store, and living quarters (on 5 Kopernik St.). (See Illustration 10.1.) It established branches in Lviv (20 Rynok Square; as of 1920 – 43 Rynok Square), Przemyśl (14 Rynok Square), and Stanyslaviv (8 Kazimierz Square). The company survived until 1939.[26]

---

[23] This name figured in the advertising of the company, e.g., *Dilo*, no. 31 (1894): 2.

[24] TsDIAL, f. 428, op. 1, spr. 55, vol. 1:44-53.

[25] "Statut 'Ryznytsy' Tovarystva zareiestr. s obmezhenoiu porukoiu v Sambori. Sambir dnia 25 maia 1893," TsDIAL, f. 428, op. 1, spr. 5, folios 1-10.

[26] Information on the company can be found in the records of the Auditing Union of Ruthenian Cooperatives, TsDIAL, f. 428.

We can get an idea of the spectrum of products offered by the company from its price list published in 1907[27] as well as from inventory documents. One of the inventory descriptions of the Ryznytsia store in Lviv lists the following products of sacral needlework: "a violet *epitrachelion;* fringes; ribbons; tassels; towels; a *phelonion;* silk humeral veil (for the benediction service); pairs of banners (*fany*) in white, red, blue, green, burgundy, black, yellow; a pair of banners of different design (*khoruhvy*); black, blue, bright, violet, red *phelonia;* silk tassels; an *aer.*"[28] The company also repaired old *phelonia* and accepted orders "for the embellishment of churches."[29] The advertisements of Ryznytsia, which were systematically published in Galician periodicals practically from the first years of the company's existence, played an important communicative role, not only for customers but also for potential benefactors.[30]

An important aspect of the company's activities was its social program, namely, supporting the poorest widows and orphans of Greek Catholic priests, whose unenviable straits had become the subject of significant social discourse. Thus, according to Ryznytsia's statutes, its supervisory council was to donate 40 percent of its annual profit for charitable purposes: 20 percent for the widows' and orphans' funds of the three Galician eparchies and 20 percent for poor churches.[31] The company not only employed priests' widows and orphans (there were always eight to ten workers in its workshops), but it also set up living quarters: in March 1898 the Shelter for Widows and Orphans of Greek Catholic Priests was established in Sambir.[32]

Similar in its range of activities was the cooperative company Dostava (also known as the Merchant-Industrial House Dostava), founded in 1905 in Stanyslaviv "with the aim of concentrating the trade in church goods in Ruthenian hands."[33] The price list published by Dostava in 1906 describes in detail the company's wares in the terminology that was current in Galicia at the turn of the twentieth century. It indicates what products

[27] *Tsennik ryz, sosudiv i knyh tserkovnykh tovarystva "Ryznytsia" v Sambori* (Sambir: Shvarts i Troian, 1907).

[28] TsDIAL, f. 428, op. 1, spr. 58, vol. 4:178-89.

[29] TsDIAL, f. 428, op. 1, spr. 61, vol. 7:170.

[30] *Dilo*, no. 31 (1894): 2.

[31] TsDIAL, f. 428, op. 1, spr. 5, folio 3.

[32] Nataliia Kolb, "Material'ne zabezpechennia vdiv i syrit hreko-katolyts'kykh sviashchenykiv u Halychyni naprykintsi XIX stolittia," *Istoriia relihii v Ukraini. Naukovyi shchorichnyk* 1 (2006): 327.

[33] The quotation comes from an advertisement for Dostava published in *Iliustrovana Ukraina* (Lviv), no. 10 (1 June 1914): on the reverse of the cover.

were in greatest demand, their parameters (such as size, colors, and prices), the most popular iconographic motifs, and the products' functional purpose. For example, we learn that individual parish priests and church brotherhoods most frequently ordered *phelonia* and *sticharia*. Other examples of the kind of sacred needlework included in it are: "*Elitons* (*ilitony*) [cloths laid over the altar cloth or *endytes* upon which the sacred vessels stood] of pure linen for the altar for 1 crown and higher depending on embroidery and lace. A shroud (*plashchanytsia*) with the image of J[esus] Christ and the troparion around it: on canvas with lyonnaise borders, fringes, and tassels, from 40 to 55 crowns depending on size, with bullion added 65-85 crowns; on silk material 100-150 crowns; decorated with embroidery 200-300 crowns and higher. A shroud depicting the interment of the body of J[esus] Christ and also depicting St. Josaphat, the Mother of God, Mary Magdalene, Salome, Martha, St. John, and Nicodemus costs 10-20 crowns more."

Correspondence contained feedback from Dostava's customers. Fr. Kyselevsky, pastor of Teliache, wrote: "I am completely satisfied with the *phelonion* you sent. I will gladly recommend Dostava to my friends, but what testifies most positively about Dostava is the *phelonion* itself." Fr. K. Mykolaievych, pastor of Kapustyntsi, wrote: "The renovated *phelonion* is so magnificent that it is hard to believe that it is a remake." Fr. Pavlo Petrytsky of Teliache wrote: "The church brotherhood sincerely thanks you for the good and solid production of our *phelonion*. We are asking now for a pure linen *sticharion*.... May God be with you."[34]

The company opened warehouses in Stanyslaviv, Lviv, Przemyśl, and also Winnipeg, Canada. The primary director was Fr. Vasyl Lytsyniak, and the associate director was Ivan Petrushevych, who moved to Canada after the branch of the company was opened there in 1913. During World War I, when the directorate and almost the entire personnel for various reasons found themselves outside Galicia, "our employee Mrs. Karanovychivna"[35] played a significant role, renewing the Dostava store in Lviv in 1914. The company had a permanent workshop for making vestments in which eight women worked.[36] In the postwar period, one of the important components of the company's activities was rebuilding destroyed churches.[37]

---

[34] Ibid., 10.
[35] TsDIAL, f. 301, op. 1, spr. 2, folio 3.
[36] Ibid.
[37] TsDIAL, f. 301, op. 1, spr. 2, folio 5.

The Interaction of Sacral and Folk Needlework

Sacral needlework always developed in close interaction with folk art, but at the end of the nineteenth century there was a paradigmatic change in the relationship. This period accelerated the penetration of folk elements into sacral culture, since at this time church institutions assumed the role of agents and leaders of the national renaissance. We can see this clearly in the examples of sacral needlework preserved in Lviv's Museum of Ethnography and Art Crafts (MEKhP), photographs of which are published here for the first time. A cruciform cover and an *aer* were liturgical cloths for covering the Holy Gifts during the *proskomedia* rite. (See Illustrations 10.2. and 10.3.) A decorative cloth and an altar cloth were meant to embellish the church. (See Illustrations 10.4. and 10.5.) With their chosen imagery, they are products of the

Illustration 10.2: A cruciform cover. One of the liturgical coverings with which a priest covers the communion chalice. Source: MEKhP, f. "Promyslovi tkanyny," inventory no. EP 38 287.

religious understanding that consecrated liturgical items should be placed on specially prepared cloths. The *phelonion* is the outer garment of the priest's vestments. (See Illustrations 10.6 and 10.7.) It symbolizes the scarlet robe which the soldiers put on Jesus during his passion. The *epitrachelion* is a component of the priest's vestments worn around the neck. (See Illustration 10.8.) It is composed of two strips of cloth that fall freely over the other vestments and symbolizes the divine grace and spiritual power to perform divine services and administer the sacraments.

The collection described above comes from the region of Lviv, and the items in it were made in the first half of the twentieth century. All the pieces conform to a single ornamental style and were made for use in a

Illustration 10.3: An aer. The largest of the liturgical coverings for the Holy Gifts. Source: MEKhP, f. "Promyslovi tkanyny," inventory no. EP 38 292.

Illustration 10.4: Decorative cloth. Source: MEKhP, f. "Promyslovi tkanyny," inventory no. EP 38 291.

single church. They were sewn of home-made linen, but for the *phelonion* a heavier cotton material was used. The embroidery was executed in satin stitch and cross stitch. The key ornamental motif was a branch of flowers with a stylized cross in the center. Most of the items have a border sewn on, consisting of a strip with a geometric pattern. As to the color scheme, which has important significative connotations where items for sacred rites are concerned, it is, in this case, multicolored. According to the decisions of the Lviv synod, a priest could use such vestments for daily services.[38] We might also note that representational embroidery, which was so characteristic for liturgical items in previous centuries, is here entirely absent; instead, floral and geometric ornamentation dominates, i.e., designs borrowed from folk patterns. As Martha Bohachevsky-Chomiak correctly noted, folk-motif embroidery "became identified with the Ukrainian rite as opposed to the

---

[38] *Chynnosti i rishenia*, 187-89.

Illustration 10.5: Altar cloth for covering and decorating the main altar. MEKhP, f. "Promyslovi tkanyny," inventory no. EP 38 289.

more elaborate silk stitching of earlier centuries."[39] When we look more closely at the illustrated items, we realize that we are not dealing here with mere copies of traditional motifs, but with a creative, constructive, and quite masterful folk reimagining of sacred handicraft.

An early twentieth-century church periodical called the adornment of churches "the authentic vocation of Christian maidens."[40] It was most often women from the families of Greek Catholic priests who took up this activity, and for them "church aesthetics had social and national significance."[41] These activities quickly took on an organizational dimension. Thus the primary aim of the women's society associated with the Dormition church in Lviv (in 1878, the organization was named the Society of Ruthenian Ladies) was to take care of the decoration of the church.[42] Among the obligations of the Marian Sodalities (or Marian Societies of Ladies), which were extremely popular prayer societies, was the adornment of churches.[43] In 1894 the Lviv-based Ruthenian Women's Club initiated a program of preservation and

[39] Martha Bohachevsky-Chomiak, *Feminists despite Themselves: Women in Ukrainian Community Life, 1884-1939* (Edmonton: Canadian Institute of Ukrainian Studies, University of Alberta, 1988), 51.

[40] Hnat Mykhailovych Ts-skyi, "Zadachi s'viashchenychoho k zhinotstva v nashii tserkovno-suspil'nii pratsi," *Nyva*, no. 13 (1911): 387.

[41] Bohachevsky-Chomiak, *Feminists despite Themselves*, 50.

[42] *Entsyklopediia istorii L'vova*, vol. 2, ed. A. Kozyts'kyi (Lviv: Litopys, 2008), s.v. "Zhinochyi rukh" by Oksana Malanchuk-Rybak.

[43] Lesia Uhryn-Salyk, "Mariis'ka druzhyna zhinok v Rohatyni," in *Rohatyns'ka Zemlia. Zbirnyk istorychno-memuarnykh, etnohrafichnykh i pobutovykh materialiv*, vol. 1 (New York: Ukrains'kyi Arkhiv, 1989), 430.

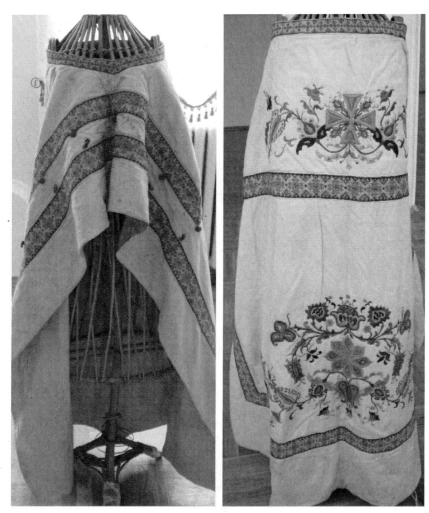

Illustration 10.6–7. Phelonion. MEKhP, f. "Promyslovi tkanyny," inventory no. EP 38 282.

popularization of folk art.[44] Cooperating with some moderate Polish women's organizations, the club raised funds and collected items for exhibit for the all-Galician exhibition of folk art and also organized an exhibit of samples of folk ornaments, embroidery, and sacral needlework.[45]

---

[44] Bohachevsky-Chomiak, *Feminists despite Themselves*, 91.

[45] *Providnyk po vystavi kraievii u L'vovi z osoblyvym ohliadom na viddil etnohrafichnyi i na pavil'on ruskykh narodnykh tovarystv* (Lviv, 1894), 49.

Illustration 10.8:
Epitrachelion. MEKhP, f.
"Promyslovi tkanyny,"
inventory no. EP 38 284.

Olha Bachynska-Tyshynska (1875-1951) was one of the first women to engage in the study, collection, and promotion of folk embroidery on a professional basis. She developed an enthusiasm for folk art already as a child, thanks to her parents, and retained it through her whole life.[46] In 1915 Olha and her husband Ilarion Bachynsky worked in the Austrian refugee camp in Gmünd on the preparation of an exhibit of Ukrainian embroidery for the War Aid Exhibition in Vienna.[47] As Iryna Pelenska recalled: "During the war there were a lot of our people there in great poverty and psychological depression. Olha Bachynska found a way to make contact with the women. It helped that at that time Dr. Ilarion Bachynsky was a reserve administrative officer who worked on the board of the camp. Three hundred of them embroidered, at good wages, wonderful original patterns from their locality."[48] The exhibit showed patterns from twenty Galician counties and one Bukovinian county, "from which these women refugees came, who were able to embroider patterns either from items they brought with them or from memory."[49] Later Olha Bachynska-Tyshynska used this collection in teaching rural youth; she organized embroidery groups, especially under the aegis of the Society of Servants and

[46] Romana Savchyn, "Stryis'ka Berehynia -- Ol'ha Bachyns'ka," *Ukrains'kyi rodovid* (Lviv: Ukrains'ki tekhnolohii, 2001), 85.

[47] Ilarion Bachyns'kyi, "Ukrains'ki vyshyvky na videns'kii vystavi," *Dilo*, no. 33 (1916): 1-2.

[48] Iryna Pelens'ka, "Nashe orhanizovane zhinotstvo," in *Stryishchyna. Istorychno-memuarnyi zbirnyk*, vol. 2 (New York: Ukrains'kyi Arkhiv, 1990), 23.

[49] Bachyns'kyi, "Ukrains'ki vyshyvky," 1.

Domestic Female Laborers.[50] In 1926 she gave the collection of embroidery patterns to the National Museum in Lviv.[51] Osypa Bobykevych (1862-1950) mentions in her memoirs an interesting episode in which rural women in Radekhiv used these patterns for sacral embroidery: "Using Olha Bachynska's patterns, the girls embroidered on grey linen the image of Jesus Christ, and on the other part the image of the Mother of God. This was a beautiful, practical adornment for the square pillars."[52]

Another interesting aspect is the question of personal symbolism incorporated into sacral needlework. We get an insight into this from the memoirs of Mariia Kuzmovych-Holovinska (1904-86). She came from an old priestly family and was herself the wife of the pastor of Zarvanytsia, Vasyl Holovinsky. We learn indirectly from the memoirs that Mariia Kuzmovych-Holovinska was a highly qualified artist who invented original patterns and organized courses on embroidery and lace-making for girls in Zarvanytsia.[53] She also was in charge of the sewing of vestments and decorative towels (*rushnyky*) for the church, and she picked the colors of the threads for embroidering *sticharia* and *epitrachelia*.[54] She assigned girls from neighboring villages to embroider towels for the church: "With these towels Sister Melaniia decorated the dark pillars near the icons of the Heavenly Mother and the Crucified Jesus. The church was rather dark because of an ancient mural, so the white embroidered towels somewhat enlivened it."[55]

In her characteristic emotional manner, Mariia Kuzmovych-Holovinska explained the internal symbolism with which she invested the embroideries she made for the church. For her, it was connected with a profound, spiritual experience of maternity. The birth of each new child was also a battle for her own life: "I also beseeched the Crucified Jesus for the grace of life for the little child, for myself. - I will embroider a cloth for underneath the Most Holy Mysteries on the main altar. [...] Placed on the corners of the cloth was a pattern with multicolored little crosses. For Natalochka. [...] Out of gratitude for the happy arrival into the world of a son, for whom I prayed, I embroidered a pillow for the Gospel Book on

---

[50] Pelens'ka, "Nashe orhanizovane zhinotstvo," 22.

[51] Svientsitskyi, *Dvaitsiat'piat'-littia Natsional'noho Muzeiu*, 23.

[52] Osypa Bobykevych, "Spomyny" (typescript), Arkhiv Instytutu Ukrainoznavstva im. I. Kryp"iakevycha NANU, 45.

[53] Mariia Kuz'movych-Holovins'ka, *Zarvanytsia. Lystky spomyniv* (Toronto: Dobra Knyzhka, 1972), 57.

[54] Ibid., 57, 72.

[55] Ibid., 72.

the main altar, red poppies on green cloth. For Andriiko."[56] She also mentioned how "one woman sent Fr. Vasyl a *phelonion* embroidered in blue on white linen out of gratitude for the Divine Liturgy he celebrated for her, since her entreaty was heeded. She thanked the Mother of God for the grace she received."[57] Mariia Kuzmovych-Holovinska's memoirs allow us to see beyond the external and into the internal world of sacral needlework, i.e., into the individual motivations, concrete life circumstances, and personal symbolism of this creativity.

Conclusions

Our text has attempted to analyze the phenomenon of sacral needlework through the lens of the construction of a national canon at the end of the nineteenth and beginning of the twentieth century. It looked at the role of collecting, museums, and the institutionalization of sacral needlework. In the latter connection, special attention was paid to the organizations Ryznytsia and Dostava, which were the first specialized manufacturing centers that dealt professionally with the production of sacral needlework in Eastern Galicia in the modern period. With the help of archival documentation, it has been possible to reconstruct the spectrum of products of sacral needlework that were current in Galicia at the turn of the twentieth century, their parameters, their most popular motifs, their functional purpose, and more.

The second half of this study allowed us to become more acquainted both with some of the personalities promoting sacral needlework and with particular examples of this art. The reciprocal relations between sacral and folk needlework were explored in the illustrations of individual items preserved in the Museum of Ethnography and Art Crafts in Lviv. The study also looked at various women's organizations and particular individuals who contributed to the study, popularization, and transformation of embroidery into organized crafts and industry.

---

[56] Ibid., 42, 89.
[57] Ibid., 90.